SCREEN
MEMORIES

WOMEN ARTISTS IN FILM

Roswitha Mueller and Kaja Silverman, Series Editors

THE HUNGARIAN CINEMA OF
Márta Mészáros

SCREEN
MEMORIES

CATHERINE PORTUGES

INDIANA UNIVERSITY PRESS
BLOOMINGTON ● INDIANAPOLIS

Photos courtesy of Hungarofilm, Budapest.

Manufactured in the United States of America

Library of Congress Cataloging-in-Publication Data
Portuges, Catherine.
    Screen memories : the Hungarian cinema of Márta Mészáros /
Catherine Portuges.
        p.   cm.—(Women artists in film)
    Includes bibliographical references and index.
    ISBN 0-253-34558-8.—ISBN 0-253-20782-7 (pbk.)
    1. Mészáros, Márta—Criticism and interpretation. I. Title.
    II. Series.
    PN1998.3.M47P67 1993
    791.43'0233'092—dc20   92-2359

1 2 3 4 5   97 96 95 94 93

CONTENTS

ACKNOWLEDGMENTS

The idea for this project began in 1983 during my first visit to Hungary, the country my father had left in 1936 and to which he never returned, when I was invited by Antal Bókay, Chair of English and American Studies at Janus Pannonius University in Pécs, to participate in an international conference on psychoanalysis in Central Europe. I thank Professor Bókay and his colleagues for initiating what became an ongoing collaborative program in cultural exchange—the kind of transformative experience that led me to discover "the other Europe." Murray Schwartz, former Dean of the Faculty of Humanities and Fine Arts of the University of Massachusetts, made it possible for me to accept that invitation; I am deeply grateful for his continuing professional support and unfailing confidence. The Graduate School of the University of Massachusetts provided Research and Summer Travel Grants for trips to Hungary which enabled me to enjoy outstanding cooperation from filmmakers, archivists, scholars, and journalists.

The generosity of spirit and hospitality of Márta Mészáros and Jan Nowicki culminated in the series of interviews presented here; invitations to join the director and her colleagues for working sessions at Mafilm Studios/Budapest during post-production work on *Bye Bye Red Riding Hood* and *Diary for My Father and Mother* allowed me to experience the atmosphere of extraordinary professionalism and familial camaraderie that characterize the director's endeavors. I am indebted to the expert staff of Hungarofilm for screening facilities and services that permitted me to view all the Mészáros films available in the Hungarofilm/Budapest archives, and in particular to Katalin Vajda, Vera Surányi, Lia Somogyi, and István Várady for arranging screenings, dialogue books, stills, and documentation. (Prints of Mészáros's earliest documentaries that were unavailable for screening are noted in the filmography.)

Conversations with other filmmakers, including Miklós Jancsó, Gyula Gazdag, Károly Makk, György Szomjas, Judith Elek, and László Sántha, provided invaluable insights into the dynamics of Hungarian visual and political culture. To Pál Schiffer I am especially appreciative for continuous support and friendship.

The historical context of this study was enhanced through visits to the Hungarian Film Institute, a collection of rare prints of great historical interest, under the aegis of its director, Vera Gyürey. Invitations to the twenty-second and twenty-third Hungarian National Film Festivals in February 1990 and 1992 greatly enriched my understanding of Hungarian cinema and its importance to East-Central European cultural life.

The Hungarian Consulates in Washington, D.C. and New York, the Museum of Modern Art, Facets Multimedia, New Yorker Films, and Kino International provided 16mm prints and videocassettes of Hungarian and other East European cinema. Kevin Tierney of Les Productions la Fête (Montreal) furnished stills, videocassettes, and interest in the project.

Hungarian specialists in psychoanalysis and literary history, both in Paris and in Budapest, offered professional advice and personal observations, among whom Judith Dupont, Eva Brabant, Ádám Péter, Vera Létai, and Pál Pataki are especially worth notice. Professors Yvette Biró, Ivan Sanders, Tamás Ungvári, and István Deák provided perspectives on Hungarian history and cinema at early stages of the book. Professor Tamás Aczél shared his views of the political culture of the Rákosi era (1948–56) and of the life of a writer in exile. To Jerry Carlson, film and television producer as well as cinema studies professor, I am indebted for a shared passion for Hungarian cinema and for the opportunity to participate on his CUNY-TV cable series "Cinema Then, Cinema Now."

Graham Petrie's *History Must Answer to Man*, the first and still most distinguished history of Hungarian cinema in English, taught me how to think about the subject; I thank him for an invitation to present materials from this project in Canada for the conference (and subsequent book) "Soviet and East European Filmmakers Working in the West." The late Frantisek Galan's invitation to the first panel on East European cinema at the Modern Language Association was an important source of encouragement; he will be missed. Helene Keyssar offered a forum for presenting parts of this work for the Communication and Women's Studies Departments at the University of California, San Diego; Kathleen Woodward enabled me to consolidate portions of the project for the Literature and Philosophy Conference "Bodies: Image/Technology/Text" at the University of California, Irvine; and Scott Nygren invited my participation on the panel "Representations of Democracy in Eastern Europe" at the 1991 Society for Cinema Studies Conference.

I thank Bella Brodzki for the opportunity to formulate my thoughts for her book *Life/Lines: Theories of Women's Autobiography* and Mary Russo for her gracious invitation to present a segment of this study for the Harvard conference on "Nationalisms and Sexualities." I am especially indebted to Kaja Silverman for making possible this contribution to the International Women Filmmakers' Series for Indiana University Press.

Vincent DiMarco read the manuscript at several stages; I am thankful for his comments and support. Eva Rueschmann deserves credit for excellent research assistance on filmographical and bibliographical materials, and Dennis Porter for support through the Center for Studies in Contemporary Culture. To Don Eric Levine, special thanks for his detailed critique, and to my graduate students in Comparative Literature, thanks for their forbearance.

Alexandra Juhasz and Marietta Pritchard shared experiences of our common Austro-Hungarian heritage in ways that have enriched this study. Diana Diamond, Helene Keyssar, Greta Slobin, Wendy Smith, Madelyn De Maria, and Janet Rifkin provided the enduring friendship that makes such an endeavor possible. Special thanks to Richard Pini and Karen Hendrickson.

For his anthropological expertise on the language, customs, and cultural history of Hungary, and for translation and research, I am deeply grateful to László Kürti. This book is dedicated to my family—Lisl Füredi Steckler, Tom Füredi, and Cyndi Füredi—and to the memory of my father, Paul Füredi, who left Hungary during the advance of fascism and who would, I like to think, have enjoyed this symbolic return home.

SCREEN
MEMORIES

1 INTRODUCTION

Since this book began to take form, the momentous events in Eastern Europe have inevitably forced changes in its original direction and emphasis, prompting a recasting of earlier thoughts in light of contemporary cultural politics.[1] Initiated by an encounter with Márta Mészáros's work in the early 1980s for a symposium on gender and visual representation, this book bears the imprint of Mészáros's own East-Central European culture—her habits of mind and speech, and her vision of the cinematic and ideological context in which she has worked for thirty-five years.[2]

I had begun at that time to examine the interplay between fiction and autobiography in texts by French women writers, an inquiry that later came to embrace first-person narrative cinema as well and culminated in my essay "Seeing Subjects: Women Directors and Cinematic Autobiography."[3] Previous preparation in modern French literature had led me to do a psychoanalytically oriented study of gender in the work of French New Wave directors and subsequently enabled me to enjoy relative freedom as a comparatist to move beyond the boundaries of a single national cinema or literature.[4]

In an effort to integrate these perspectives, I began nearly a decade ago to interview filmmakers and writers, endeavoring in these dialogues to articulate the place of subjectivity and cultural meaning in their projects. At the same time I sought to discover the site and consequences of the speakers' image-making activity. Why, for example, had they chosen to work primarily against the grain of mainstream commercial cinema, or to cross the borders of their own nationalities? By engaging with these filmmakers in a narrative of the individual, cultural, and artistic concerns that inflect their work as artists of a particular gender, generation, racial or ethnic background, and professional formation, I hoped to reflect as well upon the interview as a contemporary cultural form and to assess its value to film directors whose own subject positions are often obscured.

Márta Mészáros

In so doing I suspected that, in that privileged terrain which is the space of autobiography, both subject and reader/spectator experience what Lacan has called "correct distance" and Winnicott "potential space": the safety of apprehending a textual object without fear of either the suffocation of excessive intimacy or the detachment of too great a separation.[5] Guided by a sense of primary responsibility to the filmmaker and to the cultural context Márta Mészáros inhabits—that of East-Central Europe—this study privileges the director's account of her own subjectivity as one of the few East-Central

European women directors whose work has reached international audiences, and whose status is that of a senior colleague and model for many international women filmmakers.

Like many of them, Márta Mészáros came of age in the postwar generation.[6] A woman of extraordinary dynamism, independence of spirit, and sense of purpose, she has succeeded in achieving and sustaining an autonomous and highly respected position within the parameters of the formerly centralized—and preponderantly male—Hungarian film establishment.[7]

In her documentary film *Travel Diary* (*Utinapló*, 1989), filmed for Hungarian television during a return to the Soviet Union in 1988–89, Mészáros recalls her years as a film student at the State Institute for Cinematography (V.G.I.K.) in Moscow where, despite the extreme privations of the early 1950s, an atmosphere of creativity and intense productivity prevailed. There she was taught that Braque, Chagall, Modigliani, and Picasso, while "decadent," were nonetheless worthy of close study. Mészáros reminisces with former colleagues, admitting that her sense of those times is "operatic: everything was *red* at the V.G.I.K.!," and recalling the internationalism, the constant exaltation, and the sense of mutual responsibility that compensated for the material poverty. Tarkovsky, Konchalovsky, Chiaureli, Chukrai, Gerassimov, Romm—these were her mentors and colleagues. Mészáros herself conducts some of the interviews, intercutting rare footage of the period: "I'm still trying to find the secret of what happened at that time," she admits, showing a montage from Romm's *Vladimir Ilyich Lenin*—a film Stalin used to celebrate the day of Lenin's death, each year causing a different Leninist to be blacked out of the picture.

Recalling early movie-going with her mother, seeing Beria in newsreels of the Seventeenth Party Congress, Mészáros disputes facile characterizations of the 1950s as a time of stagnation in light of the creative atmosphere that reigned in the academy. For the first time in her professional life, in *Travel Diary*, Mészáros is herself the subject of on-camera interviews during this journey to Moscow, Leningrad, and the town of Frunze in Khirgizia, where she lived with her parents between the ages of two and eight. More than once in this intimately autobiographical film essay, she alludes to the difficulty of talking about those years and acknowledges a passion to discover their secrets. Beneath the film's disarming title, suggesting a travelogue, *Travel Diary* reveals the director's courage in returning, in her early 60s, to the scene of her own traumatic past. Her demeanor is at once reluctant and excited, contemplative and irreverent, as she permits her camera crew to record conversations with local audiences exposed for the first time to her films. She acknowledges the difficulty of verbalizing the horrors of the early 1950s—the death of her parents, the atmosphere of terror and silence that reigned over her youth—yet as an adult she recognizes that those years were responsible for the difficulties of the present. Her Russian subjects in *Travel*

Diary comment on the philosophical depth of Hungarian cinema, its film language previously unimaginable to Soviet filmmakers: "Through Hungarian film, and the Diaries, we realize how much we have been deprived."

In the third section of *Travel Diary*, filmed in Frunze, a woman stands up in the audience after a screening of *Diary for My Children* (*Napló gyermekeimnek*, 1982), thanking Mészáros for having given her the chance to hear the truth forty-one years later, she says: "I felt you took this material from my private life . . . my grandfather was also purged in '38." Mészáros is visibly moved by the restrained yet forthright tributes of actors, painters, and workers whose lives had been touched by her father. She is overcome to learn that one of his fellow artists had set aside a small bronze sculpture for the day when his daughter would surely return to claim it.

Standing outside the house where she lived with her father until his arrest, she recalls the neighborhood children who died in the war, including a little boy who was her "first love." Many others came to live in the house, including the leading communists of Hungary and some of Stalin's future henchmen—Révai, Nagy, Rákosi, Gerö. Mészáros recalls sleeping in shifts with other children on the living-room rug, sharing the fate of the local intelligentsia and bureaucracy, with the exception of the elite cadre. She reflects on the ironies of her father's arrest in 1938, when only a few years later the top Hungarian leadership from Moscow came to live in the same two rooms; she recalls that, as a little girl, she slept there on the floor next to Szofi Nagy, daughter of Imre Nagy, with whom she spent hours looking out the window at swaying branches. Mészáros interpolates here photographs of herself seated next to her parents on the sofa. During a dinner in her honor hosted by a famous Khirgiz writer, Mészáros speaks of the whispers, lies, avoidances of yesterday; the visit has, she states, made her understand why people feel the need to visit the graves of their parents.

Mészáros's personal narratives of her life and filmmaking career emboldened me to learn how, coming from a cinema considered "minor" by the West, she had nonetheless succeeded in transcending the limitations of that cultural marginality. Referring to Mészáros several years before, Agnès Varda told me she had remembered a moment from *Riddance* (*Szabad lélegzet*, 1973) in the course of shooting two of her own films in California in the early 1980s, *Murs Murs* and *Documenteurs*. The scene in question foregrounded a woman taking a shower, alone and oblivious to the world. "She simply needs the water," Agnès Varda explained, in the course of speculating on the ways temporality is represented differently by women directors. That exchange compelled me to investigate further the cinema of women directors of "the other Europe" or the "Second World"—a cultural field that still remains on the borders of Western film theory and history.

The recognition of this marginality prompted my desire to extend our field of inquiry as film scholars beyond the Western ethnocentrism that is equally impoverishing to filmmakers, students, scholars, and general viewers. Despite significant progress in pedagogical and scholarly attention to Third World and other national cinemas, the substantial contributions to film of East-Central Europe or the "Second World" continue to be relatively untheorized and rarely taught in the West—all the more perplexing in light of the political reconfiguration of Europe and the parallel cultural reconceptualization now taking form. There is some reason to believe that this neglect may be repaired, if only by virtue of the potential commercial and cultural exchange value of a more globalized film industry, once the film industries undergoing privatization are able to compete in the international market.

Paradoxical though it may seem, the politics of location and the border crossings that mark contemporary East-Central European cultural practice solicit a rethinking of prior assumptions about nationality in the visual media that extend to other regions as well and that accord fuller weight to the representational world than it has yet received from postmodern critiques. Interpreting the national in "the new Europe" of 1992 risks the ever-present dangers of cultural misreadings, projected appropriations, and, for that matter, outright incomprehension. Tempting though it may be to surrender to the lure of the "free-market" fervor that threatens to dominate global cinema for years to come, we would do well to recall other historical migrations and dissolutions that ultimately paved the way for the multiethnic cultures that global cinema has become. It is thus perhaps not surprising that post-glasnost Soviet cinema outstrips in availability of prints and marketing tactics its smaller former East-bloc counterparts, ironically mirroring their former political relationship.[8]

The complexities of locating historical as well as current materials—feature and documentary films and videos, filmographies and reviews, scholarly analyses and mass media criticism—for developing curricula and advancing research of the culture of East-Central European cinema have, at least for the moment, been exacerbated by uncertainties in the cultural-political scenes of Poland, Hungary, Czechoslovakia, Yugoslavia, and the post–Soviet Union.[9] The Twenty-Seventh International Film Festival in Karlovy Vary, Czechoslovakia in 1990, featuring films produced by Czech and Slovak filmmakers in exile as well as a number of "unshelved" films banned after 1968, suggested future possibilities for focusing international attention on these national cinemas, as did the Seventeenth International Film Festival in Moscow in 1991.[10] In a similar effort to bring little-known cinemas to larger audiences, the 1990 American Film Institute Los Angeles Film Festival reserved a screen exclusively for films from Eastern Europe as part of its tribute to "Hollywood Glasnost," while the 1991 Berlin Film Festival, held for the first time in close cooperation between East and West, featured films never before seen by either side.[11]

The following chapters are intended as a contribution to this movement within international cinema to redress the imbalances that have so long determined the politics of production, distribution, and reception.

If a freer circulation of visual information from Eastern Europe is now within reach, the potential for exploration of its national cinemas within academic discourse is also substantially increased. Central to this study are the contributions and consistent international influence of a pioneering woman director whose work—and that of her counterparts represented in this series—warrants a more thoroughgoing assessment and sustained visibility than it has to date enjoyed.

When Mészáros first came to international prominence in the 1960s, "la politique des auteurs"—the now much-maligned auteur theory—enjoyed substantial influence in continental and Anglo-American film theory. And, while the terrain between individual authorship and such contemporary issues as the intersections of nationality and sexuality have come increasingly to occupy our critical agenda, the status of women directors who do not necessarily claim their own work to be specifically "feminist" or "women's cinema" deserves special consideration with regard to Eastern Europe.[12]

Now that East European women are, because of historical events, better positioned to enter more fully into debates—including those on gender—on an international scale, they are beginning to claim their own contestatory discourse. And, like the smaller former East-bloc nations that are in the painful process of moving toward market economies and away from the central control that for decades regulated the production of word and image, they too will undoubtedly insist on the right to explain and theorize their experience in their own ways, rather than accepting formulations imposed from without.

An urgent issue for contemporary film theory arising from the position of East European filmmakers is that of realism, the status of which, like that of *auteur* theory, is problematic. Western film theory might well have too quickly trivialized—if not discarded altogether—the practices of realism in cinema as unworthy of the postmodern condition. But for Eastern Europe, its uses may have very different meanings. Many intellectuals, for example, have had little access to Western publications over the past several decades; moreover, Stalinist prescriptions of realism—"socialist realism," for instance—deformed and neutralized its possibilities. Filmmakers working under such constraints nonetheless required viable solutions to their esthetic, political, and subjective realities. This impasse opened a space for cinematic autobiography—neither entirely fiction nor entirely documentary—that at once privileged the individual *auteur* and encouraged the multiple possibilities of a realism freed from the artificial homogeneity and seamless perfection of socialist-realist or Stalinist film esthetics. Those qualities rejected by Stalinism—human ambiguity, the rough edges of daily life, the unsolicited promptings of memory—are in fact the very stuff of autobiography, and in particular of women's autobiography.[13]

Autobiographical essays by male and female filmmakers may of course also serve as critical pronunciamentos;[14] published interviews in film journals and on videocassette likewise incorporate statements of artistic philosophy and cinematic practice.[15] Current research in the visual arts reflects an increasing awareness of the need for studies that locate historically questions of spectatorship as well as the politics of production, technology as well as textuality. And the proliferation of recent publications on national cinemas indicates, among other things, the importance of that topic in determining the ramifications of distribution and reception.[16]

Accordingly, this study is an effort toward recognizing such developments through a focus on the cinema of Márta Mészáros in the context of a restrictively known national cinema over a span of several decades. In view of the growing complexity of production and consumption of the moving image, and the concomitant urgency to account for the diversity of their enactments, my methodology integrates readings of Mészáros's films, her life, and its cultural contexts in ways that mean to be at once historical, autobiographical, cultural, and cinematic. Mészáros is rare among women directors in being able to claim a thirty-five-year directorial achievement that encompasses documentary, feature, and musical genres, and that integrates within those genres both autobiography and history. That she is also a woman working in a country that has alternately considered itself communist, statist, socialist, and democratic is even more remarkable. To account for and hold in balance these interlocking historical, cultural, psychological, and social dimensions, their relationship to each other and to the totality of Mészáros's *oeuvre*, each chapter is structured on close readings of individual films and liberally interspersed with Mészáros's own commentary.

For Western audiences generally unfamiliar—at least until recently—with East-Central European culture, interconnections between historical events and their cinematic representation often seem tenuous at best. Mészáros's Polish contemporary, the director Andrzej Wajda, offers what may be taken as a statement of purpose for our consideration of East European cinema today:

> Films made in Eastern Europe seem of little or no interest to people in the West. The audiences in western countries find them as antediluvian as the battle for workers' rights in England in the time of Marx. Thus our efforts here in Eastern Europe have nothing to show audiences in the West who look upon the world they live in as permanent. Those of our Eastern European film colleagues who have chosen emigration can—if they are young and talented and after they have spent years in the West—come up with some works of startling beauty, such as Milos Forman's *Amadeus*, but they will not find audiences attuned to the same concerns that we in the Eastern bloc feel are vital. And that is a pity, for I am certain that those concerns are not ours alone but apply to the world at large, or will in the very near future.[17]

Wajda's prophesy resonates uncannily with regard to the problematics of nationality and emigration in the case of Mészáros. In the life of many directors there has often been a decisive moment that determines and demarcates the future. In the case of refugees fleeing Nazi Germany and Nazi-occupied Europe, such as Jean Renoir, Fritz Lang, Max Ophuls, and Billy Wilder, their motives have been primarily political, as were those of the earlier wave of Hungarian directors, such as Alexander Korda and Michael Curtiz.[18] But other significant factors may also guide a filmmaker's decision to risk working in a foreign language or an unfamiliar culture. For Mészáros, 1968 proved to be such a moment. In the West, the upheavals of the May events in France and the cinematic experiments of filmmakers such as Jean-Luc Godard struck a sympathetic chord with youth movements around the world, in concert with the American antiwar, civil rights, and women's liberation movements. At the same time in the "other Europe" (perhaps more accurately called the "new Europe"), "Prague spring" witnessed Alexander Dubček's efforts to implement "socialism with a human face," while in Hungary the "new economic mechanism" opposed centralized Stalinist policy, effectively positioning Hungarian society en route to a Western-oriented economy whose apotheosis was realized in 1990. A time of intense, if too brief, revolutionary artistic activity in Eastern Europe as well, this era is remembered, among other things, for the originality of Věra Chytilová in Czechoslovakia, Jerzy Skolimowski in Poland, Dušan Makaveyev in Yugoslavia, and Miklós Jancsó in Hungary.[19]

That same year Mészáros, then 37, released *The Girl (Eltávozott nap)*, the *first* feature film directed by a woman in the history of Hungarian cinema. It is not without interest that a decade later the leading actress of Mészáros's *Nine Months* (1976) was filmed during actual childbirth as part of the film's narrative, a daring departure in a cinematic tradition little given to such unsparing yet empathic portrayals of women's lives, in a country governed as much by patriarchal as by socialist ethics. These "firsts" might well have warranted—and would very likely have received—critical attention had they been generated by a Western artist, or, arguably, by a male director. Originating as they did in a country defined by cultural and linguistic insularity, however, their meaning in the context of feminism and women's cinema passed unnoticed at the time. In view of Mészáros's acknowledged influence on other women directors and her largely unacknowledged influence on Hungarian cinema, it is not merely as an innovator that she merits recognition. Her integrity of vision, consistent mastery of ambiguous and complex emotions, rigorous refusal of sentimentality and overstatement, together with an unfailing independence of spirit and action, exemplify the best qualities of international women's cinema. Her omission from the index of several major film reference texts is, therefore, all the more surprising, and indicates the need for further research such as the studies inaugurated by this series on the production and sites of reception of other directors.[20]

By the 1970s and early 1980s, Western feminist film critics had begun to claim Mészáros as a maker of "women's films." Such assumptions, valid though they may have been from Western perspectives, are not, however, shared by Mészáros, a problematic to be addressed in the following chapters. For if we are truly to validate feminist claims that authenticate and honor subjectivity and difference, we must consider the vexing question of the critical appropriation of "second world" realities by "first world" formulations, despite the integrity of the appropriators' intentions. Such colonization, however unwitting, of the cultural products of a small, marginalized nation in the service of theorizing its discourse within the conceptualizations of a dominant Western discourse—oppositional though it may be in the context of its own mainstream—risks misreadings and misapprehensions. Not unlike other European women whose art is taken to be unquestionably "feminist" by Western audiences, Mészáros regards the designation at best with skeptical ambivalence. To be sure, in common with many of her European women colleagues, Mészáros's concerns with the experience of women have been consistently manifested in her films; nevertheless, she prefers to maintain her own sense of freedom from any *a priori* or *a posteriori* categorization, perhaps as a result of having worked throughout her life under the imposition of externally imposed ideological categories.[21]

Whereas many Western women filmmakers have structured narrative and documentary films on the pre-oedipal, Mészáros instead negotiates female subjectivity in the context of the Oedipus complex. The maternal figure, as in the case of the Stalinist Magda, is often constructed as a "bad mother," a withholding or punitive presence that may appear harsh to the Western viewer accustomed to a more covert aggressivity. This tendency can discomfit contemporary Anglo-American audiences, who expect a woman director to oppose conventional movie stereotypes of women at odds with each other by creating more "positive" images in their place. And such discomfort is all the more complicated when it is the father who is most deeply cathected as the object of the daughter's desire. Mészáros insists upon this point:

> When you write about me, it's important to point out that, in Eastern Europe, films ought to be made not only by male directors. I don't want to make speeches about women's emancipation, because I'm not part of that movement, but [filmmaking by women] represents a different kind of sensitivity. If you interpret my films as strictly political, you see that I approach power relations differently from the way they are portrayed by male directors. Not because my films are necessarily better, or theirs worse, but because they are different. One must be aware of this.[22]

But this "different kind of sensitivity" (understandably interpreted as "feminist" by many conscientious critics) cannot be read accurately without a sense of the historical meanings of femininity and masculinity in the Hungarian psyche and its cinema. Toward that end, I begin by briefly setting the scene of the Hungarian cinema, proceeding to an overview of the critical reception of Mészáros's work in Hungary and the West that suggests the rather surprising lacunae and distortions to which her work has been subjected. In reconsidering her works' status, I take up the intersections of cinema and autobiography by theorizing their relationship in light of current debates on the positionings of the gendered speaking subject. Detailed descriptions are provided of films that have received little or no exposure to Western audiences.[23]

The spectrum of images conjured up by contemporary Hungarian cinema ranges from the sweeping, deserted "puszta" of Jancsó's avant-garde films to such denunciations of Stalinism as Pál Gábor's (1978) *Angi Vera*. More recently, Péter Gothár's youth-oriented social critique, *Time Stands Still* (*Megáll az idö*, 1982), has been echoed by István Szabó's *Colonel Redl* (1984), a meditation on the break-up of the Austro-Hungarian monarchy, and *Mephisto* (1981), a searing critique of the artist's plight under the culture of totalitarianism, in this case Nazism. These are, to be sure, only a few of the currently better-known productions from an industry of great vitality, experimentation, and independent spirit. Such characteristics of Hungarian filmmaking are more than evident in a country where fiscal considerations have assured consistent annual production of some two dozen feature films, a situation that has already altered as studios are increasingly decentralized and privatized.[24]

Western, and particularly American, audiences and critics tend to consider Hungarian—and, for that matter, most East European—films to be excessively political, solemn, even cynical, qualities deemed undesirable by those whose filmgoing pleasure is measured by successful escape from precisely such affects or conditions.[25] Politics are, of course, inescapably inscribed far more pervasively in Hungarian cinema than in its Western counterparts: most of its films of recent vintage bear the traces of its wrenching political history. And the difficulties of sustaining a proud national identity over the course of its thousand-year history are celebrated tropes of artistic and intellectual discourse, filmmaking included.

From the time of its first newsreel in 1896, the Hungarian film industry has been one of the most venerable in Europe, and it was among the first to be nationalized, in advance even of the Soviet Union, in 1919.[26] Regular feature production was initiated in 1912, and during the short-lived Council of Republics (from April to August, 1919), the state-owned industry produced some thirty-one films. The defeat of the Council by the combined forces of Admiral Miklós Horthy and his Western allies, however, returned the industry to private ownership; Hungarian film workers such as the director Sándor (Alexander) Korda and the theoretician Béla Balázs were exiled to the West. There followed a period of prodigious, if commercialized, productivity throughout the 1920s and 1930s, represented primarily by inferior imitations of Hollywood. By 1941, the young director István Szőts had made *People of the Alps (Emberek a havason)*, generally considered to be the outstanding film of the pre-liberation epoch. The studios suffered substantial damage during World War II, and the transitional postwar years were marked by massive reconstruction. The outcome of these efforts were two films of international distinction, Géza Radvány's *Somewhere in Europe (Valahol Európában*, 1947) and Szőts's *Song of the Cornfields (Ének a búzamezokrol*, 1947). The first feature after the "renationalization" of the industry, *The Soil under Your Feet (Talpalatnyi föld*, 1948), inaugurated the genre of lyrical realism which was to become a hallmark of Hungarian cinema in the 1950s.[27]

In order to respect the complexities of this national film culture, and to resist reductive nationalist stereotypes, it must be acknowledged that Hungarian audiences also seek pleasure, escape, and humor, albeit of a rather darker variety than that favored by Hollywood. With the recent rise of Western coproductions and joint ventures and the massive incursion of Hollywood product, this tradition is obviously in transition. Yet the scope of Hungarian contributions to what we know as "Hollywood" bears ample testimony to the history of this complex Central-European sensibility, as evidenced in the work of Michael Curtiz, Alexander and Zoltán Korda, Béla Lugosi, and Miklós Rózsa, among others.[28] In Hungary, the film industry has, quite apart from those films known in the West, also produced a substantial quantity of light-hearted, sophisticated dramas, many of which are based on literary sources such as the novels of the aristocratic Gyula Krúdy or the populist Sándor Csoóri. Perhaps more than in West European cinemas, there is a strong tradition of close alliance among the arts in Hungary, and it is no less unusual to find high-quality films written in collaboration with novelists than filmmakers—of whom Miklós Jancsó and Péter Gothár are among the most notable—working regularly in the theater.

Along with its uniquely specific emphasis on the past, Hungarian cinema also bears the equally ubiquitous traces of the rural culture that has played such a powerful role in that country's history, in particular the populist nationalism evident in films such as Ferenc Kósa's *The Other Man (A másik ember*, 1988) and Sándor Sára's *Thorn under the Nail (Tüske a köröm alatt*, 1988). In its long and martyred history, Hungary's Central-European and Habsburg heritage combined with its socialist past to create a uniquely contradictory, even tragic national portrait, yet one stamped by a fierce and uncompromising individualism. History is everywhere implicated; in the words of the Hungarian tragic poet Attila József, himself a victim of extreme poverty, schizophrenia, and ultimately suicide, whose poem of an orphan's solitude is cited in Mészáros's *Diary for My Loves (Napló szerelmeimnek*, 1987), "Accepting the past is struggle enough."

A woman of vision, tenacity, and spirit, Márta Mészáros's most powerful strategies for survival and continuing creative success within the oppressive decades of post-Stalinist Hungary are, I suspect, the desire and ability to write about and film the times through which she lived and, in so doing, to accept—and understand—her own past. No less important is the fact that her "first" career was that of documentary filmmaker, with over one hundred films to her credit, a record that alone exceeds that of many filmmakers' lifetime achievement. Éva Pataki, her frequent collaborator and scriptwriter, attributes Mészáros's success in part to a passionate, even-handed interest in people:

> It's very important to say that she is interested in everyone, from the waiter in the commissary to the lighting engineer and the hairdresser—everybody . . . she knows everything about everybody, who is divorcing, who is expecting a baby, everything. When I started working with her I was inexperienced, yet she treated me absolutely as an equal.[29]

Beginning in the late 1960s, Mészáros began to make feature films, insisting on shooting scripts whose main protagonists were female and doing so in ways that appeared radically different from those to which Hungarian audiences were accustomed. Both privileged, in the public eye, on account of her marriage to Miklós Jancsó, while simultaneously judged in comparison to him, she dared to subvert official versions of sexual equality under state socialism by portraying the domestic as well as economic struggles of working women and men. It is perhaps no coincidence that a number of other Hungarian women directors such as Livia Gyarmathy, Judit Elek, Judit Ember, and Marianne Szemes first distinguished themselves in documentaries and short subjects. Among them, however, Márta Mészáros was the first to succeed in a full-fledged "second career" as a feature director. This pattern invites speculation about the implications of preparation in documentary for other filmmakers and the varieties and effects of the presence of documentary footage within fictional narratives, a topic taken up in chapter six. More specifically, the challenges posed by her cinema are attributable in part to her experiments in documentary praxis within the fiction film through the exploration of techniques of re-enactment, questioning of "objectivity," and departure from more classic techniques of cinéma vérité.

Perhaps in part because of this crossover tendency, since 1978 Hungarian film production has been unmistakably informed by a strong autobiographical and retrospective tendency that utilizes contemporary pictorial, technological, and narrative modes to recreate and reevaluate recent history. Together with established film artists such as Pál Gábor, István Szabó, Károly Makk, and Péter Gothár, Márta Mészáros has been honored at international festivals, setting the stage for other women directors attempting to press beyond the artistic, political, and gender boundaries that have prevented such historical examinations from taking place. No less important have been the activities of these and other filmmakers in bringing about reforms in the centralized organization of Hungarian filmmaking as a whole, placing the artists themselves, within newly formed independent studios, at the center of film production.

Suppressed under the aegis of Stalinist internationalism, conflicts—social, psychological, and artistic—between culturally based inscriptions of gender, sexuality, and politics are now emerging, albeit in the guise of a Western-oriented audiovisuality that appears to be an inescapable consequence of decades of official censorship.[30] Instances of this crisis are visible in the cinematic body politic through the unfolding of an oedipal drama in which the former State as father, having both infantilized and shielded its subject-children through a centrally funded cinematic apparatus, is now abandoning a national cinema ill-prepared to function as a free-market economy.[31]

This privileged locus is also the site of reenactment of an older dialectic of sexuality and nationalism denied or foreclosed by postwar materialist priorities. Joining the growing list of "limited corporations" that characterize Hungary's postcommunist transitional moment, the culture of cinema must reinvent itself if it is to survive under a new order. Such recent films as *The Documentator* (*A Dokumentátor*, 1988) *Sexploitation* (*Aszex*, 1990), and *Fast and Loose* (*Könnyű Vér*, 1990),[32] however, suggest that some Hungarian filmmakers have responded to liberalization by embracing the more commercially viable trajectory of soft-core pornography or, at the very least, eroticized spectacle. Long banned by the Communist Party as a symptom of the more decadent aspects of Western capitalism, pornography is now graphically displayed in publications found at local kiosks, and X-rated videos constitute a growth industry.[33]

The future of Hungarian cinema and the consequences of the transition from centralized state support to privatization (with its concomitant over-dependence on foreign capital) remains for the moment uncertain, even for established filmmakers.[34] What, we must now ask, are to be the subjects of cinema in a society whose filmmakers have developed highly refined methods of encoding opposition and subversion within the very texts subsidized by the governments they opposed? Perhaps a more open discourse of social and cultural realities, in which gender issues can be foregrounded, will now be legitimized.

Among the directors who have addressed the intersections of state ideology, sexuality, and everyday life—rural and urban, workplace and domestic—Márta Mészáros stands virtually alone in consistently collapsing gender and national identities. She has been alternately dismissed or misread in the critical literature as a "realist" or a "feminist," marginalized as a "documentarist," or omitted entirely. With the notable exception of France, where her work has long been recognized, few studies of Hungarian cinema evaluate Mészáros's cinema in depth. Michael Jon Stoil's *Cinema Beyond the Danube: the Camera and Politics* (1974), for instance, contains no reference at all to her films. In the anthology *Post New Wave Cinema in the Soviet Union and Eastern Europe* (1989), David Paul refers to Mészáros's *Nine*

Months (1976) as "by no means the first of director Mészáros' feminist stories. The uncompromising naturalism of the final scene is consistent with the film's realism throughout—as it is characteristic of Mészáros' feature work in general—and the subject matter, an intimate story about contemporary people, is also typical of Mészáros' *oeuvre.*"[35] István Nemeskürti's classic study *Word and Image: History of the Hungarian Cinema* (1974) refers to Mészáros in the same sentence with two other women directors, Judit Elek and Livia Gyarmathy, saying that "as women, these three directors are naturally interested in the position of working women, the subject of many of their films."[36]

As a further indication of her marginalization both in Hungary and in filmmaking more generally, Mészáros's name is missing entirely from Károly Nemes's *Films of Commitment: Socialist Cinema in Eastern Europe* (1985), an "official" version of Hungarian film history. In refreshing contrast, Graham Petrie's valuable *History Must Answer to Man* (1978) argues that "Mészáros has a fine understanding of the unspoken tensions between men and women, and also of the moments of insight and tenderness that bring a genuine, though temporary, understanding." He goes on to suggest, however:

> Though her films are rarely exciting visually, they are functionally effective in presenting personal relationships and in using background and setting as an indication of the characters' states of mind. Nevertheless, some very real problems remain. The main one is the strange disparity between Mészáros' concern for realism of detail, for presenting ordinary, unexceptional people in their everyday working and living environment, and the wildly implausible progression of her plots.[37]

Nevertheless, Petrie's serious discussion of Mészáros at an early stage of her career merits further attention, and I shall return to his and other evaluations in later chapters.

The limited typologies of "realism" and "naturalism" often proffered in the place of interpretive analysis cannot, I think, do justice to the complexity and richness of Mészáros's films nor, for that matter, of East European cinema in general. While the relationship of Mészáros's cinema to realism and feminism will be taken up in more detail in the following chapters, one aspect of her "realistic" approach merits mention here. Among the remarkable developments throughout contemporary Eastern Europe has been its citizens' courageous reappraisal of the Stalinist era and its aftermath.[38] In the vanguard of this movement, filmmakers have found ways of proposing a new order by representing on screen that which individuals could scarcely permit themselves to imagine privately. When, for instance, in *Diary for My Loves* (1986) Mészáros portrayed the funeral of László Rajk—thereby implicating the "unburied" Imre Nagy and his martyred colleagues of the uprising—she could not have suspected that the longed-for burial of the heroes of 1956 would take place only three years later, nor that it would receive the massive media attention it earned around the world. Accordingly, chapter six is devoted to a treatment of the Stalinist era and its reassessment by Mészáros and several of her contemporaries. There, I analyze the phenomenon of these "retrospective narratives" as a manifestation, among other things, of a kind of "collective mourning," one consequence of the long period of repression endured by Hungarians under Stalinism. I interpret Mészáros's Diary films as a model of cinematic representation that integrates documentary and fiction in an autobiographical mode as a means of resisting "official forgetting," the totalitarian efforts to obliterate and distort the past. Such films, I argue, also serve as a form of public discourse that continues to play an important role in the recent changes in Hungary and elsewhere in East-Central Europe, articulating in image and word that which was, for decades, repressed from popular consciousness.[39]

A groundbreaking force in this autobiographical/historical cinematic effort, Márta Mészáros's extraordinary accomplishments in documentary and feature film took place within a national film industry whose structure—despite collegial and critical opposition—enabled her to produce regularly for more than three decades. Feminist studies of the interrelationship of cinema by women directors and gender have rarely been privileged to boast such historical sweep in the lives of their subjects.

Consequently, we will want to consider how reading Mészáros's controversial status as cultural Other may lead to a confrontation with the Self. As the Cold War ends and the East Bloc is no longer, we must be particularly concerned with the analysis of these interrelationships: Mészáros's *oeuvre* poses a direct challenge to our Western tendencies to isolate or privilege biography, image, gender, culture, or text without accounting sufficiently for their complex interplay. Today in what was formerly the socialist People's Republic of Hungary, the attention of young people is concentrated on questions of historical responsibility for the difficult present they face, while filmmakers of Mészáros's generation continue to reflect upon mourning and remembrance, the historical lies and unfulfilled promises of the revolution and the 1956 uprising. With the approach of a European community of the 1990s, and in view of Hungary's drive to be a part of that community, it is a privileged moment for understanding the dynamics of this transitional visual space between collective discourse and gendered subjectivity.

2 A CINEMATIC AUTOBIOGRAPHY
The Documentaries

From the film academy professors who rejected the "excessive" realism of an early documentary film on Hungarian peasants to studio officials and censors made uneasy by her audacious choice of subjects, Márta Mészáros's professional career has often encountered incomprehension, derision, and overt opposition. Yet even during the anxious years of Stalinist repression, when few of her colleagues dared to challenge representational discourses that controlled the regime of the gaze, Mészáros refused to "forget." Milan Kundera's formulation from the perspective of a Czech writer in exile seems to speak for her as well: "Forgetting is a form of death ever-present in life: but forgetting is also the great problem of politics. When a big power wants to deprive a small country of its national consciousness, it uses the method of organized forgetting."[1] If, as the noted historian István Deák has remarked, Stalinism "lies on the Hungarian national conscience like a horrifying nightmare,"[2] Mészáros's film project has empowered viewers to awaken from it by deconstructing the realities of the present while appearing to be overwhelmingly preoccupied with the past. The political and personal context in which she matured—childhood and adolescence in the time of Stalin—set the stage for a highly refined documentary approach to cinema. A thematics of uncovering hidden truths, coupled with multiple representations of departure, bereavement, mourning, and return, are discernible in all stages of her work and cannot be disconnected from her own life story. From early documentary essays on the effects of urbanization on rural Hungary to popularizations of scientific subjects, from biographical and esthetic portraits of painters, sculptors, and other artists to studies in cultural and political history, her work has in some sense always been about the past, a form of what I call "retrospective narrative" in which the interconnections among personal experience, political ideology, and national identity that later became the hallmark of Eastern European cinema are foregrounded. The "organized forgetting" pressed upon small nations of the former East bloc—a methodical obliteration of national cultural identity in the service of a supranational socialism—was in fact resisted by other filmmakers as well. Hungarian cinema has earned its international reputation as much for its formal innovation and avant-garde experimentation as for the poignancy with which filmmakers have interpreted the meaning of history, as evident in the rural populist narratives of Károly Makk and Zoltán Fábri, Gábor Bódy's epic *Narcissus and Psyche* (*Nárcisz és Psyché*, 1980), and István Dárday and Györgyi Szalai's *The Documentator*.[3] Mészáros's career covers four distinct moments in Hungarian cinema: the brief period of liberalization between 1953 and 1956; the rise of auteurist cinema in the 1960s; the development of the avant garde, notably at the Béla Balázs Studio, from 1965 to the present; and the "new wave" of the 1970s and 1980s.[4]

In highlighting Mészáros's tendency toward retrospective narratives, I am guided in part by the psychoanalytic literature on mourning and grief that suggests the acceptance of the present may be thwarted by incomplete mourning for what has been lost in the past. A mourning group, whether conscious or unconscious of the specificity of its loss, behaves like a bereaved individual in the strategies upon which it relies to replace that loss. Holocaust survivors, Germans with respect to the legacy of Nazism, and Vietnam veterans all create symbolic objects such as monuments, religious artifacts and shrines, or texts linking them to the departed persons, country, or hopes. Likewise, those like Mészáros who grew up under Stalinism create corresponding cultural representations of a group self through retrospective narratives. Hungarians coming to terms with the consequences of the post-Stalinist period may thus be seen as engaged in a delayed mourning ritual, having been previously denied validation of private and shared grief by official communist party denials of historical and personal events they themselves experienced.[5]

Throughout her cinematic *oeuvre*, Márta Mészáros interweaves documentary, fiction, and autobiography at once as historical document and as a form of self-analysis. The interplay among these temporal and spatial registers is, in her view, anchored in early experience: "Each one of us is formed by our childhood and past. . . . At the time when my country's new society was in its childhood, I was a child too. Once an adult, each of us must face up to our past and childhood."[6] Eastern European artists have, to be sure, been both constrained and at the same time empowered by the often conflicting demands of political realities and artistic expression, in contrast to their Western counterparts. Paradoxically, however, while the insistence on prevailing socialist-realist esthetics and central governmental control provided a point of opposition for artists in small East-bloc nations such as Hungary, they also served to unite those similarly affected by otherwise disparate political and cultural perspectives. Those like Mészáros, whose identity was formed both in tandem with and in opposition to that of the nation, were positioned to feel accountable as well for the country's fate, especially in Hungary where film production maintained a steadily visible—albeit small—international profile.[7] One might suppose that this paradox informs, to a great extent, the often rueful and even ruthless interrogation of society, past and present, that characterizes much of postcommunist East-Central European intellectual life. In order to produce a text under conditions that demand denial and deception, the artist who continues privately to pursue an internal, subjective analysis whose status is officially deprecated by the State is working under pressures rather different from those encountered in the West.[8]

Disguised as historical drama or masked as private fantasy, remnants of the "double life" well known to former Soviet and East-Central European culture continued to haunt its cinematic practice as recently as the close of the 1980s. The schism between the language of outward conformism and that of inward dissent, which has also been called a form of "inner exile" or emigration, persisted despite the gradual perestroika that overtook Hungary well in advance of its more violent manifestations in neighboring countries. In "Mourning and Melancholia," Freud writes:

> The occasions which give rise to the illness extend for the most part beyond the clear case of a loss by death, and include all those situations of being slighted, neglected, or disappointed, which can import opposed feelings of love and hate into the relationship or reinforce an already existing ambivalence.[9]

The narrative and visual strategies of Mészáros's cinema—documentary, fiction, and autobiography—arouse spectatorial identification with such mourning. Her interrogation of a nation's loss of self-esteem under Stalin and post-Stalinist regimes is at the same time an alternative to much East European "literature of inwardness" in its subversion of the very state structure under which it was produced.[10] Mészáros's "retrospective narratives," then, are marked by the pull of the past and the absences at its center:

> I consider myself absolutely Hungarian. . . . At the same time I was undoubtedly exposed to many other influences . . . my attraction to things Slavic, I think, will remain with me throughout my life. One can love one's homeland from afar just as well . . . I have always been excited by the problems of roots, of how one is sought after and found by one's homeland. . . . This subject is traced, one way or another, through all my films, including the Diaries.[11]

Articulated by someone whose life has been so intimately bound up with the trajectory of her nation, the director's observation suggests the inextricability of autobiography and cinema, and the degree to which their interplay solicits a more sustained theorizing than it has thus far received either in autobiographical literature or film theory. We would not go too far, in fact, in suggesting that the intersections between cinema and autobiography define a neglected area of inquiry, one which, in contrast to its literary counterpart and to other film genres, is only now beginning to be recognized.[12]

In forms that range from home movies and diaries to dramatized narrative reconstructions and cinéma-vérité self-portraits, autobiographical films invite critical attention on numerous levels, the most pertinent of which to Mészáros's work are the mélange of fictional and documentary modes and the representation of gender. The whole fabric of Mészáros's cinema, for that matter, offers a paradigm for extending our inquiry into the analysis of individual autobiographical films, the points of convergence between autobiographical literature and film—their ethics, economics, and psychology—and the cultural issues that define the terms of their creation and reception.[13]

To appreciate more fully the ways in which Márta Mészáros's cinema offers an extraordinary window at once on postwar Hungarian life and on the possibilities of autobiographical cinematic praxis, we do well here to reflect a moment on the limits and possibilities of the autobiographical subject as constructed by and in cinema. In his classic essay "Conditions and Limits of Autobiography," George Gusdorf discusses the search for the "specific intention of autobiography and its anthropological prerogative as a literary genre." In so doing, he differentiates between a recapitulation of the individual's externally articulated self and a more internal, interpretive search for self-knowledge, arguing that "autobiography is a second reading of experience, and it is truer than the first because it adds to experience itself consciousness of it." Although this statement was intended to refer primarily to literary genres, Gusdorf's conception of autobiography nevertheless encapsulates as well the dialectic between present and past that undergirds the autobiographical gesture in cinema, the desire to "situate what I am in the perspective of what I have been."[14]

The proliferation of narrative autobiographical films by feature directors stands as eloquent testimony to the adaptability of the genre for visual as well as literary artists. Among the very first motion pictures, after all, were the "home movies" of the Lumière brothers, domestic tableaux of their own family members dining together or feeding the baby. And films that take as their subject aspects, albeit often disguised, of the director's life have long been a hallmark of popular cinema; we have only to think of Ingmar Bergman and Federico Fellini, François Truffaut and Woody Allen, to be reminded of the more openly narcissistic qualities of the autobiographical impulse.[15] The efforts of these and other directors—most of whom, the reader will have noted, are male—are tantamount to a "canon" of mainstream autobiographical film, from *Annie Hall* to *Scenes from a Marriage* to *All That Jazz*.[16]

These and other first-person narrative films overlap with literary autobiography by virtue of the motifs usually associated with that genre: a pressing—and often long-delayed—urgency to narrate a family history; a wish to offer "reparation" to those one has presumably harmed or disappointed; and a longing to be reconciled with powerful "objects" from the past, a phenomenon which may be interpreted as a stage in the normal human process of mourning for what is lost. The psychoanalyst Roy Schafer understands this need for reworking one's internal relationship to primary individuals from one's past by proposing that in psychic reality "the object is immortal," suggesting that, from the subject's standpoint, "there can be no thoroughgoing object loss."[17] Representation of such internal experience, reconstructed and fantasized in visual and auditory registers, may permit the subject of cinematic autobiography (who may also simultaneously be narrator/director/actor) to rework object loss and hence reconstruct identity.

For today's postdeconstructionist spectators and readers, cinematic representation—autobiographical or otherwise—of a subject position is necessarily conditioned by heightened attention to postmodern notions of authorship.[18] Rather, the construction of "self" through symbolic discourse—be it written or oral language, painted surface, or electronically transmitted sound—is shaped by the discursive practices of individuals in their infinitely varied subject positions. In other words, the inscription of self comes into being and is communicated by means of its inextricability from the discourse in which it is founded. The autobiographical written or spoken word—and, for that matter, its filmed counterpart—thus implicates the subject in an act of fragmentation, a splitting between the writing self and the one that is written. A useful example comparable to that of Márta Mészáros, and illuminating for our purposes here, may be found in Nathalie Sarraute's autobiographical text *Childhood*, where Sarraute's use of a double as an interrogating voice that repeatedly shadows the primary narrator embodies this split. Sarraute thereby reminds the reader that even—better yet, especially—the memory of an autobiographer may well be as untrustworthy as the unreliable narrator of modern literature, at precisely those moments when the text threatens to overwhelm by its seductive strategies. In Michel Foucault's phrase, words are "insuperably inadequate" to the task of conveying visual memory, for the image is eroded or distorted by the very effort of translating it verbally:

> It is well known that in a novel narrated in the first person, neither the first person pronoun, the present indicative tense, nor, for that matter, its signs of localization refer directly to the writer, either to the time he wrote, or to the specific act of writing; rather, they stand for a "second self" whose similarity to the author is never fixed and undergoes considerable alteration within the course of a single book.[19]

While a verbal narrative of one's life falls prey to the distortions, repressions, and transformations resulting from human subjectivity and the fallibility of memory, there is evidence from psychoanalysis that images are more directly linked to the internal experiential world. As Ingmar Bergman has noted: "I take up the images from my childhood, put them into the 'projector,' run them into myself, and have an entirely new way of evaluating them."[20] The same may be said of Márta Mészáros in her role as professional picture-taking witness—one of the more provocative social roles of contemporary life—who exists in a kind of double exposure, a permanent state of resistance to and implication in self-presentation, and to which the distinguished tradition of Hungarian photography abundantly attests (one has only to remember Moholy-Nagy, Brassaï, Capa, and Kertész, all of whom were, like Mészáros, disdainful of an overclarifying self-consciousness). But these concerns transgress national and gender boundaries to raise fundamental concerns with regard to the interconnections among the politics of authorship, the dynamics of representation, and the nature of spectatorship.[21]

In this sense, then, Mészáros combines narrative techniques, visual styles, and thematic concerns that address the historical and political exigencies of the moment of their making. Central to her method in its diverse expressions is a commitment to enact what she has stated to be the *responsibility* of the adult individual to discover his or her identity by confronting the childhood self, an activity that demands at times a somewhat ruthless invasion of one's own memory, an audacious confrontation with one's own decisive moments. Whereas the desirability of coming to terms with one's identity by knowing who one has been—what family background, ethnicity, political identity—is virtually a given of contemporary social discourse, in Mészáros's case it is also a psychological necessity, a personal need to "fill in the blanks" of Stalin-era history. To this obligation she addresses herself consistently throughout the decades of her filmmaking.

Márta Mészáros spent a substantial portion of her childhood in the Soviet Union after her parents emigrated there in 1936, having been born in Budapest in 1931. Her father, László Mészáros, a distinguished sculptor and a man of strong communist convictions, was the prototype of the "old communist radicals" later portrayed in her Diary trilogy. For his commitment to pre-Stalinist communist ideals, he was arrested in 1938, prosecuted in one of the "show trials" of the period, and executed. Her mother, also a talented artist, died in 1942, four years after the birth of Mészáros's sister, when Mészáros was eleven years old.

In 1960, she married the Hungarian film director Miklós Jancsó, with whom she raised three children (two of whom, Nyika and Zoltán, are cinematographers), and from whom she was divorced in 1973.[22] Of Jancsó, Mészaros has said:

Jancsó made me Hungarian. He taught me what this country is all about. Without Jancsó, my return to Hungary would have been much more difficult. At the same time we had a very close association: we thought about the same things, worked on the same things, helped to keep each other's souls intact. We were married for fourteen years, and this association was broken off by him. We divorced. Here I was with all the children who took up my time; I had to pay attention to them, bring them up. It wasn't easy, but if you have to, you can do it.[23]

Mészáros's search for missing parents or parental figures, and a concomitant quest on the part of many of the adult protagonists for children lacking in their lives, is predominant in every period of her work. In the Diary trilogy, set for the most part in Hungary in the 1950s, this dynamic operates both on the biographical, historical level and as a metaphor of separation from—and the longing for fusion with—primary love objects, as her protagonists seek reparation and reconciliation with lost family members as well as national identity. In keeping with these details of Mészáros's life, the first part of the trilogy, *Diary for My Children*, is set in postwar Hungary. Its point of view is that of the director's younger alter-ego, who has returned there in 1947 with members of the revolutionary communist underground exiled for a decade in the Soviet Union. The young Juli, played by Zsuzsa Czinkóczi, the nonprofessional actress previously cast by Mészáros in *The Two of Them* (*Ők ketten*, 1977) and *Just Like at Home* (*Olyan mint otthon*, 1978), occupies the principal role in all three parts of the Diary trilogy.

The group is welcomed by Magda, now an influential cadre in the Hungarian Communist Party, but who, together with the older man Juli calls "grandfather," had been a member of the underground movement living in the Soviet Union with Juli's family. Magda's character is drawn from Mészáros's own foster mother, a rigidly punitive woman for whom her feelings were equally ambivalent. Juli's aversion to this powerful "aunt" is palpably obvious from the start: the uneasy quality of their encounters recalls those of prior "surrogate" mother-daughter dyads in *Adoption* (*Örökbefogadás*, 1975) and *The Two of Them*, without, however, the redemptive sensual intimacy that ultimately wins out in the earlier films. Ushering the disoriented young woman into her bedroom in Magda's comfortably appointed apartment, Juli rejects the older woman's awkwardly unfamiliar gesture of affection:

MAGDA: Why do you always turn your head away?
JULI: I don't like to be stroked. . . . Why don't you have a husband?
MAGDA: I did, but he divorced me . . . a long, long time ago, when I was young.
JULI: Didn't he love you? . . . Didn't you ever want a child?
MAGDA: I didn't have the time. But maybe it's not too late. You can be my child.

When situated within the discourse of contemporary Western feminism, this exchange might be expected to culminate in an alliance between two women isolated by historical circumstance, their generational differences allayed by a shared sexuality. But Mészáros does not permit such bonding to take place: quite the contrary. Her posture rigid, Juli moves beyond Magda's reach to the window from which she sees an old building being demolished by a wrecking ball, clearly a reminder of the destruction of the past taking place as the new socialist Hungary is created. At that instant, she recalls herself as a child in flashback as she cries out: "Mother (*Anyu!*), wait for me." Her radiantly youthful mother, in flowing summer dress and long hair, a sharp contrast to Magda's severe uniform, grasps the child's hand as the camera remains stationary, coolly observing the receding image of their closeness. It is a scene of pre-oedipal, blissful union, mother and daughter alone together in harmony with the striking beauty of the landscape, far from the film's present-tense starkness.

In contrast to the dreamlike material of the autobiographical Diary films, Mészáros concentrates in her earlier feature work on the realities of women struggling to achieve both autonomy and intimacy, compelled by less than favorable circumstances—loneliness, divorce, unwilling partners, or infertility—to seek a daughter or mother. The insistent motif of *Diary for My Children* is not, however, primarily a wish for the "good enough mother" or daughter lacking in the protagonists' lives.[24] Instead, the entire Diary trilogy is structured around an absent, idealized father, its most consistent trope. Aspects of Mészáros's male characters seem to constitute paternal elements or part-objects, a reference perhaps to the false paternalism—indeed, the deformed patriarchal system—of Stalin and his associates, whose propaganda was specifically directed toward the vulnerabilities of those seeking the comfort of surrogate and illusory paternal strength in the Party's ideology.[25] With regard to her depiction of male characters, Mészáros has noted:

> All I did was to show how they saw things and reacted in terms of the stereotypes established in them for centuries. I have never seen more weak, miserable, cowardly and intolerable men than in the films of Bergman and Fellini. But that's accepted because the directors are men. If a woman showed a fraction of that impotence in her male characters, she was immediately labeled a feminist! Besides, considering that men have helped me throughout my life, I have no reason—or right—to be "against men." It's simply that women and men see the world in different ways. Both sides have to be open.[26]

Mészáros reinforces the alliance—at once political and emotional—between lovers and fathers by casting Jan Nowicki in both roles in the Diary trilogy. After her first meeting with János, when Juli glances back at him after they have parted, she recalls her father in flashback in an identical position of affection toward her, as we hear her child's voice crying "Father!," a cry that reverberates throughout the trilogy and is only partly mirrored in representations of the mother/daughter bond.

Nevertheless, Juli's mother is represented as a nurturing, sensuous woman, adored by her daughter. When her friend Tomi asks Juli to describe her mother, she responds: "Red hair, green eyes, tall, sad, happy, unlucky, and lovely. She drew, sang, and spoke four languages. . . . we were always together. I went to school and sometimes we went to see a film together." Photographs of Mészáros's mother bear resemblance to this description, and the director acknowledges that these qualities were hers as well, including the four languages she spoke as a child.[27] During her narrative, we see mother and daughter together at an outdoor movie projection in the Soviet Union, Juli being affectionately reassured that the actors who have been killed will reappear again in another film. Juli's clandestine passion for cinema, carried out at great risk to herself and in spite of Magda's threats, may be understood to be linked to this earlier shared pleasure with her real mother; it affords her the only locus of independence available under the strict guardianship of Magda.

Cinema as privileged, eroticized space, the movie theater as a zone that promotes fantasy and dream—these are the associations established by the narratives of Diary for My Children and Diary for My Loves that link an adolescent girl's desire with her eventual choice of profession, the autobiographical film with its author.[28] The authorial voices of Mészáros within and outside the cinematic text, as well as the maternal voice of the author's mother, are thus enacted through a complex series of temporal and spatial references.[29]

As Juli's account of her life acquires narrative momentum, she recalls for Tomi's benefit her pregnant mother summoning her: "She stood in front of the house, her stomach huge. She could hardly stand the pain. We walked to a hospital far away in another village." The mother's face contorted in pain, we see her attended by solicitous, white-clad nurses as the little girl waits alone on the steps outside, covering her ears to drown out her mother's piercing screams. Juli continues her monologue: "The baby died. We were always together." This representation of pre-oedipal intimacy, ruptured by the death of an infant, is re-cathected throughout Mészáros's work through the figure either of childless women or motherless children.

As Juli explains that her father was arrested soon thereafter at dawn, the camera cuts to a stand of pine trees on a steep mountain enshrouded in fog in a symbolic reference to disappearance and death.[30] Terrified and helpless, Juli and her mother watch the police enter and search the house. As they take her father away, he looks into his daughter's eyes and departs with the words: "I'm going away now. I'll come back in a few days. Why don't you say something? Look after your mother." The child's mute disbelief is registered in a gaze that suggests the magnitude of the betrayal she is about to endure—having heard what will likely be the first of many lies—and that implies that she will resolutely refuse to accept their claims to truth.[31] After a passionate final embrace with his wife, Juli's father ceremoniously drapes the head of an unfinished clay sculpture as the camera lingers on the art work.[32]

The thread of Juli's interrupted narrative, delivered in a restrained, at times solemn tone, takes up again the trauma of her mother's subsequent illness. As she speaks the line, "I visited her every day and took her soup and black bread," we see her as a child peering into the hospital window from the wall below, learning of her mother's death only by the sight of her empty bed in the six-person ward. In shock and unable to express her grief, she rides home alone in a horse-drawn cart; there, her mother's body is laid out for burial, surrounded by her father's sculptures of female nudes. "I didn't go to her funeral," she explains, "I didn't feel she was dead."[33] In the next cut, wind whistles through tall pines in a misty fog as Juli sits alone on one of three grave mounds, marked only by flowers: "The war came, everyone was crying—children, women, men. But I didn't die—I remained alive." The guilt of the child survivor and the inevitable depression that accompanies it are delicately inscribed in this restrained comment from a child abandoned— albeit unwillingly—by both parents. Mészáros's understated directorial strategy calls attention to the irreducible and undeniable subjectivity of such an experience while leaving open wider possibilities for spectatorial identification with the memory of objective historical events. In this way, her project complements that of other filmmakers of her own generation and younger, engaged in the work of reconciliation and reassessment of the past.[34]

In contrast to Juli, Juli's father, portrayed in soft focus and celestially bright lighting, emerges on screen as larger than life, the heroic sculptor at work in a monumental stone quarry as a flock of birds circle overhead. Tenderness and physicality are emphasized in a subsequent sequence of idyllic familial contentment, the splendor of the sylvan setting at odds with the child Juli's wistful vision of her parents embracing on a blanket under the trees. Mészáros's lyrical musical motif heightens the mood of eroticism suffused with anticipatory dread as Juli's father lovingly carries his wife into the mountain lake and the camera tracks back to reveal the fragile happiness of this tiny, vulnerable family, lost in the vastness of the landscape. Later, in a frightening scene out of a totalitarian nightmare, Juli awakens from a deep sleep, having dreamt of her father just as the police arrive to seize János. That moment is intercut with a flashback to her father's arrest as the young child looks on in mute rage and humiliation.[35] Although Mészáros is reluctant to discuss details of her early life, it is clear that she lived through precisely such violent moments in which the authority of the state—whether legitimate or otherwise—intervened in family life at an early age, with predictably dramatic consequences.[36]

Like her protagonist Juli, the young Mészáros was enamoured of movies, spending hours at the cinematheque instead of in class.[37] After graduation from secondary school in Budapest, she applied to—but was rejected by—the Hungarian Film School, from which most aspiring directors, cinematographers, and screenwriters eventually graduate. With support from her foster mother, like Magda a high-ranking party member, Mészáros was able to fulfill her longing to study filmmaking with her acceptance by the Moscow Academy of Cinematographic Art (V.G.I.K.), where her mentors included Soviet theorists and filmmakers such as Chauduri. It was only after the end of the 1956 revolution that Mészáros—like Juli—returned to Hungary. In her interviews with me, she recalls her experiences at the Soviet Academy in these terms:

> My own general cultural education in Moscow was very good; it was the time of Stalin, of course. But the film education wasn't so good. The Moscow Institute was, financially speaking, quite impoverished, and there weren't enough cameras or film stock for our needs. But I began making documentaries immediately in 1955, and continued to do so for many years. Altogether I completed about one hundred documentary films; this was my real education.

The year of her homecoming signalled the production of Mészáros's documentary diploma film, *A History of Albertfalva* (*Albertfalvai történet*, 1957), a study of a small Hungarian town that was to become a model for her later documentary work. Over the next ten years, she worked for the Budapest Newsreel Studio, producing some two dozen short documentaries, most of which focused on the arts or popular scientific subjects.

Between 1958 and 1959, Mészáros spent substantial periods in Romania, making films for Bucharest Documentary Studio and traveling extensively in the ethnically mixed, remote countryside of its northernmost region, Transylvania.[38] From this period of her film career, the only extant documentary concerns religious Hungarian villagers in Transylvania.[39] A short subject entitled *Life Goes On* (*Az élet megy tovább*) was made in 1959 in Bucharest. But these early travels in the picturesque mountainous terrain so cherished by Hungarians provided images and experiences that were to reappear later in the Diary films, and especially in *Bye Bye Red Riding Hood* (*Piroska és a farkas*, 1989).

Throughout the late 1950s and early 1960s, Márta Mészáros produced numerous films with the Hungarian documentary studios and for educational television. Even such seemingly straightforward, "nonpolitical" realist work was, however, not unproblematic, as she told me in a 1988 interview:

> At that time my family was so poor: I needed work, my children were small, Jancsó was between films, and work was absolutely necessary for me. I made a number of educational, nature, and science films. Some of my art documentaries displeased officials because they were produced in the early 1960s when avant-garde art as such was not recognized, and films such as the Szentendre school

and the piece on Jenő Barcsay were considered too controversial. . . . The old hard-liners favored the realist school that perpetuated in many ways the socialist-realist tradition.

Aside from the popular science and nature films of her documentary period, Mészáros has concentrated primarily on the topics of childhood, youth, and visual artists. Her best work in that genre are a 1962 film on the painter János Tornyai, and *Miklós Borsos* (*Borsos Miklós*, 1967), a short subject on one of Hungary's greatest sculptors who lives and works on Tihany, a peninsula on the shores of Lake Balaton.

Two beautifully composed short subjects, *Colors of Vásárhely* (*Vásárhelyi szinek*, 1961) and *Szentendre: Town of Painters* (*Festők városa*, 1964), extend the scope of her vision to the artists' colonies in which many Hungarian sculptors, painters, and craftspeople live and work. Mészáros's prize-winning 1962 documentary *A Town in the Awkward Age* (*Kamaszváros*) is a chronicle of the difficulties of a new socialist town, and anticipates the director's later investigation of state policies in feature films such as *The Land of Mirage* (*Délibábok országa*, 1983). *Blow-Ball* (*Bobita*, 1964), a twenty-two minute documentary investigation about an unwanted child of divorced parents, likewise takes up a concern that becomes central to Mészáros's future filmmaking. Finally, perhaps most important of all her documentary projects is a cinematic homage to her father, the sculptor László Mészáros. Unlisted in official Hungarofilm filmographies, the film nevertheless warrants closer reading than the other documentaries of this period, for its very subject is paradigmatic of Mészáros's entire cinematic *oeuvre*.

In Memoriam: László Mészáros (1978) is prefaced by Picasso's credo: "Love is my art: that is the basis for my existence." We see first a self-portrait, then a photograph of the handsome László Mészáros as a female voiceover reads his daughter's words:

> His art died in 1938 when they took him away. I don't remember much of my father, so I am trying to re-evoke his image through this film. I want to re-create his life and trace his thoughts, to follow the road that made him a talented Hungarian sculptor.

It is rare enough for an East European film artist to portray such an openly personal subject with the support of the state production apparatus, and surely rarer still when the subject was the victim of execution as an enemy of the state. The exhortation to remember, to re-evoke, to re-recreate is therefore accorded special significance by this autobiographical project, and the viewer becomes a party to the inscription of Márta Mészáros's own life by means of this *memento mori* to her father. László Mészáros was born on September 18, 1905, in Kőbánya, a gritty working-class town of factory smokestacks and crumbling fences. His circumscribed world was not unlike that of many Hungarians of his class: his own father had worked as a foundryman in the nearby steel mill of Csepel Island, a famed stronghold of radical workers' movements which remains a district of Budapest.[40] The factory milieux portrayed by Márta Mészáros in her early feature films, in fact, draw heavily upon that background, offering an insider's view of the workplace. Thanks to a small inheritance, Mészáros's mother was finally able to move her family to Kispest, a suburb of Budapest, where she ran a small cafe/grocery shop. In such modest circumstances, the young László, one of six brothers, worked in the family business, spending summers on a neighboring farm where he grew to love the *puszta*, the peasants, horses, and fields that were to form the characteristic images of his sculpture.

In Memoriam describes in loving detail a countryside of thatched-roof, whitewashed houses, sun-swept wheat fields, and wild horses in the pasture. On the thick walls of the cottage where László Mészáros once lived and worked, hand-hewn farm implements ornament the walls like artworks, and the hills nearby are dotted with the traditional carved wooden graveposts of the peasant community. The opportunity to read this film with a prior knowledge of the director's feature work allows the viewer to observe in retrospect how gracefully these images—the "screen memories" or bedrock of Márta Mészáros's attachment to rural landscape—are threaded throughout her work. The alternating currents of peasant culture and the dynamic rhythms of the urban landscape punctuate Mészáros's films, as in her first feature, *The Girl*, with its close attention to the subtle detail of rural culture.[41]

To the dissonant accompaniment of Central Asian musical instruments, Mészáros's narrator recites the sculptor's accomplishments: a description of his first exhibition in 1928 begins, in a visual style typical of the director's earlier art documentaries, with a shot of the figure of a peasant woman seated in darkness. The lighting is turned up until the scene is fully illuminated, while the voice of the noted Hungarian artist István Dési Huber judges the work to be that of a preeminent twentieth-century Hungarian sculptor. The narrator then reads from a letter written by László Mészáros to his family when the young sculptor received a scholarship to Italy, explaining his artistic odyssey as a quest for "a new language . . . difficult to discover and to combine with one's own . . . [that breathes] in harmony with life." The restrained tone and compositional perfection of the film convey the filmmaker's empathic vision of the young father whom she scarcely knew, yet whose artistic spirit and committed political beliefs undeniably came to shape her own. Although these words are quoted on the soundtrack from the sculptor's writings, they seem to speak as well for the scope and motivation of his daughter's cinema:

> What is closest to my heart is the ordinary man, the proletariat, for I cannot and do not want to deny my own origins. Machinists, steelworkers and chimney sweeps, architects of all that surrounds us, reap no rewards in this life. But to

me they are pure and saintly, for working people are as beautiful as great rivers, priceless jewels full of life. . . . I cannot betray myself, cannot speak through interviews. What I hope most of all is that my sculptures speak for me.

In Memoriam: László Mészáros provides links missing from the story of Márta Mészáros's life by clarifying the reasons for her father's departure to the Soviet Union after his Italian sojourn. The narrator (ostensibly Mészáros's "voice") explains that popular interest in the origins of Hungarian nationality and ethnicity had led him to seek his ancestors in Central Asia and Siberia. Traveling there in 1931, the year of Márta's birth, he became enamoured with the icons and paintings, the folk architecture of Russian wooden churches, and the vastness of the steppes, which found their way into his art. Invited to establish the first academy of sculpture in Central Asia, László Mészáros was also active as an architect and interior designer. An admirer of Roman and Etruscan art, he fused folk motifs with elements of the peasant craftsmanship he appreciated, amalgamating them to create a characteristic style in statuary and portraiture. Mészáros composes her homage to his creative genius to a soundtrack of Mongolian, Turkmen, Khazak, and Uzbeki musical motifs that demonstrates her command of authentic folk traditions and an unusual cinematic musicality. The Central Asian villages resemble those of Transylvania, with their wooden houses and cultivated fields; these references to her father's world are extended and re-envisioned by Mészáros in the later Diary trilogy, just as motifs from her documentary period found their way into her earlier features. While it is obvious that artists often rework ideas at different developmental stages of life, Mészáros's approach tests itself systematically in a current work that serves as a laboratory for the next, to be developed and explored more fully thereafter.[42]

The film's intensity is dramatized toward the conclusion, when Mészáros's female narrative voice speaks of finding the house in which her beloved father lived and worked, another motif to be thematized in the paternal search of the Diary trilogy. On the night when the Russian police arrested him, the thirty-three-year-old Mészáros is said to have smiled, thinking it all a mistake, for he had planned to travel to Japan, America, and then back to Hungary. The viewer has been well positioned to experience the poignancy of the director's restrained anguish at the extinction of this young and talented man, an artist longing to continue his work. *In Memoriam* concludes with an epitaph that speaks to the interconnections among memory, history, and autobiography: "We must remember him . . . if we do not preserve his memory, his life and art will become part of our forgotten past."[43]

Through Mészáros's tribute, László Mészáros becomes an exemplary—even typical—case: a young East European artist with deep political convictions exiled, suppressed, and finally put to death by Stalinist forces. Of his fate Márta Mészáros says:

"No one really knows what happened, why they took him away. . . . Old painters and sculptors there say they learned everything from him . . . but at that time his opinionated personality, his tendency to speak out when he saw injustice being done, made him vulnerable to the Stalinist purges. The real question is: what happened to him? Did they take him to Siberia? Did they kill him? I don't know . . . official papers say only that he died in 1945. . . . But I'm going back to Moscow, now that the archives are opened, and I'll find his files.[44]

This unswerving dedication to the preservation of her father's memory, this refusal of the obliteration of historical memory—especially that of ordinary people in small East European nations—for the benefit of future generations, defines Mészáros's cinema, speaking beyond the personal to the most important political and cultural issues of our time.

3 FAMILY ROMANCES
The Early Features

In *Women Directors: The Emergence of a New Cinema*, one of the few studies in English to survey systematically East European women directors, Barbara Quart asserts, correctly in my view, that "Mészáros works from 'a woman's angle' . . . though [she] deals with male characters with considerable compassion, also frequently seeing the world through their eyes."[1] The implicit paradox of this statement points us toward the larger question of culturally grounded differences with regard to feminist interpretation, an issue taken up in chapter 1, and calls attention to the contradictory reception of Mészáros's films. East Europeans, influenced perhaps by the critical realism of György Lukács, tend to view her work in terms of the complexities of male-female relations, whereas Western and, in particular, feminist critics emphasize more exclusively her representation of the female condition. The noted Hungarian critic György Szabó is at pains to clarify the contradiction:

> Beginning with *Adoption*, there is a new perspective at work here that is based on the exposure of vulnerability between the sexes. This perspective embodies a wider judgment on social and historical conditions, yet it is also specific to our current situation in Hungary. To liberate ourselves, Mészáros contends, we must develop qualitative human relations. Therefore she justifiably opposes the label "feminism" for, as she says, ". . . even in specific women's problems, I am searching for the possibility of a more total human development." But on the other hand, the label 'feminism' is justified, at least here in Hungary, because her perspective is exclusively limited to the scope of male-female relations.[2]

From whose perspective, then, is "the label feminism" justified? Barbara Quart specifies that:

While *Nine Months* is clearly a feminist film, there is no idealization here, and no ideology, but the incalcitrant [*sic*] contradictory stuff of life and art, to which Mészáros always remains true. . . . As in *Nine Months*, the themes are directly feminist, though Mészáros denies she is a feminist. . . . At the same time, again, Mészáros' men characters are mostly hopeless. . . . The feminist note in Mészáros gets sounded even more strongly in the later films, *Nine Months* and *The Two of Them*. . . . But whatever the strong pull between women, the men in Mészáros' films are at once sympathetic and impossible figures.[3]

The debates at the center of these interpretations recur throughout Mészáros's career but are particularly resonant in response to her first group of features: *The Girl, Binding Sentiments* (*Holdudvar*, 1969), *Don't Cry, Pretty Girls* (*Szép lányok, ne sirjatok*, 1970) *At the Lorinc Spinnery* (*A lőrinci fonóban*, 1971), and *Riddance*, five important films made between 1968 and 1973 by a filmmaker whose documentary career had already made its mark. With the release of *Riddance* in 1973, Mészáros (now 42) also ended her marriage to Miklós Jancsó, Hungary's most celebrated and innovative director. There is reason to suspect that the timing of these events may have been more than mere coincidence, as Mészáros steadily earned a reputation independent of her more famous husband. The tiny community of Hungarian cinema, with its overlapping friendships and enmities, does little to ease such an autonomous move by a woman filmmaker, making her achievement all the more exceptional.

Gender relations are, to be sure, problematized in each of these films. But sexuality is always carefully contextualized within the ongoing crisis of Hungarian life, for Mészáros does not allow the viewer to escape from the consequences of that context. Hungary's involvement in three revolutions within as many generations, and the grievous losses it suffered in both world wars, must not be overlooked as contributing to this pervasive sense of crisis.[4] Set against such relatively constant national trauma, the persistence of loss is a frequent narrative trope: "Nothing's Lost" (Minden megvan), proclaims the title of a contemporary Hungarian short-story collection, an incantation against despair, as images of absent fathers, lovers, brothers, and sons fill the pages of contemporary East-Central European literature.[5] Representations of loss are no less a motif of postwar Hungarian cinema: Kézdi-Kovács's *When Joseph Returns* (*Ha megjön József*, 1973) and Károly Makk's *Looking at Each Other* (*Egymásra nézve*, 1982), Sándor Simó's *My Father's Few Happy Years* (*Apám néhány boldog eve*, 1977) and István Szabó's *Father* (*Apa*, 1966) are but a few examples that chronicle the often unmourned losses of human life, land, international esteem. Each of these films in fact is structured upon a paternal quest: whether undertaken through the socialist state apparatus or by means of an interrogation of generation and gender, the past is inescapably summoned to task.

Freud has suggested that the most important event of a life—and here he specifies a *man's* life—is the day of his father's death: "By the time [his own father] died his life had long been over, but at a death the whole past stirs within one."[6] And several years later, in his preface to *The Interpretation of Dreams*, the text Freud considered to be his most important and valuable, he writes:

> For this book had a further subjective significance for me personally—a significance which I only grasped after I had completed it. It was, I found, a portion of my own self-analysis, my reaction to my father's death—that is to say, to the most important event, the most poignant loss, of a man's life.[7]

The vast literature on the history of psychoanalysis attests to Freud's use of his own object-world as the crucible for a subsequent theoretical elaboration and to his self-analysis as a cornerstone of the psychoanalytic technique and method. Such formulations were inevitably informed by his personal obsessions and those of Victorian, patriarchal Vienna and continue to be revised, rejected, and reinterpreted by practitioners and scholars of every persuasion, in particular from Lacanian perspectives in film theory.[8] Contemporary psychoanalytic critics have, to be sure, provided compelling critiques of the ways in which masculine bias (at once unconscious and culturally constructed) permeates Freud's work and is, for that matter, central to certain psychoanalytic theories of psychosexual development. And the neo-Freudian emphasis on the power of the paternal to the exclusion of the pre-oedipal continues to occupy feminist psychoanalytic theorists today.[9]

That Freudian hypotheses with regard to the centrality of the paternal figure and to the "normal" course of mourning are the subject of continuing psychoanalytic debates serves to problematize these considerations for our understanding of East European culture, Hungarian cinema, and the work of Márta Mészáros in particular. On the cultural level, the inability to mourn has been viewed as an implicit awareness that such mourning may be experienced as an acknowledgement of responsibility for the crimes of the state. In perhaps the most influential European work on the subject, Alexander Mitscherlich and Margarete Mitscherlich explore the interlocking psychological reactions of guilt, shame, recognition, and forgiveness in postwar Europe.[10] For Mészáros, personal and national losses of great magnitude were sustained at an early age, with the death of both parents and exile from her country. For her, filmmaking serves as a necessary stage in the process of reintegrating losses, the "normal" mourning for which is truncated or displaced, and which may be inexpressible in other forms. "I am fortunate," she states, "to have the opportunity, through my films, to psychoanalyze myself, and so to communicate what I think and feel."

At once a vehicle for self-analysis and social analysis, exploration of the imaginary and work of mourning, Mészáros's cinema is also an intervention in the East European grief-work of the post–Stalinist period, a departure from concealment, paranoia, and the disturbed and often abusive communications that are among its legacies.[11] Distinguishing between mourning and melancholia, Freud suggests a wider application to the reworking of object loss: "In melancholia, the occasions which give rise to the illness extend for the most part beyond the clear case of a loss by death, and include all those situations of being slighted, neglected or disappointed, which can import opposed feelings of love and hate into the relationship or reinforce an already existing ambivalence."[12]

Although the clinical dimensions of this theory originally concerned the trajectory of an object relationship, when transposed to the cultural sphere it describes well Hungarian filmmakers' preoccupation with an incompletely integrated past. For, in Freud's analysis, melancholia differs from mourning in a single feature: "a fall in self-esteem": "In mourning it is the world which has become poor and empty; in melancholia it is the ego itself." Mészáros's self-analytic method enabled her, like Freud, to rework and therefore mourn the private grief of early paternal loss and her country's public travail.[13] While Freud's theoretical paradigm of melancholia might also apply to a nation's "fall in self-esteem" as a result of injuries suffered through historical losses, Mészáros's authorship is more clearly, it seems to me, an instance of mourning.

In the short subjects of her early career, Mészáros had already begun to reveal a passion for representing human relationships in a state of existential crisis. *Blow-Ball* (1964), for example, a short feature about a child living alone with his mother in grim circumstances, portrays the son's thwarted needs for affection empathetically but without sentimentality, in a style that becomes in short order typical of Mészáros's unflinching gaze. The child's rejection by his remarried father, rendered in touching moments when the camera tracks his solitary play beyond the wall of the house, seems to confirm his existence as more burdensome than pleasurable to either parent.

A similar disequilibrium within the family leads a lonely young female protagonist on a search for maternal as well as paternal affection, albeit on a wider stage than in *Blow-Ball*, in Mészáros's first full-length feature, *The Girl* (*Eltávozott Nap* 1968, literally translated "the sun has set"). Here, Mészáros initiates the interrogation of parentage and family history that defines her work up to that time, as she said in a 1988 interview with me:

> In my fiction films . . . I thoroughly reconstruct situations and narratives: this is not due to a "documentary" view of life. I work very hard with my actors and leave them a great many possibilities for improvisation. I never write a scenario without knowing who will play the main role, and I often write my stories in terms of the personality of the actors with whom I want to work.

This personalized approach is immediately recognizable in a visit to the set, where she works with an enviable combination of familial intimacy and consummate professionalism, as longtime collaborators will confirm.[14]

In Zsonyi, the young female protagonist, the insecurity of an unwanted child is represented by restless, anxious gestures that suggest the weight of premature adulthood, in a style reminiscent of the neorealism of Rossellini, whose child protagonists are often left to fend for themselves in the streets of postwar Italy. At twenty-four, the orphan is now a textile-mill operative, aware of her illegitimate origins and of her mother's responsibility in giving her up for adoption (a topic Mészáros explores more deeply in a subsequent film, *Adoption*). It is an unsparing portrait in which the director's eye for documentary detail leaves little room for sentimentalization or self-indulgent pity. These, she seems to suggest, are the usually tough conditions of life: no relationship is privileged, no human bond—save an enduring longing for the absent, beloved parental object—supersedes conditions of human deprivation. The girl's desire to locate her biological parents eventually leads her to find her mother, now remarried and with a new family, in a nearby village.

At a time when the quest by adoptive children for their birth-parents was not yet a matter of wide public discourse even in Western media, Mészáros's unceremonious focus on such a topic in an East European context was daring. The girl is unprepared, however, for her mother's ambivalence about the eventual encounter; the camera impartially registers the older woman's denial of Zsonyi's reality as daughter, and hence the evidence of repressed past in the interest of a self-constructed present, and it records the disappointment of the daughter.

Denial of the biographical past of the subject—Zsonyi as repressed woman/other—functions here to destabilize the narrative by interrogating the status of "official" truth claims. Lying and its consequences in fact constitute a central thematic in Mészáros's later work, as we shall see in chapters 4 and 5. Here it is embodied by the mother's strategy of avoidance by which she deauthenticates the biological relationship by introducing the girl as her niece; her husband immediately expresses erotic interest in the girl, behaving seductively toward her the following day at the traditional Sunday afternoon dance.

Fleeing his advances, the young woman returns home on the train, where she is momentarily attracted to a young man who later invites her to his room. Although she agrees to meet him, the lack of spontaneity in her expression and gestures in a medium shot during the undesired lovemaking is reminiscent of similar moments in *Riddance* and *The Two of Them*, when the camera tracks back to reveal a woman's isolation from her lover. When they meet a final time, Mészáros captures the sadness of their mechanical coupling, conveying the embarrassment and futility of erotic adventure as an escape from the deeper pain of life.

When an unidentified middle-aged man visits Zsonyi at the mill where she works, begging her to speak with him, she again complies with a man's wish, and the two meet in a deserted restaurant. The unkempt stranger informs the girl that he knew her parents and has presented himself to her in acknowledgement of her written inquiries. We sense through the girl's guarded face that his romantic story is itself a lie, portraying as it does a great—and ostensibly fabricated—love between a man and woman, both of whom are now dead. She pays the tab and offers to help him, and her manner suggests that she suspects that *he* may be her father. One might conclude that Mészáros is implying that an inadequate father is better than none at all, as she herself suggests indirectly by making the alcoholic father in *The Two of Them* simultaneously appealing and impossible. Although little of this is conveyed by dialogue, the allusive direction evokes an unspoken—if precarious—communication between "father" and "daughter," as indeed it does in her subsequent films when the father/daughter dyad is primary.

In the final sequence of *The Girl*, Zsonyi is quickly attracted to her blond partner at the factory clubhouse dance, and although the couple's embrace at the conclusion is ambiguous, Mészáros creates for them an atmosphere that, at the very least, lacks the unhappy solitude of so many of her cinematic lovers. In the end, a sense of the precariousness and unpredictability of post–Stalinist life is counterbalanced in *The Girl* by the protagonist's determination to attain a degree of contentment, however minimal, in spite of the overwhelming odds arrayed against her, both by familial deprivation and sexual exploitation.

Mészáros's subsequent film, *Binding Sentiments* (1969, literally translated "the moon's aureole") constructs a narrative based on a classic triangle with oedipal overtones. The widow of a famous economist who has died tragically, her son, and his girlfriend are enclosed in a psychological tyranny reminiscent of Sartre's play *No Exit (Huis Clos)*. Edit, the widow (played by Mari Töröcsik, one of Hungary's finest film actresses), is morbidly preoccupied by memories of her recently deceased husband, the absent, "underwater" quality of her posture and demeanor virtually a clinical symptomatology of pathological mourning. Impatient with her depressive state and heedless of her mental anguish, the young couple try unsuccessfully to redirect her energies to the present. But Edit resists their attempts to lock her up in the country house they share, and Mészáros loses no opportunity to juxtapose the vitality of the younger woman with Edit's sadness.[15] Mészáros employs Edit's shattering realization that she had been less than happy with her husband as a parallel to the marriage of her friend Mancika, also a widow, just as in *The Two of Them* she compares the loveless bourgeois marriage of Mari with the destructive passion of Juli and her husband: "I don't remember my husband anymore," Edit confesses. "Sometimes I take his photograph and keep looking at him. I can't remember his face. You want to cry now, don't you, but you can't." Their private sorrow calls forth the more public suffering of a small East European nation unable to mourn its losses while in the grip of the "organized forgetting" of Stalinist ideology.

The fear of forgetting, Mészáros thereby suggests, is equal to the desire for oblivion, just as Alain Resnais's *Hiroshima Mon Amour* (1959) instantiates the conflicting polarities of memory and desire.[16] In that film, Emmanuelle Riva's memory of her dead German lover, murdered by a French bullet on the last day of the war in occupied France, is repressed for fifteen years until a new lover—this time Japanese—reawakens its memory for the first time. But Edit is not granted the transitional space in which to come to terms with her belated reappraisal, as she is confronted by the condolences of friends and colleagues such as the engineer Gyuri, whom she has not seen in fifteen years and who now abuses her with unsolicited remarks:

> He always pretended as if nothing had happened. Nothing. Though he knew lots of things had. He was right on course to become a great economist but he became a party functionary. . . . You are the beautiful, sad and honest widow who's having a fit of conscience. You wanted to live well, in comfort, in peace. But you never achieved peace because there's no peace inside you.

It is well documented that the values and discourse of Stalinism—the "double life" of words uttered without conviction or silenced by fear of reprisal—led many to abandon individual ideals in order to survive as "party functionaries," and Mészáros effectively utilizes the "personal" narrative to comment upon social reality. Unlike Resnais's heroine, however, Edit is deprived of the healing catharsis of new love or, for that matter, honest friendship. She is a kind of zombie, as if shellshocked by the dawning disparity between past and present, emotional truth and social appearance. Mészáros weaves into the personal narrative threads that lead outward to a wider political commentary, especially a critique of members of the party elite, a technique developed further in the Diary trilogy. In so doing, she subverts the very central authority that subsidized film production, a strategy perfected as well by other filmmakers whose work was regularly subjected to the censor's judgment. When Edit discusses the disposition of her husband's estate with her son Istvan, he seizes the opportunity to accuse her of having lived her entire life as a lie:

> ISTVAN: Mother, this is your affair. But you have to do this to the end. For the sake of my father's memory. . . . I won't let you hurt father's memory because, unlike you, I loved him.
> EDIT: That's true . . . we had nothing in common except that he cared for and kept me and we didn't get a divorce. It was he who was against it.

Disharmony and misunderstanding between men and women, mirroring as they do the larger politico-economic picture that defined the decade of Mészáros's first features, are here given voice for the first time in depth. The litany of disappointment and the female protagonists' resistance to the insufficiencies of their male companions and families evoke an ambiance of futility.

Only Edit's neighbor Margit shares her sense of loss by confiding that her own husband had also died a decade earlier, leaving her with nine children to raise, while Margit's daughter mourns the lost opportunity for a university education. Foreclosure of possibilities is thus added to death as a legitimate source of mourning: Mészáros consistently refers without judgment to the abusive domestic lives of her characters, as when Margit admits that her husband had been an abusive alcoholic. Workers or professionals, they are trapped in a tight circle of pain. But she allows the women a moment of respite together at Margit's house, where they encourage each other to drown their sorrows:

> Margit: If you loved him—drink. And if you didn't, drink!
> Edit: You think I'm a coward . . . well, that's what I am. I put up with my husband, I didn't get a divorce, I didn't have the guts to do it. But at least I know, I do know what I am like. . . . You just want to marry István because you went to bed with him. Because he's clever and handsome. But I know my son is just like his father.

Escape from the deceptions and anguish of domestic life, albeit fleeting, is nevertheless essential to a renewal of courage on the part of her female protagonists. *Binding Sentiments* concludes with the heroine's refusal to play the role of "gendarme" for her fiance's mother; despite her lover's entreaties, she decides to return to Budapest alone.

Refusal to compromise with a psychologically abusive or immature lover becomes a powerful stance for Mészáros's female protagonists with *Adoption* and *Riddance*. They enjoy no illusory "happy endings," no flight from the responsibility for their choices. The compulsion to repeat the errors of the previous generation is thus confronted, at the cost of status, stability, and companionship, in a diegetic universe of "no exit" and "no end."[17] Generational conflict, alcoholism and abuse are, in Mészáros's early features, an unpleasant fact of life in Hungary. Similarly, Vasily Pichul's Soviet film *Little Vera* (*Malen-kain Vera*, 1989) deconstructs, in nineteenth-century naturalist theatrical style, the economic and psychological ties that bind a contemporary Russian working-class family in the Soviet city of Zhdanov's grim urban landscape.[18]

Without the social, political, or artistic endorsement of many of her contemporaries, Mészáros represented in films of this period the bitter consequences of gender inequality, the intimately painful—and repressed—aspects of Hungarian life that were not addressed in otherwise excellent films by her colleagues. Her 1970 feature film *Don't Cry, Pretty Girls* offers a compelling portrayal of the intersections of working-class life and popular culture as Juli leaves her provincial home with her brother and fiance to work in a Budapest factory. She lives in the subculture of a workers' hostel with other young people separated from their parents and regional roots, bound together primarily by their function in the industrial economy.

The opening sequence, shot in cinéma-vérité style, shows a group of young male workers carrying their drunken older colleague to the factory showers in the same Csepel Island steel mill where Mészáros's grandfather once worked. On the soundtrack a popular song of the late 1960s celebrates a mythologized happy family, while urban youth are depicted at a mass rock concert, even more enraptured by the spectacle than their Western counterparts. Sung by Illés, a top rock group of the time, the lyrics lament such material realities as the lack of affordable housing and recreational areas for youth ("a place to make love with my girl"). In a clever reversal, members of the band photograph the audience; the protagonist Juli, attracted by the appealing atmosphere of the club scene, is torn between her fiance and the attractive, seductive Géza. There is no doubt where Mészáros's sympathies lie: the cinematic apparatus is clearly on the side of the young crowd angrily confronting police who harass them at an impromptu party in a crumbling, abandoned building slated for demolition.

Unlike Péter Gothár's *Time Stands Still* (1985), a retrospective reconstruction of the same period, *Don't Cry, Pretty Girls* is itself contemporary with the realities of international youth culture and rebellion against the parental world. The oppositional culture of rock music is given its due as a harbinger of social dissatisfaction; Mészáros's masterful use of lyrics and melody itself constitutes the contestatory statement she clearly intends to make.[19]

Perhaps in part because of the censorship exercised on Hungarian films of the period, Mészáros resorted to lyrics to intensify the audacity of her social critique. By the early 1980s, however, liberalization in Hungary had reached a moment when considerably more pointed accusations could be made within the narrative itself. *Don't Cry, Pretty Girls* features Kex, another highly influential rock group,[20] performing an *a cappella* version of "With All My Heart" by the modernist poet Attila József as the young people listen reverently:

> I have no father and no mother,
> I have no God, I have no land,
> neither cradle, nor a cover,
> nor kiss, nor lover's hand.[20]

The sense of utter desolation evoked by the poem speaks for a culture that in many ways paralleled that of the poet, also young, poor, working-class, fatherless, and abandoned by the state.[21] Echoing American youth-culture films of the 1950s and 1960s, *Don't Cry, Pretty Girls* offers a rather more optimistic denouement than many of Mészáros's films. Recognizing her fiance's feelings for her, Juli marries him in the presence of their friends, while

Géza attends the wedding accompanied by another in what we are meant to assume will be an unending series of girlfriends. The camera pans the "pretty girls" crying at the sad festivities, concluding that class and regional affinities supersede those of romantic love and individual desire.[22]

At the Lőrinc Spinnery (1971), a short documentary with dialogue, nonetheless warrants mention in this discussion of Mészáros's early features. A highly focused, beautifully textured study of three of the one thousand Hungarian women working in the Lőrinc spinning mill on the outskirts of Budapest, it represents a gesture of return to the director's love for documentary even as she approached wider recognition as a feature filmmaker. The film interweaves the lives of the three workers by allowing them to speak in their own voices. The first advises other women to remain faithful to their jobs, as we see close-ups of legs and hands working, and hear the deafening roar of weaving machines and the overseer's whistle. The camera quickens its pace to approximate the speed-up of workers on the line and the physical demands of the work itself, a primary motif of Mészáros's representation of factory workers.

The camera pans laterally to capture the motion of the looms while the forewoman admits in voiceover that she is trapped by a job so fatiguing that, by evening in the hostel, she has no energy left for anything but rest. We later see her at home alone in her kitchen, stirring a pot on the stove: "I went home for my holiday, I didn't go away anywhere. It's cheap and I like it . . . until I find somewhere else I'll have to go on living here . . . perhaps I'll get married some day." Her narrative stands for those of other voiceless factory operatives with minimal leisure time, many of whom also formed a part of the "second economy" of small private enterprises tolerated by the socialist government in desperate need of fiscal growth.

The second interview is set against the sight and sound of weaving machines as the woman explains her attachment to the factory in which she has virtually grown up:

> Why did I stay so long? Because the people here always stood by me and helped me whenever I needed it. I've been working here for twelve years . . . there's a good creche and nursery-school, so I never had any problems with the children. I could keep up with the job, and besides, they let me go on studying. I took my finals from the factory, and I'm still studying. I've got a factory youth-league flat; we members who did voluntary work and had a good record could, for a low deposit, secure a league flat.

Having joined the Communist Party six years earlier with the encouragement of the party secretary, she describes her progression from propagandist at the age of twenty-one to branch secretary: "I put all I had into it. . . . I feel I have stood the test." Her statement contrasts powerfully with other testimonies by party members such as those interviewed in Pál Schiffer's documentary, *Magyar Stories* (1988), in which the speakers—mostly male—renounce their former affiliation or admit to a sense of futility and waste.

In the next shot the woman is depicted at her weaving machine, her hands a blur of movement. Her account indicates satisfaction with her life and acceptance of its deprivations. When a younger, more attractive woman is questioned, she admits to considering herself lucky to be working in the cleanest shop: "My work absorbs me, I love it. I've been living at the girls' hostel since 1968 and I like it . . . it's one more link with the factory." Describing the minutiae of her daily life—up at 5:45, reading after work, followed by a film or a play, dancing with her boyfriend when he has a furlough from the army—she wonders whether she will marry, surmising that other men think her to be "a bit of a tart" because she works "in that place": "I like boys who are clever and not conceited, and who don't look down on me for being a spinner. Some of them do, you know, so now I don't tell them. I tried lying once but I'm not a good liar. They look down on me because I'm a manual laborer." Proud though she may be of her accomplishments in the party, the spinner is nonetheless relegated, in the minds of her male co-workers, to the ambivalently cathected status of sexually promiscuous woman. In Mészáros's construction of sexual politics, the claims of state socialism notwithstanding, it is still the woman who is scorned and who bears the burden of self-loathing. We see the young worker's beauty ritual in her solitary room, as she transforms herself into the very "object" which she is expected to become, to the accompaniment of the Illés rock band, used again here to speak for the alienation of youth and the indifference of the state.

The desire for upward mobility, the denial of class origins, and the conflict between genders occupy Mészáros in her 1973 feature, *Riddance*. The title, literally translated "free breathing," evokes as well her own life situation at the time of her divorce from Miklós Jancsó, when she became more fully autonomous as a film director. Transposing the documentary material from *At the Lörinc Spinnery* into fiction form, she sacrifices neither rigorous fidelity to the factory setting nor the ethnographic details of workers' narratives, structuring the story around Jutka, a weaver in a large textile mill, estranged from her divorced mother for eight years after growing up in an orphanage.

As the credits roll, a young woman is swimming alone in a lake; she undresses while emerging from the water. Next, a precisely composed longshot of the factory introduces the viewer to shop-floor daily life, moving to a close-up on the attractive blonde Jutka as she threads her machine, looking nervously about. Mészáros's camera records the relentless motion of the weaving machines, then cuts to an outdoor cafe with a tight two-shot of Jutka and her boyfriend András, a technician at the same factory. Encircling her against a tree, he speaks insistently of his love for her, begging her in desperate tones to marry him and promising to stop drinking, increase his wages, abandon his male comrades and live together with her in his parents' house.

The camera moves to a close-up as Jutka screams, "No, I don't love you." András strikes her, slowly at first, then with increasing force, until Jutka cries out. The barrage of blows, punctuated by her screams, finally attracts the attention of the waitress who intervenes. Distraught and sobbing, Jutka stumbles off alone as the cafe patrons observe the scene with detachment.

The naked brutality of the moment is immediately followed by a cut to Jutka taking a shower, the water cascading with her tears, as the camera pans slowly from her face downward, filling the frame first with her breast, then her navel, lingering there until she turns slowly away. It is the first of many such sensual moments in Mészáros's cinema when a woman finds refuge in the cleansing solitude of a shower, the image that had so captivated Agnès Varda. A counterpoise to preceding scenes of psychological or physical distress, these scenes are remarkable, among other things, for the way in which Mészáros presents the female body, imaged—but not, I think, feti-shized—through the purificatory ritual of bathing, either alone or in the company of other women. Although the unclothed female figure was not unknown to post–Stalinist East European cinema, other Hungarian repre-sentations, among which the most celebrated are those of Miklós Jancsó, Mészáros's former husband, privileged the spectacle of the female body primarily for the delectation of a male spectator.[23] Mészáros's scenes of bathing, swimming, or showering, on the other hand, seem to be governed by a different sensibility which solicits equally, if not more strongly, the female spectatorial gaze. This sense of women's pleasure is anchored in the simple fact of physicality for itself, rather than for another, in contrast to the splitting off of self conveyed by many of her lovemaking sequences between men and women.

Next we see, in the close quarters of the workers' hostel, a close-up of Jutka's face in the mirror as she readies herself for the evening. On the soundtrack is a humorous song of the period in which female voices imitate the meowing of cats, commenting cleverly on the "boudoir" intimacy of the hostel and the ambience of female competition for male attention. In these beauty rituals, class distinctions are preempted as the young women measure each other's feminine attributes with a mixture of envy and cool detachment, for the scene could just as easily be taking place in a suburban bourgeois bedroom. As the provocatively dressed young women ride the tram to their dates, passengers stare at their sleek miniskirts with the envy and even hostility that divides the generations, a reminder of Mészáros's refusal to gloss over the persistence of difference, whether intergenerational and same-sex or between men and women.

Jutka dances with several young men at the university club, accompanied by lyrics by a popular female singer: "There's a way out / Be good to me / I loved to distraction / Now I can see / Blindfolded, I let someone else lead me / I've lived in darkness, now I can see." The lyrics comment on Jutka's moral dilemma, for as she and her friend Erzsi leave the dance, she lies to a young man who asks her name by calling herself "Kati Simon, university student." When the two women discuss Jutka's beating by her former boy-friend later that night, they are seen in semi-obscurity, whispering together conspiratorially in a shared bed. Jutka explains her revulsion to violence by admitting that she had been beaten by her mother, causing her to leave home; this explanatory moment serves to remind the viewer that women, too, must bear responsibility for oppressive behavior, suggesting that its causes are deeper and more pervasive than any facile assumptions might allow.

The next day, when a group of factory women are washing up after their shift, they complain about working conditions in an affectionately argumen-tative tone.[24] In this companionable scene, Jutka's friend Zsuzsa urges the women to improve their earning power by learning to operate new machin-ery and an older woman expresses her apprehension about changing work routines at her age. While they talk, Mészáros's camera takes time to register the variety of bodies—some lithe, others corpulent—in a take that prefigures that of Pál Gábor's internationally successful 1978 film, *Angi Vera*. There too, women of markedly different anatomical and generational identity congre-gate in the workers' shower, arguing whether or not it is "bourgeois" to appreciate an attractive body when their older party colleague reprimands them for singing and commenting playfully on the beauty of each other's breasts. In Mészáros's hands, these sequences condense a world of sensuality into small moments of free play, a "transitional space" in which "free breath-ing" is enjoyed.[25]

Zsuzsa then helps Jutka escape over the factory's barbed-wire fence to join András Molnár, the university student to whom she has lied about her back-ground. At the dance next evening, the couple takes refuge in the library next to a bust of Stalin, stealing a moment of privacy together. But, visibly uncom-fortable in unfamiliar surroundings, Jutka again leaves with her girlfriend. A long-shot of the factory follows, after which the girls leave, arm in arm, happy as always in their own company. Jutka runs, luxuriant blond hair flying, to meet her lover at the lake. We see her floating alone, enjoying the moment of respite. Later, as the lovers embrace in bed, Jutka confesses:

> JUTKA: You don't know anything about me. . . . I'm not a university student, I lied to you. . . . Sometimes when I tell the truth, they don't ask me to dance again.
> ANDRÁS: Well, what's the truth?
> JUTKA: I'm a weaver. I work at the weaving mill. I live at the workers' hostel. Should I have told you about my wages? The loom I work on? On how many shifts? It's so dull.

During this conversation, the couple is lying together, but the distance be-tween them is conveyed when, as András assures her she need not lie to him,

Jutka looks away. This turning away is coded throughout Mészáros's features as a woman's visible acknowledgement of her ultimate isolation and the unattainability of intimacy between disunited couples in lovemaking scenes.

The structure of *Riddance* is based on the alternation of factory sequences with those of outdoor activity. Mészáros returns regularly to the giant looms, and the cycle of the women workers' days and nights unfolds rhythmically. In a subsequent love scene, Jutka weeps silently, admitting that she is frightened: when she tells her friend that she is sick of constantly lying, she admits that András's refusal to allow her to meet his family demonstrates his shame at being with her. When afterward she again meets Laci, her former lover, at a dance, she goes home with him, and we find her again weeping silently during their lovemaking. Covering her breasts in shame, she confesses that, although she has tried to love him, she cannot. Their parting is mutual, and the following day, Jutka is stretched out on a chaise lounge in the garden drinking wine. "People usually renounce love," says her friend, "They don't miss it." But Jutka responds: "They don't know it, they're just sad and tired. I want to live in a different way." Jutka reminds her that love is work, not mere romance, a notion that seems far away indeed from most Western cinematic constructions of love.

Trapped between a longing for wider horizons and disdain for her own origins, Jutka further complicates the self-loathing of her class betrayal by agreeing to András's parents' wish to meet her family. For the first time in eight years, she approaches her mother, a hairdresser, but the woman refuses her daughter's request that she reunite with her estranged husband, if only for display, rejecting Jutka's offers to pay her for her trouble. Standing far apart in the street, the two women cannot bridge the chasm between them, but Jutka assures her mother that she does not hate her for what she has done. She then visits the father whom she has not seen in three years and manages to convince him to pretend to be a "real" family with his current wife. But the charade proves a dismal failure; after a protracted, exruciatingly strained meeting between the "families," András's mother confronts Jutka in the kitchen, where the women enact their traditional role as dishwashers while the men smoke and drink in the living room. Finally able to admit the truth, Jutka initiates the unveiling of each family's true class origins, in turn forcing the son to choose between the support of his "nouveau-bourgeois" parents and his working-class love. The marriage is clearly doomed, indicating the persistence of class as an overdetermining factor in Hungarian life under socialism.

In the next shot Jutka is framed by her loom, weeping as the droning machinery fills the soundtrack. In the final scene, however, she stands once more in the shower, repeating the trajectory of the film's opening sequence. Mészáros's camera trails slowly, even caressingly, down the body's surface as the water mingles ambiguously with the girl's tears.

As in Mészáros's other early features, denial of family and origins is proved to be an unbearable burden in *Riddance:* the fate of her characters indicates that improving one's lot in life at the expense of the truth destroys the soul. The film's ethnographic accuracy links it with *At the Lőrinc Spinnery* and represents a move away from the director's fascination with youth culture toward the conflicts of adulthood. The problems of alcoholism, desertion, and child abandonment, the failed attempts to repress the need for "good" mothers and fathers, lead her protagonists to embark on an endlessly repeated search for companionship and love in their attempts to repair the inadequacies of their parents. Whereas class solidarity and women's friendships remain dependable, the divisions of gender relations are intensified.

4 LOVERS AND WORKERS
The Gendered State

Adoption (1975) widens the scope of Mészáros's preceding cinematic and psychological concerns by directly implicating the state in the politics of gender. While her uncompromising yet empathic perspective is clearly informed by the documentary rigor and craftsmanship characteristic of *Riddance*, the interplay between individual desire for self-fulfillment and the forces of Stalinist ideology combine with material circumstance in the persona of Kata. Widowed, attractive, and in her early forties, Kata's life is subordinated to her job as a lathe operator in a wood-working factory. We first see her awakening alone in her narrow bed at dawn, coughing steadily as she lights the stove, showers, and dresses in what is clearly a daily litany of repeated gestures.

In visual composition and camera movements nearly identical to those of the documentary *At the Lőrinc Spinnery*, the factory shop-floor sequences pay tribute to the repetition of movement by skilled hands and fingers, but it is a tribute to the rough edges of workers' lives rather than the unified surface of Stalinist esthetics. Close-ups of bent heads, bodies moving in harmony with machines, and hoses spraying away the layers of sawdust accumulated by the shift's end alternate with facial expressions of absent concentration. The iconography of each frame conveys the industrial functionalism of the mill, the mute presence of the machine dominating the stance of its operators. But these images speak beyond the specificity of this particular factory, reaching out to a seemingly timeless universality of gender-specific work-life, a scene that might as well have been set in a nineteenth-century mill in some other industrial capital.

Mészáros's creation of these multiple surfaces and layers in *Adoption* is such that the designation of "realism" is insufficient to the work. The mechanized existence of the women workers yields quickly to point toward a more nuanced view of the protagonists' lives in socialist Hungary, and, for that matter, elsewhere in Eastern Europe at the time. When Kata, looking pale and thin, consults a physician about her condition, we expect her to be worried about her lungs. Tapping her chest, he asks why she has requested the physical:

> DOCTOR: Is it only because you sleep badly and have no appetite, or is there family trouble?
> KATA: I'd like to know whether I'm in good health and whether, considering my age, I could still bear a child.

The moment is understated and surprising: Mészáros plays on audience expectation that middle-aged widowhood cannot possibly be equated with desired pregnancy, as the doctor informs Kata there is no physiological reason for her not to conceive. Kata then goes to a cafe to meet Jóska, her longtime but secret married lover and fellow-worker, to explain that, although she still loves him, the limitations of their relationship have become intolerable to her:

> KATA: I want to have your child.
> JÓSKA: It would ruin everything. We've kept our relationship secret for years. How does a child fit into that? . . . Don't you see this would be hell for the kid? To be born illegitimate? To be fatherless?

Mészáros comments ironically on the man's equation of "fatherlessness" with "illegitimacy," his refusal to commit himself more fully to her, and the freedom afforded him by their clandestine relationship, for Jóska and Kata have managed to remain lovers in spite—or perhaps because—of their understanding that he will never divorce his wife or leave his family.

If Mészáros's narrative of a middle-aged woman living alone, dissatified with a long-term arrangement yet desirous of a child, was unusual enough at the time from a Western European perspective, in the Eastern Europe of the mid-1970s it was quite extraordinary. A review by a Hungarian critic illuminates the perplexing nature of the topic and the reaction of native viewers:

> These "documentaries" [i.e., Mészáros's features]—which, according to Mészáros's own terminology, are "quasi-realist"—show limited signs of psychological characterization, but at the same time they elevate the specific male- and "female-centric" perspective to a universal image. Hence, according to critics, her films fall into the "trap of feminism." For example, in her 1975 film *Adoption*, she again protests against loneliness by portraying the search for fulfillment through a dramatic relationship between two women. Kata is a working woman around forty, whose life is uneventful, conflict-free; nevertheless, her days pass without happiness. She has a lover who withholds himself out of fear of fatherhood. To counteract this emptiness, Kata takes in an orphan girl, Anna.[1]

Both the critic's use of the metaphor of entrapment with regard to feminism and his application of the term "documentary" to what is clearly a feature film suggest important differences between East European and Western sensibilities. Moreover, that a woman should continue a long-standing relationship with a married man is, to be sure, as common in Hungary as elsewhere, but Mészáros's unflinching depiction of the terms of such a situation—especially in its effects upon an "older woman"—neither sentimentalizes nor heroicizes the protagonists in light of any predetermined political stance. Rather, the director's dissection of the psychosocial dynamics of their relationship is forthright, refusing at the same time to devalue the couple's genuine—albeit conflicted—affection for each other. We see, for instance, the physical intimacy of Kata and Jóska through affectionate gestures in contrast to the emotional chasm separating them. In this way, Mészáros insists that complicated love relationships persist despite inhospitable circumstances, human failures, or the limitations of convention. For Western viewers whose visual satisfaction is predicated more conventionally on oedipal narratives with a satisfying closure, these "rough edges" cannot be easily naturalized.

A second narrative thread is introduced during the tête-à-tête between Kata and Jóska. A group of sullen teenage girls from a neighboring orphanage seated at a nearby table at first solicit her attention and then walk home behind her as the camera registers, with coolly detached distance, the disparities between their vivacity and Kata's fatigue. One of the girls, Anna, returns to Kata's to ask to rent a room in her house as a private space for her trysts with her young lover, Sanyi. Kata refuses unsympathetically and appears annoyed, even jealous. Another girl from the orphanage, distraught and disheveled, returns to Kata's, begging to read aloud a bitter letter of farewell to the mother who deserted her at the age of seven, alienating her from the father she still adores. The letter concludes with a phrase that suggests a daughter's anguish at the hands of an abandoning, withholding, perhaps even persecutory mother: "Mother, I'm sorry, but I don't love you . . . try to be happy." Her acknowledgement of their failed relationship is delivered without apology, and Mészáros records Kata's expression as she measures her own potential maternity in light of these shattering revelations.[2]

Mészáros's documentary realism examines the effects of familial abandonment and adoption when Kata, reconsidering her refusal to accept the young woman as a tenant, wanders through the orphanage halls in search of Anna; long tracking shots take note of bleak corridors more evocative of a hospital than a home for children. When at last Kata confides in Anna about her affair with Joska, and discovers in her an unsuspected emotional depth, she asks her to "be my daughter." But Anna replies gently that she has "had enough of parents," as the two lie together in bed like mother and daughter. In spite of her own truncated childhood, Anna encourages Kata's maternal aspirations:

Scenes from *Adoption*

KATA: A child at 43 . . . I'm insane.
ANNA: No, you aren't. But don't adopt one. Abandoned children are all
    wounded.

Emboldened, Anna then confesses her history as an unwanted child: abandonment, physical and psychological abuse, homelessness, exploitation, and
emotional instability. But by allowing her to mature into a lovely young
woman, more psychically sound than many whose circumstances are far
more fortunate, Mészáros takes a soberly empathic position toward her own
childhood difficulties, which coincided with those of her nation, suggesting
that even such seemingly overwhelming odds may be overcome through
reparative experiences at a later developmental stage.[3]

Visually, Mészáros structures the spectator's gaze around the spectacle of
a growing intimacy between the two women, while their mutual admission
of pain opens a potential space of healing between them. Through her relationship with Anna, Kata is able to summon the courage to consider adoption, even in less than ideal circumstances; at the same time, she herself
wants to assume greater responsibility for Anna in the present. In a meeting
with the orphanage director, she acts as Anna's advocate in her wish to
marry Sanyi against her parents' opposition, and she intercedes to obtain the
consent of the girl's parents: "Now her parents won't take responsibility for
what she has become . . . she could be my daughter, my friend." We are now
in a position to discern a fundamental *modus operandi* of Mészáros's directorial style: the suggestion of maternal substitution that emerges in *Adoption* is
transformed into the still more sensitive topic of surrogate motherhood as the
central focus of her next film, *The Heiresses*, also known as *The Inheritance*
(*Örökség*, 1980), further elaborating Mészáros's method of amplifying in a
subsequent film a secondary theme from a prior text. Similarly, the earlier
documentary material on woman workers, childhood neglect, and visual
artists is narrativized as fiction in her feature films.

An impromptu visit to Jóska's house convinces Kata that they too would
fail as a married couple, and she finds his unsympathetic treatment of his
own wife intolerable. Enclosed in a conventional (East European) masculinity, he reveals himself to be more patriarch than partner, and when Kata
endorses Jóska's wife's interest in working outside the home he intervenes to
suppress this rebellious solidarity. This encounter, unconventional though it
may seem to Western eyes, plays a decisive role in Kata's decision to move
on with her life without him. Yet Mészáros does not permit the viewer the
false comfort of a reductive indictment of this "hopeless cause," for Kata
continues to love Jóska in spite of his obvious limitations. A distinctly European and, for that matter, specifically East European attitude toward hetero-
sexual love is discernible in this unstated acceptance of human imperfection,
this tolerance for difficult conditions in which no facile outcome seems possible in relationships between the sexes.[4]

When Kata and Anna sit on the terrace of a restaurant, eating, drinking, smoking, and laughing, their affectionate embraces arouse the attention of male patrons, who regard them with curiosity and expressions of disapproval. Flaunting their new-found friendship, Anna declines a young man's invitation to dance and returns with Kata to her house, where Anna, having taken a shower, is offered Kata's own nightgown. In this tender gesture Kata seems to confer upon her the mixed blessing of adult womanhood: the scene parallels one in which Kata has earlier (and gratuitously) interrupted Anna's lovemaking with Sanyi by insisting on retrieving her bathrobe from their room. Resentful of the intrusion, Anna opens the door, the chiaroscuro lighting offering a tantalizing glimpse of her slender nude body. The later scene, in contrast, reveals Anna's back to the camera as she slowly slips on the nightgown, facing Kata. This transfer of intimate clothing from "mother" to "daughter" mirrors the deeper transference that has taken place between the women, for in desiring marriage with Sanyi, Anna is also in some sense emulating the widowed Kata. Mészáros presents in this way the vicissitudes and variants of femininity, demonstrating that the family of choice may be more viable than the family of origin.

Female nudity is thus represented by Mészáros as pleasurable for the spectator and the protagonists, yet devoid of prurient interest. But it should be noted that in this scene, only the younger woman is represented nude, while the middle-aged Kata is always at least half-dressed. This disparity leads one to consider traditional ambivalence toward cinematic representation of the aging female body, equated as it is with imperfection and even revulsion.[5] The anxiety of the older Kata toward a delayed maternity is thus mirrored by the discretion of Mészáros's avoidance of making a spectacle of the aging female body. This quiet intimacy nevertheless inscribes a space of repose within the cinematic text, structurally similar to Mészáros's sequences portraying women of different ages bathing alone or with a companion.[6]

The film's finale takes place at Anna's wedding, where the camera slowly pans a group of girls—the orphaned comrades of the new bride—seated around the table. Their tearful faces suggest not joy for their more fortunate sister, but sadness for themselves. The concluding shot frames Anna standing in a corner as her new groom leaves the room alone: the honeymoon, if indeed there is to be one, promises to be short-lived, Mészáros reveals, and Kata's future single motherhood is made to seem less burdensome by comparison with this image of domestic sadness.

Resolved within herself to go forward with the adoption, Kata returns to the orphanage and receives a robust, dark-haired infant: bundling the child in her arms, she is at once vulnerable and determined. As Kata prepares to board a bus for home with the new baby, we feel concern for their welfare, and the director characteristically withholds the spectator's wish for harmonious closure. Her use of the freeze-frame ending recalls the final shot of

François Truffaut's first feature film, *The 400 Blows* (*Les 400 Coups,* 1958), when, in flight from a center for juvenile delinquents, the fourteen-year-old Antoine Doinel—also an abandoned child—reaches the ocean at the end of his long journey on the run.[7] When Truffaut first used that cinematic device (now reduced to a cliché of prime-time television), it signified a combination of ambivalence, confusion, and loss—an ambiguous statement. And although it is still ambiguous here, Mészáros's film language postulates its dialectical relationship to the narrative as a whole, which has been read by a Hungarian critic as "a final sense of unremitting struggle, burden, difficulty."[8]

While there is surely merit in this interpretation, we do well, I think, to bear in mind the film's social and psychological context in order to avoid the imposition of unintended ethnocentric assumptions about gender and culture. In taking possession of the baby denied her through early poverty and young widowhood, and by virtue of an affair with a married lover unable to fulfill her desire for a child, Kata has also resisted the overwhelming prescriptions of the patriarchal post–Stalinist state. Despite Anna's caution, she refuses to be deprived of her existential freedom to enact her desire, even at mid-life, at odds with prevailing conventions of tradition and class. The final freeze-frame, then, acknowledges the persistence of her struggle to survive in a world where class origins and gender equality remains a marginal concern.[9] For Kata will remain a factory worker, not an upper-middle-class matron leading a life of leisure supported by a husband. In the eternal present of cinema, the frozen moment—what Marguerite Duras has called "the absolute photograph"—consolidates the victory of a single, older woman who refuses to relinquish her desire. Temporally and spatially, Kata's stance indicates that she has at least obtained her goal, yet its ambiguity reminds the viewer that Kata's struggle is only beginning.[10]

Before taking up the second film of Mészáros's second "period," let us consider briefly the historical and social context in which *Adoption* was produced. Between 1976 and 1977, Hungarian cinematic discourse had begun to reflect more openly such national concerns as a return to centralized control of governmental structures in the wake of the failure of the "New Economic Policy" instituted in 1968: the oil crisis that affected Hungary and Eastern Europe with particular force; a soaring inflation rate; the liberalization of travel to the West; and growing demands for Western consumer goods.

These socio-economic changes fostered an artistic milieu in which Hungarian filmakers were increasingly preoccupied with aspects of their culture rarely before examined in cinema, such as a peculiarly Hungarian melange of high esteem for national culture and history with a singularly pessimistic self-regard, a legacy of centuries of occupation, marginalization, and self-condemnation. As in *Adoption,* love, politics, independence, and dreams of national solidarity are often seen in Hungarian cinema as irremediably doomed—impossible, unrealistic, hopeless chimerae.

Linguistic metaphors may be useful in illustrating this point. The *gyász-magyar*, for instance, is a somber, even morbid perspective that assumes that, no matter where one might have begun, one will always, inevitably, finish last, vanquished by forces beyond one's control. This notion is also expressed in the common phrase "the thousand-year-old-curse," referring to the fragmentation and lack of cohesion of Hungary's martyred history. Finally, the popular proverb *sirva vigad a magyar*, or "tearful happiness," speaks to the melancholia of East-Central Europe—a temperamental proclivity for experiencing pleasure at the same time as sorrow.

These expressions are given visual forms which enable us to read more accurately the rather muted darkness of many Hungarian films of the late 1970s. János Domoky's 1977 feature, *The Sword (Akárd)*, describes the plight of Sándor Bojti, who sells his car during a Western tourist trip to purchase a priceless, historic sword that symbolizes the uprising of early eighteenth-century noblemen against Habsburg domination. Returning home, he discovers that no one, not even the officials of the National Art Museum, believes his account of the authenticity of his valuable acquisition. Jobless, his family fragmented, Bojti throws the sword into the Danube. Soon afterward, the state apparatus retrieves the object, which is to be exhibited in its rightful place—the National Art Museum. But by that time, Bojti is reduced to a state of catatonic television watching and has lost all faith in life.

Zoltán Fábri's *The Hungarians (Magyarok)*, also released in 1977, represents this typical disillusionment by portraying a small group of Hungarian agricultural workers who realize their seemingly impossible dream in the course of a job contracted on the estate of German aristocrats. After heroic struggle and humiliation, they succeed in returning to their native Hungary from Germany, only to find that historical events have overtaken their plans. The film echoes Gábor Bódy's equally morbid conclusions in his 1976 film, *American Torso (Amerikai anzix)* in the service of historical interrogation. Hungarian freedom fighters from the Revolution of 1848 emigrate to America in flight from repressive conditions on their own soil. Refusing to massacre Indians, become policemen, or join forces they see as agents of capitalism, they enlist in the fight against the Confederate Army. They preserve the ideals of freedom espoused at great cost; like the men in *The Hungarians* drafted into the army and decimated at the Russian front, they too die a noble death.

But such depictions of "hopeless causes" may be deceptive, for, as we have just seen in the case of *Adoption*, beneath the appearance of what may seem cynicism and despair, there may also be a silent quest for independence, an indirect—but no less effective—human agency asserting itself. In

Mészáros's *Nine Months*, for instance, such female agency is inserted through the character of Juli, a young iron-foundry worker toward whom unwanted sexual advances are made by her foreman, János. Oblivious to her indifference, János insistently forces his attentions upon her, proposing marriage in the course of their first evening alone. Although Juli refuses his offer, they do become lovers, and János proves to be jealous of Juli's reluctance to disclose her past. He manages to find out that she has a child, now living in the countryside with her parents, whose father is a married university professor, and his insecurity is further exacerbated with his realization that Juli, too, has academic aspirations. In spite of her discovery that she is pregnant with his child, Juli refuses to marry János.[11]

Mészáros's heroines share a resentment of the circumstances that at times induce them to fabricate stories of their past life, and Juli chooses a moment calculated to embarrass János to expose the existence of her illegitimate child. She does so in the country house János has been building for his future family, in the presence of his outraged parents, who insult her viciously. She breaks off with János after he becomes violent with her and demands that she terminate her pregnancy.

But in contrast to Jóska in *Adoption*, János shows remorse for his behavior toward Juli. He is one of what we have come to recognize as a fairly typical male character in Mészáros's films: a decent enough fellow on the surface, but subject to unmanageable feelings of jealousy (like the working-class lover in *Riddance*) toward the woman he professes to love. The doomed nature of their relationship and the couple's seemingly hopeless inability to meet each other's needs are poignantly depicted in the final moments of *Nine Months*, when the director alternates shots of Juli giving birth in another town with scenes of Janos, miserable and alone, back at work. The dramatic intensity of this sequence is heightened by the fact that the leading actress, Lili Monori, herself pregnant as the film entered production, is portrayed during her actual childbirth. Mészáros remarks:

> I never write a scenario without knowing who will play the principal role and I often write my stories bearing in mind the personality of the actors with whom I want to work. *Adoption* is badly—although literally—translated, because in Hungarian the word has a larger meaning than the precise fact of adopting someone. It also means adapting to a situation.[12]
>
> Hungarian is a very difficult language. As for *Nine Months*, it was I who wanted the title because of this last image of childbirth, which I am very fond of. But perhaps here [in France], in the vogue of feminism, it loses much of its originality.[13]

Nevertheless, the portrayal of a live childbirth in a feature film by a former documentarist was the first event of its kind in Eastern Europe. There is as well a major shift in Mészáros's work that parallels the changes in Hungarian society in the mid-1970s, and Hungarian critics such as György Szabó interpreted these interlocking social and cinematic phenomena in this way:

> Having learned from the mistakes of her previous films, Mészáros was able in her next feature, *Nine Months*, to construct a richer social tapestry, enacting social roles more comprehensively by eliminating the ghost of sentimentality, yet without completely abandoning the story's beautiful simplicity.[14]

The critic Erzsébet Magori, however, describes *Nine Months*, ostensibly from a "woman's perspective":

> The love between Juli Kovács and János Bognár, their meeting and separation, provides an excellent vehicle for contrasting different *weltanschauungen*. Thus, the love crisis of *Nine Months* is a crisis of world views. It's not really a love battle between two youths, but rather a struggle between old and new ways of thinking. Janos is in conflict with his beloved, and she with her milieu. Juli's conflict originates from the continuous contradictions between her values and those required by society in order for people to lead a *normal* life. She bears a child out of wedlock; the father of her five-year-old son is a university professor, married and with a family, but she does not seem to resent the fact that he never marries her. She doesn't really desire marriage; she wants to study. Juli's personality interests us because she acts as if women's equality existed, not only in theory but in practice. The film ends in the maternity ward. We see the mother in close-up as she gives birth. We see childbirth in all its bloody reality. But somehow this "inappropriate," natural closing scene is inseparable from the truth of life, from the beauty and ugliness of life to which the film's director is committed.[15]

Obviously, these critics disagree, and one can only speculate on the extent to which their respective gender figures in their interpretions.[16]

During the period of *Adoption*, transformations occurred in Mészáros's personal life as well. Divorced from Miklós Jancsó, she began to work with the Polish actor Jan Nowicki (whose part as János in *Adoption* was the first of many roles under her direction), who eventually became as well her life companion. Departing from her earlier fascination with youth culture, adults now figure more fully as narrative subjects, and the director experimented for the first time with the use of color stock and moved beyond the use of primarily Hungarian actors and actresses to international casts including Marina Vlady and Jan Nowicki. At the same time, Mészáros discovered Zsuzsa Czinkóczi, a schoolgirl from the rural town of Kecskemét, whom she cast in the role of Zsuzsi, Juli's daughter, in *The Two of Them*. Their collaboration recalls that between Truffaut and Jean-Pierre Léaud, his younger alter-ego in the semi-autobiographical "Antoine Doinel" cycle, a challenging cinematic experience for both director and actor.[17]

The Two of Them, Mészáros's seventh feature, concentrates on a friendship between women and is, according to the director, the first of her narrative films to have a "sympathetic male character—albeit an alcoholic—a sensitive person who sees life in its complexity and profundity." As the self-possessed director of a provincial women workers' hostel, Marina Vlady as Mari maintains her composed serenity in principled opposition to the hostel administration's inhumane regulations on behalf of Juli, a troubled younger woman still deeply attracted to her alcoholic husband.[18]

But it is Juli's daughter Zsuzsi whose point of view indicts the adult world of deception and compromise, and the child actress who plays the role, Zsuzsa Czinkóczy, subsequently becomes Mészáros's alter ego in the Diary trilogy. Despite Mari's efforts to shelter Juli and assist her in separating from her irresponsible, childlike husband, Juli finds it nearly impossible to resist him. In a darkly lit yet revealing sequence, they make love on a kitchen chair, two bodies hopelessly lost, acting out a primally brutal physical attraction.

In contrast, Mari's own deteriorating middle-class marriage has become psychologically abusive through her husband's prolonged absences and is devoid of the erotic passion that controls Juli and her husband. This difference is demonstrated in a sequence of visually shocking sexual humiliation when Mari is left lying on the floor, legs spread, by her usually passive husband after a brief, and, we are meant to suspect, typical moment of intercourse. Afterward, we see Mari, water streaming from her blonde hair, enjoying herself in a steamy shower, joined by her fully-clothed friend Juli; the two women embrace and share a moment of sensuous release through the complicit laughter that temporarily transcends even the barriers of class and gender. Mari's husband Feri, threatened by her growing autonomy, turns out to be as egocentric as Jóska in *Adoption* and Janos in *Nine Months*, while the talented János is rarely sober, abandoning all responsibility for his daughter and wife.

Mészáros is interested in the factual aspect of social situations: like the Italian neorealists Rossellini and DeSica, whose work was known to her in Moscow and Budapest, she establishes the material existence of her characters in the first few frames of the cinematic text, without superfluous dialogue. Mészáros notes that:

> In *The Two of Them*, one sees and learns that Marina Vlady is director of a women workers' hostel, one sees and learns that . . . her work is not easy. All that is a part of the construction of my films, their dramaturgy. [But] they are not at all linear; I film, I record precise moments, facts, and it's only afterwards, when the film is finished, that one can understand the conflicts that were there in those moments.[19]

Sutured into the film's editing is a rhythm of constant motion, displacement, and dislocation that instills in the viewer an insistent anxiety: "In my films I tell banal stories where nothing extraordinary happens, always more or less the same thing, except each time in a different place. Displacements nourish conflict and change." The crisis in Mari's marriage, we may then conclude, is at once the result of and the reason for having her having taken a new position. Clearly, Mészáros is fascinated by the consequences of sudden life-changes as they affect lovers, marriages, and family relations, and Zsuzsi appears as the first child-witness to the disintegration of adult relationships. In a society still attempting to build a socialist state, masculine identity is represented as victimized by feminine autonomy, and the child's well-being is ultimately compromised.

Zsuzsi is forced to confront her father's frightening physical and mental degradation in a detoxification clinic where her point-of-view shots are shared by the spectator subjected to graphic images of the stages of alcoholism. But her mother is scarcely better prepared to care for her, and the little girl is positioned as the film's most eloquent—albeit silent—condemnation of the sins of her parents' generation. While Mészáros is not a moralist, she does not flinch from judging adult responsibility, and, in so doing, indirectly charges her nation with abandoning its duties toward the young, an idea that will find its full flowering in the Diary trilogy.

The film concludes when Zsuzsi, who has scarcely uttered a word while being spared none of her parents' agony, accuses them of lying—about themselves, each other, and her. But Mészáros's ironic gaze, focused on the guilty parties, suggests that even this epiphany will prove incapable of preventing future deceptions by untrustworthy adults. Thus she remains faithful to the vision of her earlier features by testifying on behalf of those to whom the power of full speech has not been granted.

Just Like at Home (1978) again positions Czinkóczi in the child's role at the center of the narrative, and again utilizes foreign actors, the Danish-French Anna Karina as Anna and Jan Nowicki as András. An academic recently returned from the United States, András tries to renew his relationship with Anna, his former lover, who rejects his advances. Returning to his native village, he is disappointed by a reunion with the parents about whom he has fantasized, and finally becomes attached to a dog he purchases from a woman whose daughter, Zsuzsi, does not want to part with it. Going back to Budapest, András learns that he has been fired from his university post for exceeding the duration of his visa. When Zsuzsi comes to reclaim her dog, the two unlikely companions return to her village, living a fantasy life of happy childhood outings in the countryside. Here too, Mészáros compares village life with urban culture, and finds both wanting, a motif she develops more fully in *Bye Bye Red Riding Hood* (1989).

This oedipal scenario is disrupted by the intrusion of Anna into the couple's bucolic idyll: through her eyes—and, Mészáros suggests, conventional bourgeois views—the relationship of an older, marginally "masculine" man with a young girl seems abnormal, regressive, even dangerous. Undeterred, this "odd couple" travel to Budapest, where they live together while András works on a project about the fate of émigré Hungarians. Anna meanwhile continues to press him to send the little girl back to her village and to resume their "adult" relationship.[20] By contemporary standards, Mészáros's sensitive, offbeat exploration of love between a man-child and a child-mother might appear even more controversial than it was at the time, in view of revelations of child abuse and exploitation.

The films of Mészáros's second period of feature work suggest that she consistently opposed the fantasmatic idealization of femininity typical of Western cinema. Maternity, economic and sexual independence, and the arduous work of love are her primary subjects, while the ultimate failure of people to communicate about what matters most to them is inscribed in the visual composition of her work. Physical creatures, her protagonists face both the anguish and wisdom of aging, the pleasures and violence of sexuality. An intervention in the discourse of the body, her cinema of this epoch stages new scenarios of female solidarity and community.

Whatever their age and temperament, their class background or sensibility, Mészáros's female protagonists are bound together by a common fate: shared enclosure in the socialist Hungarian state. These confining and even suffocating circumstances nonetheless fail to suppress an inner world of strength and faith in themselves and others. Quite the contrary, the women's forthright and spirited resistance overcomes the very depressive male sexuality that is so often the cause of their most grievous pain. Never idealized, Mészáros's cinematic women remain unvanquished by refusing to condemn the masculine objects of their affection and suffering. Neither victims nor victors, they are instead active participants in their own fate and that of their nation.

5 BETWEEN WORLDS
The International Coproductions

If the films of Mészáros's first decade of feature filmmaking foreground Hungarian and familial identity, her cinematic work of the late 1970s and early 1980s moves beyond the boundaries of nation and gender into a "transitional" space, the British psychoanalyst D. W. Winnicott's term for a hypothetical zone of internal experience where self-actualizing creativity is said to take place. There, he theorizes, the infant engages in playful activity without jeopardizing its primal link to the mother, while at the same time gradually differentiating itself from the merged, post-natal state that envelopes and sustains the mother-infant dyad.[1]

While Winnicott's formulation was, to be sure, elaborated originally for the psychoanalyst's clinical work with infants and mothers, it has also been more generally theorized with regard to works of the imagination and cultural experience in the largest sense.[2] Whereas these psychoanalytic applications figure prominently in the lexicon of literary critics, they are underutilized by film theorists for whose project they hold possibilities not yet recognized for elaborating the intersections of autobiography, gender, and film theory.[3]

Few of Winnicott's elaborations have been taken up so widely as that of the "transitional object," popularized beyond the consulting room to include any positively cathected entity to which human beings become inordinately attached, such as a child's blanket or toy. But the trajectory of his work was such that:

> it became progressively more important to define the role of imagination, illusion and playing in the transitional area and space from which all true spontaneous gestures of self-actualization are initiated and crystallized into a personal tradition of inner reality, which is more than fantasying.[4]

In Winnicottian terms, the loss of ability to play, unfettered by goal-oriented behavior, diminishes the subject's freedom to explore the world and hence limits access to the internal object-world from which imaginative experience proceeds. It would be misleading to reduce Mészáros's activity at this transitional moment of her life as a filmmaker to that of playful fantasy, for the demands of proving oneself as an artist on a larger stage than that offered by a small native country are daunting enough, especially in the context of Cold-War ideologies. Nevertheless, the moves that prove to be decisive in shaping the future of her career are readable in light of Winnicott's spatializing metaphor.

A self-professed "outsider," it is perhaps not surprising that, in maturing as a director, Mészáros might have wanted to test the parameters of ethnic and national difference—Jewish, Polish, Russian, and Hungarian—in conjunction with those of gender and class. Her own exposure to several languages and cultures as a child, Mészáros noted in my 1989 interview with her, endowed her with an enduring sense of adventure and curiosity about the cultural "other":

> growing up in the Soviet Union, I didn't know about the "Hungarian language complex" until I learned that language. Knowing Russian allowed me to speak to many neighboring peoples, but in Hungary I gradually learned that the "Hungarian language complex" refers to the isolation that comes about because, unlike Polish, no one else speaks the language. . . . My first "mother tongue" was Italian, the second German, the third Russian, the fourth Hungarian.

Mészáros seems to have taken a lifelong oppositional stance to the limitations of a "small" language such as Hungarian which, its distinguished literary and cultural achievements notwithstanding, inevitably narrowed the range of vision and visibility possible for a serious filmmaker with international aspirations. A seasoned veteran of several cultural milieux, her departure from Hungary in the late 1970s to make films abroad enabled Mészáros to enlarge further an already complicated international identity. Taking up for the first time in her own work the complexities of transnationality as a narrative subject, she was well situated to propose the "insider's" view of ethnicity and nationality that animates *On the Move* (*Útközben*, 1979) and *The Heiresses* (1980).

Anticipating current anthropological, psychological, and political reconsiderations of ethnic identity once imagined as a natural, inherited, and permanently given, she represents it instead as flexible, constructed, and multiple: ethnicity constitutes only one—and not necessarily even the most determinative—aspect of identity, cinematic or political. In *Just Like at Home*, Mészáros had already begun to examine the profound disorientation of a returned expatriate whose solitude is unendurable both at home and abroad.

In her work of this period, the director's subtle portrayal of class differences as they affect national identity bears witness to her command of the cinematic apparatus in tandem with a critical Marxism informed by her reading of and contact with György Lukács:

> It is my conviction that the effective bringing into being of the great community of the peoples should be begun at home, with evolving our own, more limited community—of those speaking Hungarian in our case. We must reveal and—possessed of our present knowledge (long practice and bitter experience)—re-examine the particular problems of our people, first among ourselves, and then among those who have something to do with these problems.[5]

The destiny of Hungary and of Hungarians is in fact one of Mészáros's most important subjects in these transitional films: the agonizing conflict (when indeed the luxury of choice exists) between a life of exile or sharing the fate of one's people is an ongoing problematic that resonates in some ways more powerfully in postcommunist East-Central Europe than it did in the early 1980s. Emigration, deracination, and the diaspora of departures linked to the critical events of Hungarian history since the mid-nineteenth century: such is the fabric of literary and cinematic representation in which Mészáros's work is a critical intervention.[6]

Until then, a focus on the struggles of working women and men attempting to create a new society against the background of political and socioeconomic life in post–1968 Hungary had fully occupied Mészáros's cinematic energies. Exigent and austere, her mid-1970s work foregrounds female protagonists, raising issues of power in the framework of class and gender relations, in contrast to her earlier features, depicting conflicts between lovers and workers, the family and cultural institutions, young and old. Nor should it escape our attention that these films elicited critical controversy both at home and abroad; for experimentation with other cultures does not, as Winnicott might well have agreed, necessarily please those who wish us to remain faithful to our own symbolic families of origin. Although she does not consider herself a feminist, Mészáros found that the viewpoint she took, as a woman, toward her own culture led to her work being resented or ignored. When not overtly negative, Hungarian reviewers of Mészáros's films of this period adopt a rather grudging, condescending tone. The following excerpt offers one of the more balanced views:

> we see that audiences misunderstand her films and, despite the fact that they have much to teach us, are incapable of learning from these "pedagogical narratives." Hence we understand why viewers here in Hungary feel estranged from Mészáros' films, although we are naturally happy to learn of their success abroad.[7]

So pronounced, in fact, was the disparity between the reception of Mészáros and her films in Hungary and their critical acclaim elsewhere that the director found herself obliged to comment:

> The general [Hungarian] public despised *The Two of Them* (1977), *Nine Months* (1976), and *The Heiresses* (1980) because these films described people who were different from them. They called attention to democratic problems such as women's rights to independence, to live their own lives. These are especially important themes today in Hungary, for I know no other country that is so conservative about these issues.[8]

Resistance to Mészáros's dramatization of such issues is further illustrated by the fact that, of the many awards won by her films to date—at the Berlin and Chicago festivals in 1975 for *Adoption*, at Cannes and Teheran for *Nine Months*, and at San Sebastian for *Just Like at Home*—only *Diary for My Children* has received such praise in Hungary as well. While a festival prize should not be taken as the *sine qua non* of a film's value, it undoubtedly enhances the work's trajectory in the international marketplace. It is therefore not entirely surprising that Mészáros embarked next upon a cycle of feature films in coproduction with European partners and actors. *On the Move* is a Polish-Hungarian venture featuring Delphine Seyrig, *The Heiresses* a cooperative project with Paris-Gaumont starring Isabelle Huppert, and *Anna*, also known as *Mother and Daughter* (*Une mère, une fille*, 1981), a French collaboration with Marie-Jose Nat in the leading role. Mészáros's companion and leading actor, Jan Nowicki, plays the male lead in each of the films of this group, thereby continuing the pattern initiated by Mészáros with *Nine Months*.

The critical incomprehension and, for that matter, hostility that marked these films' reception in Hungary were understandably discouraging and frustrating to a director whose cinematic subject had, until then, been the very contemporary society in which she lived. But her decision to leave Hungary for a time was also influenced by other critical factors. By the end of the 1970s, a number of outstanding Hungarian films had reached the international market, the strongest among them arguably Pál Gábor's *Angi Vera* (1978), a sensitive yet uncompromising study of a young, orphaned girl who, like many educated by the party *in loco parentis*, chooses between emotional and ideological loyalties in her rise through the Communist Party hierarchy of the Stalinist 1950s.[9]

The aptly titled *On the Move* signals Mészáros's departure from Hungary for what was to become a protracted period of dislocation and even exile for the director. The film crosses national boundaries both in the conditions of its unusual coproduction with Poland and within the narrative itself; its protagonist, Delphine Seyrig (as Barbara) is a biologist who was born in Poland but emigrated to Hungary in 1939 with her mother. There she married a physician, the director of a provincial hospital and, although their marriage appears to be stable (like that of Mari and Feri in *The Two of Them*), their domestic life has stultified in the years since their children left home. Learning of the death of a close friend in Poland, Barbara suddenly leaves for Cracow to attend her funeral, an impulsive decision that enables her to detach herself, albeit temporarily, from the alienated life she has been leading.[10] The return to the country of her birth, to its language, people, landscapes, and culture, dramatically reawakens memories of the past, especially affecting when the departure has been forced by such harsh circumstance.

Barbara's ambivalent internal relationship to that past is registered in the fact that she has not seen Poland since her mother's funeral in Cracow fifteen years earlier: "I brought her coffin by train all the way from Budapest. . . . She always told me to bring her here, to the land where she was born." Although a common enough sentiment, her words here nonetheless typify a particularly Hungarian obsession with death and nationality, a deep psychic attachment to the concept of "motherland." The mother's insistence on burial in the "right place" evokes the theme Mészáros develops fully in her Diary films: the highly charged refusal of Hungarian authorities to accord proper funeral rites to Imre Nagy, leader of the uprising of 1956, just as her own father had been denied burial, leaving his daughter bereft, haunted by the uncertainty of disinformation.[11] Symbolic rituals of death and mourning, then, are visualized as both a personal and national obsession.

In Budapest, Barbara falls unexpectedly in love with Marek, a charming Polish actor, in what may be understood as a thinly veiled autobiographical reference to the director's discovery of Poland through her relationship with Jan Nowicki. They are like young lovers together, embracing, laughing, even giddy. Barbara becomes radiant under the rejuvenating power of unexpected love. The direction legitimates the couple's most impetuous actions: an impulsive trip to the country, intimate conversation with strangers at the funeral. Clearly Mészáros takes the part of those in search—no matter how desperately—for what is missing in their lives, just as she placed her camera in the service of young people's point of view in her early features.

But the couple's common East European home both unites and separates them, and the two nationalities are further juxtaposed (and eventually separated) by language and culture, as Barbara makes clear:

> Both my parents were Poles, and Marek and his brothers are also Polish. . . .
> [According to the pre-war poet Dezső Kosztolányi] the ten most beautiful Hungarian words are: flame, pearl, mother, autumn, virgin, sword, kiss, wait, heart, grave. Ten words, a whole life.

Later, pointing out Montecassino (a World War II Italian battleground of great importance to Poles) to Barbara, the seductive Marek recites the words of Polish soldiers who fought there:

Red poppies on Montecassino drank Polish blood instead of morning dew, Polish soldiers walked over these red poppies and died, but anger was stronger than death. . . . This land belongs to Poland though Poland is far from here, for freedom is measured with crosses; history knows only this one mistake.

Paradoxically from the standpoint of Hollywood, the lovers' passionate idyll is doomed, even in view of their seemingly binding attachment to complementary nationalities and cultural backgrounds. Barbara returns to her family in Budapest where, shaken by the intensity of her adventure, she receives a phone call from Marek joyously announcing the birth of his new baby. Her congratulations are forced, and we read confusion and exhaustion in her slumped posture and forlorn expression. No explanation is given: sexual attraction is its own reward, Mészáros seems to suggest, and a woman must expect to be disappointed by a man whose company she has enjoyed, however fleetingly. Still, the viewer is left with the sense that, while two mature people have reconnected with an important part of their past and found unanticipated pleasure in each other, it is the man who this time ends up with a new baby, while the woman is left to face an uncertain future, alone.

Whether *On the Move* reflects Mészáros's personal odyssey and especially her relationship with Jan Nowicki is a matter of speculation, for the director's departure from Hungary both encouraged and was prompted by the need for a freedom of personal experimentation otherwise unavailable. Just as the "potential space" of autobiography and self-analysis enacted by cinema represented for Mészáros a resistance to the external constraints of Hungarian professional and economic politics, so too did this "space" of foreign film production release creative potential. Border-crossing yielded a new love, a new home, and a new language (Mészáros is fluent in Polish); the autobiographical dimension can be traced in the artistic endeavor, inscribing private and public history within the transitional space of cinema. These issues converge in her next and, to my mind, strongest work of this transitional epoch.

In contrast to its dismissal in Hungary, *The Heiresses*, starring Isabelle Huppert and Lili Monori, received favorable notices in France for its audacious treatment of human relations, blending the subjects of class, infertility, and female friendship in the framework of nascent fascism. For the first time Mészáros evokes a time past, focusing directly on larger, more controversial historical issues than in previous films, integrating—but not subsuming—the fate of individuals within the monstrous scale of war. The period is 1936–44, portrayed in a style distinctly different from the mise-en-scene of other Mészáros films. Szilvia Perényi (Lili Monori, the working-class heroine of other Mészáros films, is surprisingly cast in this role), an aristocrat, is married to Akos, an officer in the Hungarian army. Szilvia's father has bought her a magnificent country house which she uses to please Akos, believing in the "magic of new places" and driven by the certainty that her inability to bear a child will cause her husband to leave her. Her anxiety over her personal fate both suggests and conceals the larger, looming dread of Nazism and its aftermath: mass arrests, denunciations, distortions of normally legitimate actions, and the cynical atmosphere that leads to cruel acts of self-preservation.

Soon Szilvia learns to her great dismay that her father intends to will his estate to her unborn children; when she protests, he reassures her that she is certain eventually to become a mother. Shortly thereafter, Szilvia meets Irén Simon, a lovely young woman of modest origins but a talented art student who desires the opportunity—while lacking the means—to study abroad. Irén recites these verses by a favorite woman poet, foretelling the destiny she is to face through this decisive encounter: "Fog ahead and fog behind / A hundred swans fathered me / A Saxon girl fed and raised me / A Hungarian of Jewish blood / Among Slovaks I want to live / On their soil I made my home / I became whole from many roots / Blame behind and dreams ahead." The nightmare is portrayed indirectly, as the director foregrounds the condition of anxiety (in anticipation of the Stalinist era) that occurred prior to descent into the unutterable, unrepresentable horrors of the Holocaust.[12]

Grateful for Szilvia's friendship and financial assistance, Irén believes that "the most beautiful dreams are worth nothing if we haven't the strength to make them come true." In turn, however, Szilvia begs for Irén's help:

> SZILVIA: I can't have children because I'm sterile. And I simply can't accept it. Can you understand me? . . . It's an obsession. . . . I'm prepared to do anything you want. . . .
> IRÉN: Get it out of your mind . . . it's madness. . . . Never, I won't sell my freedom.

Later Szilvia tells Ákos that she has decided to "buy" the fertile younger woman:

> SZILVIA: She has plans and dreams and she wants to study. I'll help her. . . . Irén is pretty, young, and healthy and, if she agrees, she can have a baby for us, I'm sure. . . . I've been thinking about it a lot and I'm afraid that in five or ten years you'll want children very badly and then you'll leave me, I know you will.
> ÁKOS: How can you think of such a thing? Do you think I would leave a woman, just because she can't have children? Do you know me so little?

Szilvia's dread of being abandoned recalls Kata's equally insistent desire for a child in *Adoption:* two scenarios of women from different class backgrounds linked by the common thread of inability to conceive, one for biological and the other for circumstantial reasons.

At last Irén agrees to the arrangement and, after several modestly depicted sexual rendezvous, announces her pregnancy. Szilvia suffers violently from the fact that the contractual agreement she felt entitled to initiate has failed to prevent a deep bond of affection from taking hold between her husband and Irén. Distraught at the triangulation of passions that has overstepped her plans, Szilvia nonetheless suddenly fears that Irén, on whom she now feels dependent for the survival of her marriage and family inheritance, has left for good when she goes off one afternoon to be alone:

> SZILVIA: She won't come back. She's gone and taken her child with her.
> ÁKOS: *Her* child? You're forgetting, my dear, that I have a part in all this.

Ákos finds Irén at the train station, and, as he urges her to return, she tells him that she is Jewish, but he is not surprised. In a later conversation with his wife, dressed in satin peignoir in their aristocratic mansion, Ákos informs her that, whatever may happen, Irén is his child's mother. In so doing, he reasserts his alliance with the fate of all other Jews.[13]

Tormented by ambivalence at the inexorable triangle she has set into motion, Szilvia grows increasingly hysterical, mimicking the contractions of labor, first alone in bed drenched in perspiration, next holding a pillow to her stomach as she crawls in front of the door to Irén's bedroom from which she is dragged screaming by her aunt. Meanwhile the fair-haired Irén is shown in labor in her pristine bed, draped in white satin, as Ákos lovingly caresses her swollen belly, dangling above it a gold ring on a string to determine the child's sex. The women's facial grimaces are nearly identical; Szilvia's sobs echo the birth cries of the infant, as the "real" mother weeps in quiet ecstasy. Mészáros's candor forces the contemporary female spectator to negotiate contradictory responses: while Kata's quest for a baby in *Adoption* was undertaken in part as a solace against the loneliness and alienation of her life, the birth of a child in *The Heiresses* carries quite another set of meanings. Whereas *Adoption* problematized the taboo subjects of the symbolically pregnant older woman and its history as female grotesque, and *Nine Months* foregrounded an actual birth by the pregnant actress, this time Mészáros was unable to find a pregnant actress for the role. The physicality of pregnancy as well as its powerful emotional sequellae is her subject here, played out against the background of the political and moral consequences of the incipient Holocaust. When Szilvia takes the beautiful newborn child, wrapped in Irén's shawl, to a waiting limousine, Ákos tells her to leave without him, reaffirming at once the primacy of his attachment to Irén and hence his resistance to fascism. Mészáros describes, in my 1988 interview with her, the painful intricacies of their relationship:

To me the important thing in the film was the meaning of the friendship for these two women—friendship not in its sexual but its most noble sense. One woman knows that the other woman is "sick" [*beteg*], because a woman who is barren can be considered to have a physical disability, so why shouldn't she help her out? At the same time, however, the woman in need of help comes from the upper class in which money determines everything; consequently, she exploits the poor woman and, in doing so, betrays the friendship. This was, to me, the major interest of the film.

Post-feminist Western audiences are likely to register this notion of infertility as illness with ambivalence at best; it is important, nevertheless, to weigh its meanings both to the film's narrative and to the intercultural, gendered discourse between East and West. Mészáros demonstrates in the statement quoted above an attitude toward sexuality and femininity perhaps more East than West European in its assumption that women, no matter how independent, desire, perhaps even require maternity to be whole persons. But this attitude is at the same time tempered by the transformative power accorded to the potential bonds of women's friendship.[14]

When Ákos, the progenitor, earlier screens footage of a film he has shot of the three of them at a mountain retreat, Szilvia's head and torso appear on screen while Irén is shown entering the room so that the two halves make up a single woman in the frame, in a visual fusion reminiscent of Bergman's

Scene from *Nine Months*

Scenes from *The Two of Them*

Scenes from *Just Like at Home*

Scenes from *The Heiresses*

Scenes from *Mother and Daughter*

melding of two women, also locked together *in extremis*, in *Persona* (1961). But in a gesture suggesting a desire for rupture with the past, Szilvia reacts to this recording of the "true" lovers by throwing the can of film into the fire.[15]

Prompted by the increasingly obvious anti-Semitic remarks of an old friend, Ákos admits to Irén that he has been accused of having a Jewish grandmother:

> I've been tipped off that I should look out. In some quarters they don't like the way I talk about national socialists. . . . I've infuriated the whole right-wing clique. . . . They apologized [after examining his grandmother's baptismal certificate], but said that I must understand them, as the upper rank of the Hungarian Army had to be purged of people with Jewish blood.[16]

The connection between Jews and aristocrats is of as much particular significance to the subplot of *The Heiresses* as to Hungarian history. Popular attitudes toward the acceptance of Jewish families into the ranks of the Hungarian nobility are still a matter of fierce debate, as is the extent of anti-Semitism among peasants during the interwar period. The film alludes to Hungary's borders having remained open to Jewish refugees until 1944, compared with elsewhere in Eastern Europe where deportation had begun earlier.[17] Hungarian cinema has addressed itself to these sensitive issues tangentially, if at all: Miklós Jancsó's films of the 1960s and early 1970s reworked Hungarian national history and folklore from the populist perspective of the peasantry, while *The Revolt of Job* (*Jób láza dása*, 1983), a film by I. Gyöngyössy and B. Kabay, concerns a Hungarian peasant orphan sheltered by an older Jewish couple. Today, with the rising tide of nationalism in Hungary and elsewhere in Eastern Europe and the Soviet Union, fears of recurrent anti-Semitism appear, once again, to be more pronounced, as intimated by Gyula Gazdag's documentary film *Package Tour* (*Társasutazás*, 1986). But Mészáros remains the only Hungarian director to take up this issue as embedded within male-female relationships.[18]

In so doing, Mészáros reverses popular Hungarian consciousness of Jews as manipulators of peasants and workers by constructing a narrative in which a young lower-class Jewish woman is exploited by the upper class, hence raising several highly controversial subjects simultaneously. But her examination of the rightward progress of prewar Hungarian politics[19] is paralleled by her equally pioneering treatment, bridging nationalism and sexuality, of the consequences of Irén's advancing pregnancy. Mészáros sustains her uncompromising stance toward this difficult material—heretofore virtually unknown in East European cinema—that foretells by nearly a decade the debates surrounding the American surrogacy case of Baby M. As Irén puts it:

Oh, I can't bear it . . . that my baby is only mine until it's born. . . . How can I give my child away? I can't . . . I really can't bear it.

After the baby's birth, it is not until 1944 that we next see Ákos and Irén; we are given to surmise that in the meantime they have had a second child. This second, mutually desired pregnancy leaves little doubt that theirs is a relationship of love, despite the fact that Ákos continues to live with Szilvia and the first child. But their conversation is filled with metaphors of death, and the deportation of Jews has now begun in the countryside. The lovers speak of hiding and dying together after the screening of Ákos's own film footage of the devastation of the Hungarian army at the Russian front.[20]

A subsequent sequence in the magnificent country home that was the legacy of Szilvia's father reveals little Ákos perfectly attired as an aristocratic child, sitting on an Oriental carpet, surrounded by his school drawings, and reciting the fascist slogans he has learned in class.[21] We see his father arriving to beg Szilvia's help in saving his "true family"—Irén and their second son—from the death camps by giving Irén her identity papers. But his wife refuses:

SZILVIA: I was honorable, Ákos, I paid her. The rest is not my business. It's hers.
ÁKOS: I could kill you.

Ákos snatches her papers away and returns to the country house, where he has hidden Irén, exhorting her to leave the country, but she declines: "No, we must live or die here. I've thought everything over. . . . Should we have left you? We stayed and that settles it. We either live or die."

In the final scene, heavily armed Arrow Cross soldiers enter the house, giving the fascist salute: "Get your coat, Irén Simon." "Don't touch me!" she cries out, as their youngest child flees with the aunt. The ultimate failure of their resistance and the distinctions of their respective class backgrounds have nonetheless led to a common fate, underscored visually: while Ákos is driven away by the Gestapo in a sleek black limousine, Irén is marched along the quais with a group of Jewish deportees rounded up by the Arrow Cross, their yellow stars prominently displayed. Past and future fuse in the final shot as Ákos, a gun at his neck, is driven slowly alongside the group, forced to witness the destiny of the woman he loves. Knowing they will perish, the couple's eyes meet, and the frame freezes on Irén's direct gaze into the camera as the cold Danube fog envelops her. With regard to the outcome of the drama, Mészáros declares in my 1988 interview with her:

The man, the child's progenitor . . . makes a statement by allying himself with the poor, exploited woman, the future mother—an important element of the narrative to me. I was shocked when people referred to the film simply as a story about a relationship between two women. On the contrary, this film is about three people, the third one being the man who impregnates the surrogate mother, taking a responsible step by finally joining her, and thus they *both* lose in the end.

That both have lost in the end may reveal typically Hungarian and East European attitudes toward life—the *gyászzmagyar*. Still, Mészáros clearly identifies with the love relationship—perhaps especially the "illegitimate" one—as a force that transcends the power wielded by the fascist state over the lives of individuals. Yet hers is no simplistically romantic view, for the protagonists pay with their lives for the boundary transgressions—ethical, familial, religious, traditional—they have enacted. The stark dénouement resonates with classical tragedy in Irén's choice—not without resistance and quiet dignity—of death over separation from the man and children she loves. There is, to be sure, a clear suggestion of hope that the child, the progeny of adult desire, greed, a sense of class entitlement, and "sin," may survive, and in this suggestion Mészáros anticipates the intergenerational focus of the Diary trilogy.

The degree to which this scenario may imply facets of Mészáros's own personal situation leaves one to speculate upon her identification with the two female characters, their insecurities and fears, as she herself enters into a partnership with a man with children from a previous marriage. Mészáros thus interrogates a number of issues of vital social significance at one and the same time. Without self-indulgence, the film explores the psychology and ethics of an arranged pregnancy and the putative primacy of biology over contractual agreement, as well as the further complication of these ethical and psychological issues by the onslaught of fascism.

An unrecognized precursor of Diane Kurys's highly popular autobiograph-ical film *Entre Nous* (1978), featuring Isabelle Huppert in a similar role, *The Heiresses* was never released in the U.S., and no subtitled English print exists. One can only wonder how an Anglo-American audience might have responded to this rigorous treatment of the limits and conditions of a loving relationship between women *in extremis*, and to its examination of the highly controversial topics of infertility and surrogacy. Deconstructing the anguish of a childless woman deemed inadequate by cultural, and intrapsy-chic, constructions of gender convention, Mészáros juxtaposes the socially acceptable family in need of "inheritance" and the "true" family based ultimately on love. Finally, she weaves into the fabric of this immensely complex narrative a meditation on the nature of Jewish identity, the rights of "birth parents," the toll exacted by the suppression of religious and cul-tural identity, and, finally, the convergence of ethnicity with private life and the authority of the fascist state. In its decadent, at times suffocating ambi-ance of inevitable catastrophe, contained within *The Heiresses* is a sketch for the later Diary films. Just as those films are destined to particular audiences—

"my children," "my loves," and "my mother and father"—*The Heiresses* suggests that the legacy of the world it portrays must be borne by the present generation of viewers.

Completing this transitional cycle is *Anna*. Set in contemporary Budapest, it continues the filmmaker's exploration of urban, bourgeois concerns as distinct from the more specifically working-class preoccupations of her earlier period. Its secondary (yet perhaps more important) narrative is a schematic inquiry into the period of greatest anguish for Hungarians: the uprising of 1956, crushed within weeks when Soviet tanks rolled onto the streets of Budapest. In a mode that is by now familiar, Mészáros anticipates her subsequent film by drafting, as if in essay form, the material that is next to appear as her primary text.

The motif of adoption is here reworked through Anna, a forty-year-old Budapest clothes designer living with her twenty-year-old son Péter and her lover János, a celebrated economist. In the Marais district of Paris, in the Place des Vosges, she meets a former suitor who anticipates the quest at the heart of the film by informing the woman taken aback by this unexpected encounter: "A man hopelessly in love can always find his sweetheart, even a hundred years later." Their journey from a political demonstration in Budapest's Heroes' Square in 1955[22] to the Place des Vosges in Paris inscribes a radically different trajectory from that portrayed in *The Girl* and *Adoption*, both of which portrayed the dislocation of young women traveling from their villages to the workers' hostels in Budapest. Even among the Hungarian bourgeoisie such freedom of movement was relatively rare in 1981, when travel to the West was still severely limited. Barbara is able to come face to face with her past only by first leaving the very country that gave birth to that memory.

The subsequent sequences in Budapest are set first in the clothing factory where Anna works, and next in the thermal spa of the Gellért Hotel where she enjoys a sauna, massage, and shower with her co-workers. Later we see her in flashback, sobbing in János's arms in a hospital, then in a rustic cottage with István, her first love, during the time of the uprising of 1956 when students and workers rebelled against Soviet control of their country.[23] The streets have erupted in confrontations punctuated by gunfire in the distance. In the next cut, border guards patrol the movement of refugees from the uprising as they cross into Austria, in a reference to the 200,000 who fled their country's borders during those traumatic weeks. According to the Hungarian critic György Szabó:

> The only thing separating *Anna* from its other 1982 counterparts is its use of history as a dramaturgical device linked to the present-day narrative. It promises a truthful idea according to which the past is always a part of the present and the present is inextricable from the past, an idea in which the confused heroine

of *Anna* is trapped. And if we want to find our consciousness, our identities, our place—things that Anna is seeking for herself—we cannot lose sight of the historical dimension on our horizon.[24]

Subsequent flashbacks further document the turmoil and upheaval of 1956, when decisions to flee advancing Soviet tanks were made in seconds under the threat of prison or death and without the certainty of eventual repatriation. Like many families, Anna's and István's were separated in the aftermath of the uprising; mortally wounded in an accident, István later implores his wife to tell his estranged father of his love.[25] In the ensuing chaos, families are set against one another, opposing friends of long duration as well as young lovers, parents, and children.

Taken to Vienna by the family appointed to care for her, the couple's child disappears while Anna is imprisoned for her activist role in the conflict. The uprising's aftermath, a decade of fruitless searching for the child, has left Anna in a state of perpetual mourning: "Ever since," Anna tells János, "I've looked at people in the street hoping the next person I saw would be my daughter." Reversing the odyssey of a child in search of "real" parents that drives her earlier features, Mészáros here concentrates on a biological mother's quest for the child she has involuntarily abandoned.

Certain human losses, ineradicable by time alone, Mészáros again intimates, are irreparable. We see that Anna is persecuted by the memory of her husband's death and the baby she was forced to leave behind in the chaos of revolution, and that she is haunted by guilt for her failed attempts to find the child.[26] János's efforts to learn more about her vaguely described past are likewise thwarted by Anna's reluctance to uncover painfully repressed details: "I have only known you for six months but it seems like ages. And I still know next to nothing about you. For example, I haven't the faintest idea who your first lover was." Anna answers superficially, reluctant to discuss the traumatic episode, her evasive attitude recognizable in others unable, for whatever reasons, to come to terms with wartime experiences.

Anna's vagueness leads her next to a restaurant, where she is suddenly and unaccountably drawn to a young French girl sitting at a nearby table with her exaggeratedly bourgeois parents; implausibly, Anna is convinced the girl is her long-lost daughter. When she later confides to her mother that "Anna is here," the incredulous mother takes this confession for hysteria: once again, mother and daughter are divided as they were during the uprising, when Anna's parents chose to remain in Hungary instead of fleeing to Austria.

In order to help Anna unearth the truth of her connection to the young French girl, Marie Aubier, János enlists the help of Anna's son Peter who, unaware that she may be his half-sister, becomes infatuated with her. Anna's obsessively probing requests for detailed information about the girl obviously displease the Aubier family, and they depart abruptly from the hotel where they first met. Nonetheless, the still unspoken link between mother and daughter leads Anna to Paris to continue her search. As in *The Heiresses*, the male lead (played in both films by Jan Nowicki) is a crucial figure, quietly and selflessly enabling the female protagonist to accomplish what she feels compelled to do—in this case, to locate the person she is convinced is her own daughter. Although Péter is devastated to learn that the object of his desire might be his half-sister, he does his best to place his mother's feelings above his own by relinquishing his attachment to the girl.

János joins Anna in Paris where they discover that Marie, critically ill with nephritis, requires a kidney donor in order to live. Anna decides to save her "daughter's" life by donating a kidney.[27] Still unconvinced of the fact of her biological parentage, and concerned for Anna's life once she undergoes surgery, János confronts Madame Aubier about her own narcissistic behavior toward Anna:

> JÁNOS: Don't you think you were cruel to Anna? You let her cripple herself because of a dream. . . . Is it true then that you adopted Marie in 1957?
> MME AUBIER: Why don't you believe me?
> JÁNOS: I don't believe you because you love her so much.

Through János, Mészáros questions conventional views of the family, both the capacity for love on the part of an adoptive mother and the legitimacy of the claims of a putative biological mother. Thus she asks her audience to contemplate again the nature of motherhood itself in a variant of other, similar interrogations throughout her cinema. We have seen a daughter seeking her biological mother, an infertile woman hiring a surrogate mother, an older, still-fertile woman adopting a baby, a woman giving birth on screen in the role of one who refuses marriage to the father of that child, and several daughters whose mothers gave them up for adoption or proved otherwise unable to care for them.

With *Anna*—whose lesser-used title *Mother and Daughter* seems more appropriately descriptive—Mészáros seizes upon an intercultural milieu to rework and extend her careful investigation of these variants of family and maternity. Here, notwithstanding the film's improbable moments, she compares the authenticity of biological and adoptive parentage, concluding that profound parental attachment is not necessarily dependent upon—or, for that matter, may even surpass—genetic bonding.

Although Mészáros's *The Land of Mirages* (1983) does not follow here chronologically, as a Polish-Hungarian coproduction it belongs nonetheless to the "transitional space" of this chapter. A variation on Nikolai Gogol's play *The Government Inspector (Revizor)*, it is also a witty and trenchant, if ultimately less successful, critique of social conditions in Hungary and the Soviet Union. Set in Hungary in 1883, its period costumes and decor throw into bold relief the small-town greed, corruption, and graft rampant at that time. Following the Compromise of 1867, which established a dual monarchy for the Austro-Hungarian Empire, with joint control of foreign policy, the military, and finances, Hungarians were struggling to free themselves from Austrian domination and create an independent, self-sufficient nation-state. In those controversial and calamitous decades, the newly emerging bourgeoisie and foreign business interests benefitted from a highly bureaucratized system in which extortion, bribery, and gerrymandering were common practice. The film's otherwise rather transparent contrivances are better understood when such conditions are borne in mind.

Having taken great pains to bribe government officials into diverting a new railway to his town, the mayor (played by Jan Nowicki) is informed of the impending visit of an administrator, traveling incognito and bearing "secret instructions." The town's officials are made exceedingly uncomfortable by this news, having indulged in fraudulent schemes they would not wish to have exposed. Among their gravest concerns is the failure to build a slaughterhouse and a schoolhouse for which funds, long ago diverted to personal uses, had been appropriated. Their activities are summarized toward the end of the film by Bok:

> the postmaster pilfers the letters that have money in them, the mayor makes every tradesman and merchant pay a tax, the county judge has turned the court offices into a kennel, and the schoolmaster engages the pupils in debauchery— the prettiest girls, and there are hundreds.

With the arrival of Karikás, a young visitor to the local inn, the residents believe they have discovered the interloper. Wining and dining the "ministerial inspector," they outdo themselves with offers of gifts and money, including the charms of the mayor's daughter whom the visitor, in reality a person of no official standing, soon wishes to marry. The provincial mayor rapidly imagines himself among the prime minister's inner circle via the betrothal of his daughter. Laden with the bounty of greed and deception, the young man departs on the pretext of asking for his uncle's blessing for the forthcoming marriage. In a letter to his friend opened by the nosy postmaster, the imposter has written:

> My dear friend Gazsi, I'm writing you this from the land of miracles. On my way here I lost all my money on cards . . . the innkeeper was about to have me put in jail when fortune smiled upon me. The locals took me for some sort of government inspector because of my clothes, and since then life has been milk and honey! They wait on me hand and foot, crawl on all fours before me. The idiots. . . . I'm staying at the mayor's house and the frightened officials of this town are lining my pockets.

When the "genuine" commissioner finally arrives, the corrupt bureaucrats assume—correctly, as it turns out—that he, too, will be amenable to their seductive proposals.

The Land of Mirages does not match the cinematic, historical, or compositional standards we have come to expect from Mészáros, who returns in this film to her former use of black-and-white cinematography in period settings. Nevertheless, one cannot fail to note its critique of Hungarian life in the early 1980s, at a time when filmmakers were far less able than today to address such issues directly. The film's most telling and delightful sequence reveals Mészáros's satirical touch: when the inspector is shown the purported school building, actually painted on canvas with cut-out windows from which carefully coached schoolchildren play their part in the town's seemingly limitless scenario of corruption. Although she is obviously more at home in contemporary mise-en-scene, the director's critique of mid-nineteenth-century politics, education, and human relations is at once subtly and broadly parodic.

On the Move, The Heiresses, and *Anna* testify to the power of visual representation and reconstruction of the past by proposing cinema as an instrument for reconceptualizing the narrative of history. Despite weaknesses in plot and execution, their production is no small accomplishment in a culture where Stalinism and fascism are only now emerging from the protective mystery in which they remained shrouded for decades, insulated both by distortion and omission. Under the sway of Stalinism, illusion was paraded as truth, and the party rejected and banned as "existentialist" or "decadent" books and films considered pernicious threats or presumed to advocate passivity and political inactivity.[28] Socialist Realism was the law of the land, refracted through an equally distorted ideological mirror.

The task of the filmmaker, Mészáros believes, is to counter such distortions by providing a more truthful portrayal for succeeding generations. Her *dis*placement from Hungary, then, leads ultimately to her *re*placement in the more immediate past of Hungarian history through the perspective of her personal background. While maternal and paternal preoccupations are present in important ways in this last category of Mészáros's work, they are superseded by an awareness of the larger postwar framework in which they exist. As such, these films invite contemporary dialogue on sensitive issues that are far from resolved today in Hungarian and East European society: the meaning of family, marriage, Jewish identity, and world War II. The complex movements they describe between the structural dualities of Jews and Gentiles, Hungarian nobility and lower classes, and male and female lead us to conclude that while love may be both anchor and catalyst for traversing affective and political boundaries, obstacles to it are often overwhelming. Mészáros does not allow her viewers to forget that risks of such magnitude have their consequences.

The transitional space of cinema has thus become a dialectical zone, enabling the filmmaker to re-envision current issues in light of other cultures, thereby prompting and legitimating spectatorial interrogation of issues of ethnic and national identity. East European artists, forced too often into dislocation and repatriation, know all too well the dangers both of obliterating the past and refusing to relinquish it. Caught between languages and subject to the profound consequences of living in a multicultural identity, Hungarian filmmakers such as Mészáros are inscribed within conflicting discourses; they live with a double vision, one that imparts to Hungarian cinema—as well as literature and poetry—its particular pain and glory. For if indeed there are financial and political benefits, surely, too, there are also potential costs beyond those of artistic freedom: uncertainties of artistic livelihood and future, and alienation from heritage, culture, and peers. Mészáros's displaced temporality and spatiality in this period of her cinematic production thus serves as well to rehistoricize contemporary Hungarian culture and, in so doing, to focalize the extent to which the past informs the outcome of the present.[29]

6 RE-READING HISTORY
The Diary Trilogy

In the finale of Mészáros's *Diary for My Loves*, a distraught young woman clutches the gate of the Hungarian Embassy in Moscow. Her screams grow louder as the Russian guard stationed there rejects her pleas for an exit visa. "I want to go home," she begs, as he shouts: "But your people are shooting each other, and the borders are sealed!" This emotional moment, with its imagery of confinement and political division, captures Márta Mészáros's autobiographical-historical film-making project of the 1980s, the Diary trilogy. Her most complex and ambitious work to date, these three films, made between 1982 and 1990, broke new ground in the genre of cinematic memory narratives while tracing the contours of East-Central European history over the course of this decisive decade.

Trapped in the machinery of international conflict, the exile's desperation to return home resonates for many whose lives have been irremediably altered by such circumstances, whether through interethnic conflict or totalitarian politics. But for a people in protracted mourning for persons and lands lost to an occupying invader, that image has a particular meaning. Reading backward over Hungarian history and forward to its transitional present enables the viewer to appreciate better Mészáros's contemporary—and inextricably historical—project, for this fourth period of her work evolves from such experiences of displacement and loss.

Three narrative and visual structures, already discernible in her earlier work, as we have seen, define this stage: first, a re-reading of history through individual autobiography; second, the articulation of narrative from a child's point of view, specifically that of an orphaned girl; and third, the uses of narrative fiction intercut with documentary footage, including clips intercut from feature films other than her own. In compositional method, *Diary for My Children*, *Diary for My Loves*, and *Diary for My Father and Mother* are at once a recreation of historical events and a re-reading of official versions of history. As such, although far from merely didactic, they propose interpretations that conform neither to the prevailing ideologies of the time in which they were made nor to those of the period they propose to represent. Like other East European filmmakers and writers, Mészáros confronted the complex problem of imagining artistic and philosophical strategies that would be at once comprehensible to audiences and, at the same time, acceptable to a highly sensitive censorship. By 1990, when the final segment was completed, the political and historical critique that animates the trilogy had come to be enacted in fact through the demise of the Communist state, thereby further contributing to the status of the Diary films as an active arena of post–Stalinist contestation in Hungary.[1]

The representation of history in cinema is, to be sure, a dynamic field of debate within film studies. The historian Hayden White, for instance, argues that "Every great historical narrative is an allegory of temporality," going on to submit that the past is most dramatically affected by new emplotments of history in revolutionary societies:

> who may undertake to rewrite their histories from a new political perspective, emphasizing events that had previously appeared unimportant, grasping them now as prefigurations of the new social order; events which provide the ground and the possibility of a "new kind of action" in the future.[2]

To appreciate Hungarian cinema in general and that of Márta Mészáros in particular, the Western spectator unfamiliar with East European representational systems must make an effort to sense how deeply that country has been shaped by its tormented history. The persistence of the past is, arguably more than elsewhere in Europe, especially palpable in literature and the arts. Positioned by historical events as a culture truly "Central European"—between East and West, Germanic and Slavic influences, and dictates of Roman Catholic, Protestant, and Turkish hegemony—its endeavors to become more fully a part of the West (i.e., "European,") while retaining its cultural and linguistic independence have long been matters of profound concern.

Yoked by history and geography to the Habsburg Empire and occupied after 1945 as part of the Soviet Empire, Hungary was governed with an iron hand in the 1950s by a Communist Party whose chief, Mátyás Rákosi, was empowered to eliminate perceived "enemies of the people." Through torture, imprisonment, and death, his secret police, the AVO, then AVH (Department for the Defense of the State), ensured the absence of open opposition to Rákosi's plans, a program that included forced collectivization, irrational industrial planning, terror against the "bourgeois" intellectuals, and the perpetuation of the "cult of personality".[3] Under this physically and morally oppressive totalitarian climate, the fate of the Hungarian nation remained in suspense. In a bloody but short-lived dénouement, the "first war between socialist states" took place in Budapest: the revolution of 1956.[4] Few European countries have experienced more sustained upheaval and dislocation, nor been so haunted by the memories of war and revolution.

After the tumultuous events of 1989–90, this repressive period of Stalinism is undergoing rigorous re-examination in all former East-bloc nations, and long-thwarted efforts to discover its hidden truths move forward with a vigor unthinkable only a short time ago. The arts—especially cinema—have proved to be a viable and even facilitating environment for this activity, having long been more closely enmeshed with history and politics in the East than in the West.[5] But the status of the artist has been further transformed under the influence of glasnost, allowing formerly suppressed films and avant-garde painting to assume a privileged position where once they were the pretext for grave sanctions. In this complex interplay of forces, cinematic and literary texts previously unavailable are finding eager, demanding audiences. By 1980, opposition and criticism had become so commonplace in the Hungarian press that the projection of a controversial film was no longer the audacious political act it might have been only a year earlier. Ivan Sanders, a distinguished critic and witness to the events, has remarked: "In times of crisis, literature in Eastern Europe invariably becomes politics in disguise."[6]

Relentlessly, scrupulously debated in succeeding decades, the Stalin era constitutes the raw material of Mészáros's Diary trilogy. Mészáros having been among the few who dared make of it the focus of their art, the "transitional space" she inhabited abroad had, as we have seen, led her in new directions as Hungary itself was poised on the brink of change. By the late 1970s, as she and Jan Nowicki were working in Paris, the Solidarity movement had emerged as a legal trade union in Poland, while in Hungary the economic situation was rapidly deteriorating. As semilegal forms of a "second economy" proliferated, liberalized state enterprises appeared and independent initiatives were normalized. Contestatory cultural manifestations, including punk-rock groups, spoke the dissatisfaction of youth, while neopopulist and oppositional intellectual thought were disseminated by *samizdat* publications. Grassroots activity focused on ecological and minority issues in Hungary as it had in the United States in the 1960s, laying the groundwork for the sweeping transformations at the decade's end. For a filmmaker whose work had emphasized contemporary life in her own country, it was a risky time to remain abroad.

Diary for My Children (1982)

Mészáros's experience beyond Hungarian borders, ultimately fruitful though it clearly proved to have been, precipitated the creative crisis that was to take her back to her native land. Tempted by the heady atmosphere and pursuit of international coproductions such as *The Heiresses* and *Anna*, Mészáros faced a choice confronted by other East European filmmakers attracted to the seductive—if at times illusory and ephemeral—rewards of work in the West, as she said during my 1989 interview with her:[7]

> Just before making *Diary for My Children*, I had reached the lowest point of my filmmaking career. After *The Heiresses*, I made *Anna*, another French coproduction; success had gone to my head and I thought I could make it big in Paris. Then suddenly I found myself in deep trouble: it was so serious that for a time I really didn't know what to do, how to continue. I spent time in Paris, had offers from Gaumont to make three more films. But I was paralyzed by indecision. . . . Then in his typically honest and tough way [Jan Nowicki] confronted me by pointing out: "You might make a lot of money, but you'll compromise yourself . . . you'll lose touch with who you really are. Instead, you should consider reaching back to your own roots." It was then that I realized I had to re-think everything.

Diary for My Children is, as its title indicates, above all a personal film. That its genesis was motivated by historical forces does not warrant its categorization as exclusively—nor, for that matter, even primarily—a document of history, for it is neither purely fictional nor autobiographical, nor strictly speaking a product of "women's cinema." Instead, by maintaining an intricate balance between personal exploration on the one hand and historical investigation on the other, Mészáros's cinematic method transforms and expands its autobiographical dimension by alternating sequences in which the historical context is dominant. This structure positions the viewer in a way that refuses both the more complete distancing of documentary and the more narcissistically self-indulgent passivity of conventional autobiography. In directorial motivation and structural composition, then, *Diary for My Children* and *Diary for My Loves* transcend conventional generic rubrics. We have noted the extent to which Mészáros's reading of Lukács informed her perspective of history as enacted through individuals rather than in more abstract form.[8] Most frankly autobiographical of all, *Diary for My Children* waited fifteen years to come into being, doubly censored, as it were, by ideological repression and the director's internal struggle with the powerful material that is its subject. The opening scenes of *Diary for My Children* take place in 1947 as Juli, the adolescent narrator-protagonist, is returning to Hungary from the Soviet Union with a group of Hungarian Communists, comrades of her parents exiled there before World War II. As the plane touches down in Budapest, we see aerial shots of the city, its former Hapsburg splendor diminished by war and poverty. In that stark setting, Juli's taut features and toneless voice betray her reluctance to embark upon the paradoxically privileged life offered her by Magda Egri, the loyal member of the Stalinist elite under whose sponsorship this return was made possible.

This repatriation is clearly not to be a joyous homecoming, scarred as it is by the wounds of the past—her parents' death, her country's suffering, her own contained sadness. But Juli quickly establishes herself as an independent young woman, unwilling to be seduced by Magda's efforts to win her over either to the cause of Stalin or to her own emotional needs for a comradely family. As she looks out the window of Magda's well-appointed, if somber, apartment in the first few moments of this new life, her memory is triggered by a glimpse of a ruined building just outside, about to be demolished by the wrecker's ball. In the first of many brief flashbacks, she recalls herself as a child with her real mother, a woman whose physical beauty and youth stand in stark contrast to Magda's middle-aged severity. The visual juxtaposition of women of different ages and class backgrounds, frequent in Mészáros's films, is here brought into especially sharp focus within the framework of familial and political interrelationships. A former member of the anti-fascist Comintern movement, Magda has meanwhile become a high-ranking member of the new Stalinist Hungarian Communist Party, whereas the older couple accompanying Juli have remained embattled yet faithful devotees of socialism, but critical of Hungarian Stalinism. Magda's stern appearance—severe coiffure, tall boots, and uniform—contrasts sharply with Juli's sensual, rapturous recollections of her biological mother. These contrasting images evoke an inner-world split between longing, idealized images of the "good" (dead) mother and starker views of the "bad" persecutory one, as if to embody Juli's guilt for having survived her mother's death and her resistance to Magda's seductive offer of a new life in the powerful party elite.[9]

Magda's efforts to behave maternally toward Juli arouse in her a vehement resistance that takes several forms: repeated flashbacks to childhood memories, fantasies, and reveries of her parents; a surreptitious and obsessional love for the cinema (in the interest of which Juli steals Magda's official movie passes, viewing as many as three films a day instead of going to the school for children of the party elite, to which she has undesired access through Magda's influence); and a proclivity for friends of whom Magda disapproves, in particular her new boyfriend Tomi. Only with Tomi is Juli gradually able to speak of the past. As Tomi's mother sleeps in the adjoining room of their crowded flat, Juli and Tomi steal a few moments of precious privacy, and in that intimate atmosphere Juli describes her parents in loving detail. Both were artists, like Mészáros's own parents, her mother a talented painter, her father a brilliant sculptor, both are visualized as ideally attractive and passionate. Like László Mészáros, Juli's father is arrested by the political police and presumably executed during Stalin's reign of terror. At the same time, Juli grows deeply attached to János, a chief engineer and Communist resistance member whose resemblance to her lost father is consistently underscored by the fact that both roles are acted by Jan Nowicki.

Under the pressure of her increasing estrangement from Magda, Juli fails at school; both János and Dezső also find themselves in violent confrontations with Magda on account of her intensified detachment from the values they represent: Magda's acceptance of a new appointment as a prison warden symbolizes a dangerous betrayal of them and the causes for which they have fought. Juli's efforts to find her father's brothers, ostensibly still living in the countryside, are undermined by Magda, whose henchmen forcibly return the girl to her self-appointed guardian. With the beginning of the Stalinist purges in 1949, another wave of disappearances sweeps the country, and János is arrested at his home in the presence of Juli and his wheelchair-bound son Andras, to whom Juli has grown attached through her love for János. Her tolerance of the privileged life of a party cadre no longer manageable, Juli informs Magda that she is leaving to work, like János, in an industrial plant. When, at the end of the film, she and András visit Janos in prison, they are separated from him by the omnipresent surveillance, their conversation reduced to brief, highly charged everyday phrases, their faces filled with the sadness and suppressed anger of a long-enforced estrangement. Mészáros's use of the musical motif that continues long beyond the final credits is linked to Juli's prolonged periods of waiting, underscoring the agony of her uncertainty and capturing, perhaps even more palpably than the images, the suffering of those who risked opposing Stalinist power and paid with their lives.

As Magda's position weakens with the new regime, she eventually resigns from the Security Forces. Determined to uncover the truth of her father's fate, Juli learns from a chillingly unctuous bureaucrat that, having been like János unjustly sentenced, he was posthumously rehabilitated. In a scene that conveys the pathological damage wrought on honest human communication by decades of official prevarication and doubletalk, Juli is told first that her father has been "rehabilitated," and only secondarily that he is no longer alive. The camera follows her down the corridor of the building, disclosing her fleeing figure engulfed by its massive Stalinist architecture, where she is to receive this "good" news. After a moment of respite when she gratefully accepts a glass of tea poured from a samovar by a kindly Russian-speaking woman,[10] the final blow in this inhuman exchange comes when Juli is informed unceremoniously that the whereabouts of her father's remains are unknown.[11]

The falsification and distortion of language that came to typify life under Stalin in the Soviet Union and Eastern Europe of the 1950s (the target of much black humor among intellectuals and artists) is embodied by the exaggerated courtesy and feigned sincerity of party bureaucrats and apparatchiks: when Juli, like Mészáros, tries to find out what happened to her father, she is led through vast corridors and into the rooms whose faded elegance is not completely masked by the kitsch decor of their new owners. The disparity between Juli's genuine sorrow and the fake politeness of the officials who inform her that her father has been "rehabilitated" is made more grotesque still by their announcement that he is dead. Historical displacement of the narrative to the 1950s does little to disguise Mészáros's critique of the Kádár regime that was in power when the film was made, and it is meant to convey opposition to the present as well as the past, as is often the case in works by East European artists denied the right to overt denunciation or even indirect critique of the political world in which they live.[12] Less accustomed than East-Central Europeans to a transhistorical deciphering of the filmic text, the Western viewer is, of course, in danger of misreading highly coded inferences that permeated cinematic production in the Stalin and post–Stalin eras, and whose meanings were instantly understandable to native audiences. The problematics of reception and spectatorship raised by the possibilities of cultural and political misreadings are the subject of much contemporary film theory, and are taken up in the next chapter.[13]

Juli's exhausting struggle against such massive official obfuscation is conveyed by the determined posture and expressionless face of public compliance not uncommon in Eastern European cinema. As she leaves the office building with its monumental spatial proportions to continue her search, she sees herself in flashback as a vivacious, freckle-faced child eating fruit in her father's studio, gazing raptly as he sculpts. In the following scene, she is an adult observing him from outside his studio window, and in the next embraces him tenderly. Mészáros's use of such temporal condensation recalls the language of dreams and fantasy, the timelessness of the unconscious wherein stimuli originating in the present condense with long-buried psychic material as though it, too, were of the same temporal order.[14] In so doing, she provides a strategy for visualization of emotions for which no words seem adequate, the emotions preserved in the unconscious where, according to classic psychoanalysis, time ceases to exist. Living in Magda's elegant apartment, Juli attends the school reserved for privileged children, where students arrive in chauffeur-driven limousines, resort to elaborate cheating in class, entertain extravagantly with imported wines and food, and dramatize Communist youth rituals in the hallways under a trompe-l'oeil triptych that reflects the face of Stalin, Lenin, or Rákosi, depending upon the viewer's position. Heroic party anthems ring out over the loudspeaker, while at home high-level party-cadre guests dine on fine china and a Russian samovar is displayed on the table as Magda proudly demonstrates the lighting of a crystal chandelier, once the property of counts and bankers.

These blandishments of Magda's privileged world are meant to win over Juli at the cost of an artifically constructed equilibrium; this she steadfastly rejects in order to preserve her familial identity, an autobiographical "construction" she is constantly urged to forget by Magda and her cohorts. When Juli remembers or fantasizes about her mother and father—and those processes are left ambiguous by Mészáros's use of flashbacks indexed by the lyrical theme music—she is engaging in the mourning process that ultimately assures her ability to resist Stalinist homogenization of her personal history and subjectivity.[15]

In contrast, Magda, having withstood the rigors of prison and torture in the radical communist underground, stands for historical revisionism. "We've won," she tells Dezső, "but our enemies are everywhere . . . they smile and nod but they're awaiting their chance. But we're not giving an inch." Juli asks Dezső, a former fighter in the working-class movement and hero of the proletarian revolution of 1919, to clarify what happened to him and to Magda in 1949:

> DEZSŐ: I don't know anything . . . I didn't do anything . . . she's been given a very difficult job—prison governor.
> JULI: My father was taken to prison.
> DEZSŐ: That's different—how often have I told you not to talk about it?

In despair, defeated and enraged by the years of duplicity, Dezső strikes Juli, ostensibly in punishment for her repeated truancy from school and the resistance it enacts, but more obviously for her dogged insistence on learning the truth of the past. Magda intervenes, only to be accused in turn of committing torture as a member of the secret police. Dezső confesses to having been beaten as a child by his father with a wet leather strap, admitting the punishment enhanced his respect for his father. Mészáros reveals enough of the history of these protagonists of her parents' generation to indicate—for the benefit of younger viewers uninformed of these historical events—the complex psychological bonds of power between victim and victimizer, the subtle melange of pleasure and fear that characterizes their protective stance toward the very actions of which they are also ashamed. This familiar litany of evasion, defensive self-exculpation, and complicity in deception is, Mészáros suggests, shared by others of their generation, as Magda demonstrates in an article she dictates that mirrors both her relationship to the party to which she has devoted her life and the Stalinist mythologizing project of the 1950s: "The Red Army arrived in Hungary not as a conqueror, but as the friend of the Hungarian people, their liberator from the yoke of German fascists. . . . The Soviet . . . commanders brought order and organization to the villages and towns."

Emerging concurrently with this narrative are flashbacks of Juli's childhood memories and dreams that increase in duration and frequency as the film progresses, in much the same way as in Resnais/Duras's *Hiroshima Mon Amour*. At times the screen grows eerily bright as a haunting melody, the signature of Juli's past, replaces diegetic sound. Thus does Mészáros indicate the fallibility and subjectivity of memory and fantasy, the dreamlike mental operations of condensation as opposed to recollection and retrieval, the point of view of the five-year-old child's helpless witnessing of her father's arrest and disappearance. The selectivity and obsessional quality of these sequences are visualized in repetitive patterns that suggest the timelessness of the unconscious, the process of mourning in which feelings attached to lost loved objects and traumatic past events remain virtually untouched by time when they are not reworked internally. Mészáros also uses such moments to suggest a connection between Juli's fondness for movies—a Winnicottian space of fantasy and imaginative play—and her stubborn refusal to surrender to Magda's authoritarian demands. For the comforting anonymity of her participation as viewer allows Juli to rework these troubling losses through cinematic representations and to indulge a provisional escape from the present in rapturous viewings of Greta Garbo films and exotic newsreels, far from the dreary oppressiveness of the Stalinist present.

These moments link Juli's past and present experiences, combining the psychological (subjective memory and fantasy flashbacks) with the ideological (documentary footage of the period). Mészáros thereby implicates the viewer in the process, soliciting participation in the self-constructing dynamic of cinematic autobiography. But her account of the past ruptures contrived unity, facile substitution, or spectatorial reassurance, as in the films of her earlier periods. Parental "remembrance," idealized though it may be, is summoned in the service of resistance to Magda and all she represents—her wish to colonize Juli as surrogate daughter and to recruit her for the Stalinist project. Here the trajectory of the filmmaker's personal memory, articulated through the dynamics of the protagonist, conflates uncannily with the socio-political circumstances of national history. Juli's resistance is supported by János in her determination to remember her parents:

> JULI: I don't want to forget my mother and father, and that's what Magda wants.
> She acts as if they never existed. And I can't forget them.
> JÁNOS: You're right, you shouldn't forget them. . . . I think of my family
> too . . . they were killed in an air raid in a bomb shelter near the
> factory where I worked during the war.

The two embrace following their disclosure of the private—and hence subversive—fraternity of memory, which triggers a flashback of Juli in a similar posture tenderly embracing her father.

Addressed primarily to the post–1950s generation, these intergenerational and retrospective narratives are also intended, as Mészáros indicates, to educate. The filmmaker's effort to counter the silencing indifference of Hungarian youth toward officially sanctioned versions of their own political culture constitutes her active intervention in the dynamics of historiography. The illusion of unequivocal ideological commitment is purchased, Mészáros goes on to suggest, by zealots such as Magda at the expense of a double repression: denial of the complexity of the past, and pretense of knowledge of history. A discussion among party cadres in Magda's apartment points to the consequences of such internal splitting; Ilonka speaks of her experience in the Soviet Union when political exiles were forced to work in factories:

ILONKA: I talked with the women weavers there; well, those women clean the house, cook, raise their children after nine-hour shifts, but they accept it. They have an unbelievable self awareness.

ISTVÁN: But it's only unbelievable if you don't know they have faith in the party and are forming it. . . . The workers understand the tense international situation. They support the party unconditionally. Comrade Rákosi, too, of course.

Coercive political solidarity, Mészáros makes clear, is in conflict with individual subjectivity: propagandistic documentary footage of celebrations for Stalin's seventieth birthday, when Stakhanovite workshop members extoll their production quotas far in excess of the requirement, is inserted as bitterly ironic commentary, as are the ubiquitous busts of Lenin, statues of Stalin, and red stars atop official Communist Party buildings. Still in pursuit of information about her father and uncles (whom she has reason to believe are still living in the countryside), Juli completes another useless application, a bust of Lenin perched on Magda's desk continuously visible in the frame. This emotional confrontation is a turning point in the film, foregrounding Juli's—and Mészáros's—steadfastness in the face of "organized forgetting:"[16]

MAGDA: All we know about your father, Juli, is that he disappeared [in the Soviet Union] in 1938.
JULI: That's not true.
MAGDA: Yes it is.
JULI: You're lying.
MAGDA: All right, I'm lying.
JULI: Everyone knows everything here, Magda. Even here, among us, every other person has a relative who disappeared or who is dead. Does everybody lie then?
MAGDA: You don't understand, Juli. There are feelings and impulses here. But that's history, historical necessity.
JULI: Why didn't they arrest you?
MAGDA: That's none of your business.
JULI: But it is! You're alive and you say nothing. Is there a reason?
MAGDA: Yes, there is a reason, as you say. . . . But you wouldn't understand.
JULI: I'll understand if you explain. But you say nothing. . . . I'm not writing down lies.
MAGDA: I'm not going to argue. You fill it out as I say. That's an order.
JULI: You can't order me to do that.
MAGDA: Juli! Do you really hate me so much? Why?
JULI: I feel sorry for you, Magda.

The tension culminates in a masterfully directed moment that throws into bold relief Magda's desperate suppression of the "facts" and Juli's refusal to collaborate in the charade of denial: through her oppositional stance she—and the spectator—implicates herself in the fate of her country.

Mészáros uses the factory machines, temporarily still, as a backdrop for staging a lunchtime encounter between Juli and János as he reminisces about the young Magda, a "lovely girl, just as we imagined the word 'woman': full of life and all brains! . . . How we believed in the future then!" His evocation of the idealism of young militants in the flowering of the early movement leads János to recount the story of his arrest and imprisonment together with Magda in 1929, their escape in 1932, and his departure for Paris and hers to Moscow—two divergent paths that led both back to Budapest. Their conversation refers back in turn to an elegant dinner at Magda's apartment when Istvan and János discuss the "bourgeois" mentality said to typify the Western path:

> ISTVÁN: You aren't aware that ideological commitment is the most effective force.
> JÁNOS: An émigré life in the West was no bed of roses either. . . .
> ISTVÁN: But no one's sure what you did there.

Now circumspect, János tries to supply the missing pieces of history Juli seeks, and in so doing acts as the film's pedagogical presence, speaking in the place of the silenced. Paranoia—"there are traitors among us"—is thereby contextualized and historicized, and gives weight to Juli's final break with Magda:

> JULI: I asked you to find my relatives. But you didn't.
> MAGDA: Yes, I even met them. They're not our kind of people. They're behind the times, religious. I couldn't share their outlook.

Mészáros demonstrates, through Magda, that in the totalizing ideology of Stalin, everyone who deviates—family members included—is dispensable.

Diary for My Children was shelved for over a year and released only after excision of two scenes deemed unacceptable by Hungarian censors. The first was a sequence from *The Fall of Berlin* (*Padenie Berlina*, USSR, 1949), a massive fresco made at the height of the "personality cult," in which Stalin, dressed in pristine white uniform, his arms filled with red roses, descends from a white airplane. In his condemnation of Stalin at the 1956 Party Congress, Nikita Khrushchev exhorted: "Let us recall the film *Fall of Berlin*. In it only Stalin acts, issuing orders from a hall in which there are many empty chairs. . . . Stalin acts for everybody."[17] The second excision was a sequence portraying the funeral of László Rajk which, according to Mészáros, was taken to be an indirect inference to the secrecy surrounding the burial of Imre Nagy.

When Juli first steals the cinema pass from Magda's desk drawer, she watches, enraptured, a classic Hungarian film, István Szőts's *People on the Alps* (*Emberek a havason*, 1942). The clip shown is a poetically moving, finely wrought sequence portraying a Székely woodcutter and his wife in the mountains of Transylvania baptizing their baby with frozen holy water brought home by the father in his pocket. In a magnificent pine wood, they present the child to the natural life of the forest. The cinematic illusion is highly suggestive to Hungarian audiences, for whom Transylvania occupies a mythic cultural role as ancient home in a territory long disputed with Romania. It should be noted that Márta Mészáros's own film possesses the very qualities of sobriety, documentary precision, and refusal of melodramatic devices that are discernible in the sequence she quotes.[18]

The third clip of the "film within a film" that is the subtext of *Diary for My Children*—as well as Juli's apprenticeship to a filmmaking career—is a fashion show newsreel that heightens the very class antagonisms meant to be effaced by the new socialist order. Again it is the party elite who are entitled to enjoy such perquisites at a time when most Hungarians lived in severe hardship, even deprivation. Well-dressed "bourgeois" women, carefully coiffed and made-up, applaud politely along with Magda and Juli as the latest imported styles are modeled, culminating in a promenade of the traditional bridal gown. Mészáros uses the scene to great, if subtle, parodic effect by indicating the panoply of feminine attributes deemed appropriate for a "true" Hungarian Communist woman of the party elite. The filmmaker cuts next to a shot of Juli alone in her room, applying cosmetics in a scene reminiscent of the young factory girls' preparations for a night out in the workers' hostel of *Riddance*. Taking pleasure in her nascent sexuality, Juli adjusts the décolletage of her lacy slip to resemble the actress's pose in a photograph pinned to her mirror.

In the following clip, Greta Garbo as Mata Hari, gorgeously seductive beyond gender containment, exhibits the same vamping gestures in a nightclub, the soundtrack nearly identical to the 1930s bar music of the previous fashion-show newsreel. As Juli watches longingly from the theater balcony, her unadorned beauty seems to be commented on by that of the Hollywood screen goddesses she seeks to emulate, while at the same time a cool detachment is discernible in her knowing eyes. Taken together, these clips constitute a kind of commentary on the film itself and a counterpoise to the main narrative, in which the imaginary is given full play; the pre-oedipal bliss shared by Juli and her mother is recaptured at the cinematheque, promising both refuge and eventual professional identity to the abandoned girl.[19]

Mészáros intercuts documentary footage to underscore the tensions between individual and collectivity, past and present. Two sequences occurring consecutively near the beginning of the film illustrate her technique. In the first, the principal protagonists are gathered at a peace rally; the camera cuts from the gathered masses (shown in newsreel footage) to the speaker, Révai (a powerful figure of the Hungarian "Gang of Four" of Rákosi, Farkas, Gerő, and Révai himself—the highest ranking members of the Central Committee and the Hungarian government), and then to members of the party elite.[20] Close-ups of Magda and János, against a backdrop of Stalin's portrait, alternate with close-ups of individuals present during the actual speech, which are in turn interspersed with shots of Juli and other youthful Communists. Mészáros closes the sequence with a reprise long shot of the masses before cutting to a scene between Juli and Magda. This dialectical structure, foregrounding historical figures who alternate with fictionalized and autobiographical personages, conveys the director's (historically accurate) prediction of the ultimate victory of the Hungarian people over Stalinism, as the Stalinist Révai harangues the crowd:

> Were we strong when Rajk was in our ranks wearing a mask? And did we grow weaker when we tore his mask off and cracked down on his gang? Is that weakening? We exposed him, tried him in court, condemned him and we will liquidate the Tito spies of the imperialists!

Mészáros's directorial vision is not, however, limited to intercutting documentary with fiction. At the cinémathèque, repeatedly skipping school to indulge her secret passion, Juli and her friend Tomi see a Danish film, *Child of Man*, in which a young girl, abandoned by her unmarried mother, becomes a servant in the home of a wealthy farmer who subsequently seduces her and whose wife abuses her. In this sequence, the girl resets the hands of a clock and is punished for "lying to your mother." As the three screaming children look on, she is subjected to a violent beating and banished to the scullery. This sequence prefigures Juli's confrontation with Magda and her punishment by beating for failing at school, administered on Magda's orders by István, a former leatherworker recently appointed ambassador.[21] The final film clip, from *Singing Makes Life Beautiful* (*Dalolva szép az élet*, 1950), a feature production about the 1950 National Choir Festival, is an example of a typical socialist propaganda film popular at the time. The chorus is photographed singing in unison, while banners of Stalin and Lenin smile down on them from massive socialist-realist architectural models. In this hilarious clip, a conductor/composer triumphs over his bourgeois counterpart thanks to his careful mastery of the thoughts of Zhdanov and Lenin. As the Hungarian film critic István Nemeskürty observes:

> In the sphere of cinema it followed that directors with an inadequate political education avoided raising real problems; they confined themselves to directing the film demanded by the script. That is how a Soviet marching song became the principal musical motif of *Singing Makes Life Beautiful*, the rhythm of which was drummed by Kálmán Latabár, happily on the . . . sill of an office window.[22]

Quite the opposite is true of Mészáros's cinema, which loses few opportunities for "raising real problems"; her insertion of this clip heightens the viewer's awareness of the difference between propaganda and historical investigation in filmmaking.

Diary for My Loves (1987)

"Father, I'm writing this diary for you, so that if you're still alive, you will see what I was like," writes Juli Kovács, now 18, in the opening moments of Diary for My Loves:

> I think a lot about my mother, her eyes, her red hair, and sometimes I can even smell her. "Grandmother and Grandfather" are almost real, although not quite. They brought me home from Moscow, but there's only one person I really love: János. They took him away too, just like you. I don't understand anything. . . . I'm tired.

Juli has fled the oppressive Magda Egri without her consent, and is now sharing an apartment with a woman friend, a worker in the local textile mill. The party mistrusts Juli as it does others who do not serve its cause, especially those who have returned from the West. Magda has repeatedly questioned Juli's attachment to János and her devotion to her father's memory: "We cannot trust even ourselves," she warns: "You can't know how they contaminated you. . . . How can you love a man who betrayed our cause?"

Juli's expressions of lassitude in the face of Magda's relentless opposition to her attachment to her father and to János may be symptomatic of the mourning process: in spite of her obvious sadness, she is empowered by assimilation of the introject of the dead person into herself. Writing in the diary—like Mészáros's decision to make the series of diary films—commemmorates her loss while serving as a gesture of atonement and remembrance. Her abandonment as a child by a much-idealized father is consistently represented visually in flashbacks to her younger self in harmony with a devoted parent, which may also mask Juli's more terrifying "screen memory" of watching him dragged away as a frightening traitor. The figure of János is condensed and superimposed, visually and narratively, with that abandoning figure: this multiple representation also parallels at a cultural level the paternal imago of the Stalinist state.

Having left Magda, now a colonel in the State Security Corps, Juli applies again for admission to the Hungarian Film Academy but is ultimately rejected in a cruelly humiliating interview. "Do you have any idea what it means to be a filmmaker?" they ask, citing Lenin's dictum that "film is the most important art." In defiance of their challenge, and despite her misgivings, Juli subsequently accepts Magda's influence in obtaining a scholarhip for her to study economics in Moscow, where she had spent her childhood. Mészáros conveys the excitement of the early socialist years when Juli journeys by train to Moscow with a group of young comrades selected for the privilege of studying in the U.S.S.R.—the folk songs and uniforms, the smiling Soviet women handing up apples to passengers through the windows, the portrait of Rákosi hung on the wall. Once arrived, Juli convinces the academic officials in Moscow to allow her to exchange places with a film student; during her acceptance interview with the State Institute of Cinematography, behind the administration's raised podium hangs a banner echoing the same words of Lenin pronounced by the Hungarian officials—''Among all the arts, to us the most important is film''—as one administrator observes sarcastically that ''even girls'' are sent by party authorities to the film school. Although they consent to ''help the Hungarian comrades,'' it would seem after all that the Soviet state's claims to sexual and class equality were at best disingenuous, if not dishonest.

In alternating sequences between Budapest and Moscow, Mészáros evokes Juli's ambivalence and sense of dislocation at taking up the Soviet challenge, and in so doing captures the political tensions between the paternalistic socialist empire and its lesser satellites that led eventually to the ''failed'' uprising of 1956. The former splendor of baroque buildings, now transformed into drab party headquarters, comments ironically on the corruption of a Soviet regime that has imposed itself against the will of the Hungarian people, heightening the ominous, mournful tone of the Budapest sequences in *Diary for My Loves* that convey Juli's depression and that of her nation. But when Juli is befriended by Anna Pavlovna, a beautiful Russian actress and thrice Stalin-prize winner, she is able to confide her desire to find the house where she had lived with her family in Moscow before the war. In Anna, Juli feels she has found a sister and a mentor, and their bond enables her to enjoy close friendships with female students at the academy. In one such moment of intimacy, she lies in bed with a classmate, the glow of their cigarettes flickering as they trade confidences.

The viewer is drawn into the excitement of Soviet cinema, and for that matter of film study, through tantalizing glimpses of Eisenstein's *Potemkin* and other classics projected on the screen as the students attend lectures. Together Anna and Juli find the house of her past. As Juli stands in the courtyard watching neighborhood children at play, she remembers having been mocked for being a Hungarian child because her country's leader, Mátyás Rákosi, was short and bald, unlike the towering paternalistic figure of Stalin (who was actually small in stature). Anna's celebrity and strength of purpose, her flamboyantly high-handed treatment of the petty bureaucrats and the uncooperative commissars who create obstacles at every turn, offer Juli a model of integrity and courage, when for example Anna deflects the cloying advances of party servants by offering them a glamourous autographed portrait.

Taken together, Anna and Magda seem to represent two possible strategies for women of their generation in the Stalin era. Magda—severe, secretive, repressed—sacrifices personal life, friendship, and family for the good of the party, while Anna's status is enhanced by her generosity: in love (she is shown in a romantic scene with her handsome younger husband who carries her upstairs); in work (she encourages other young students to achieve their artistic goals); and in opposition to abusive officials given liberal powers to destroy the lives of those who fail to adhere to the party line. In this equation there is no question where the director positions herself and many reasons to suspect that she resembles the admirable—and vulnerable—character of Anna.

Torn between Budapest and Moscow, Juli grows increasingly depressed by the rigid, paranoid ambience of 1950s Stalinism, threatening to disappear from Magda's life forever unless she arranges a meeting with András, János's son. As they lie in bed together, András shows Juli a letter from her father that had been smuggled out of prison. Reverently she presses it to her lips, gazing out the window to the garden wall beyond as the mournful melody of a Transylvanian farewell lament plays on the soundtrack.

The Stalin/Rákosi propaganda hailing Soviet/Hungarian friendship is made vivid in clips from documentary footage of a Stakhanovite Hungarian worker who had outproduced all others for Stalin, attaining 3,000 percent above the prescribed quota. Mészáros handles this material in ways that enable viewers untutored in the intricacies of Stalinist ideological refinements to appreciate its excessive aspects: the massive configurations of assembled people; the loudspeakers exhorting to action; the larger-than-life socialist-realist posters and monuments that embody the gigantic scope of the Soviet empire. Again Mészáros uses archival material to intensify the contradictions between such ideological pronouncements and the ''double vision'' of those who, willingly or not, must live under Stalinism according to their own precepts.

The dramatic news of Stalin's death by cerebral hemorrhage is announced over the school's public address system as Juli and her schoolmates take their morning showers. With the exception of Juli, who resists this symbolic accommodation to Stalinism, the girls stage a spontaneous ceremony in honor of the departed patriarchal imago, offering words of praise and apprehension for the future as they recall having received news of other, more personal deaths. During the grandiose burial ceremonies, a funeral requiem sounds its dirge in a dramatic reconstruction of his interment, as the camera cuts to Magda and Juli joining the procession sutured with documentary footage of a speech by Imre Nagy. The new leader extolls Stalin's achievements and praises his countrymen for following the ''right path,'' while Juli tracks the demonstration with her camera.

This post–Stalin thaw permits Juli at last to receive permission for a visit with János, who has been imprisoned in Budapest on false charges of anti-party activity. Her attachment to him enables Juli to recover the courage to continue her film studies, and she profits from her time in Hungary by shooting an openly critical documentary film about the poverty and misery of peasant life there. When she returns to Moscow, her Soviet professors reject the work: "A director should see beyond reality," they insist, offended by her refusal to adhere to the party line. The film academy professoriate, wearing the severe uniforms of the party elite, is shot from low-angle perspectives seated on a podium high above the students who must traverse the seemingly endless spaces of Stalin-era interiors before being granted an audience. Mészáros thus loses no opportunity to parody the oppressive, widely detested power of communist party leaders and bureaucrats. Elsewhere as well in the Diary trilogy, the kitsch iconography of the ubiquitous red star atop official buildings imparts an oblique critique of the Stalinist mentality. Displaced to a postcommunist moment, the contemporary spectator would be positioned to read these parodic elements as historical curiosities were it not for the fact that Mészáros consistently links them to a core narrative of great emotional depth.

The making of *Diary for My Loves*, then, is in some sense an act of defiance against those who did not believe Juli (nor perhaps Mészáros herself) capable of becoming a filmmaker. At the same time, the film constitutes a kind of apprenticeship in the art of becoming a director, as well as an insider's view of Soviet and East European cinema in the 1950s. We follow Juli's career from her first agit-prop piece, "We Vow to Fight the Imperialists," to the documentary on Hungarian peasants rejected by the film board for excessive "realism," a coded reference to the socialist-realist esthetics that the party loyalists embodied. The "realism" that arouses their ire—and, later, that of Mészáros's critics—is indeed a merciless indictment of the failings of the Soviet system and of the party apparatchiks in Hungary who shamelessly shifted course according to the prevailing winds from Moscow. When Juli tries to film women workers in a textile factory, their male boss opposes her but the women collectively support Juli; they argue effectively against him, and when her friend Erzsi admits to having had an affair with him, she confesses that he had her fired even though he was "a good lover." This moment recalls Pál Gábor's *Angi Vera* (1978), set in the same period, in which an ambitious young woman becomes sexually involved with her Communist Party school teacher and then denounces him for betraying his professional calling. Mészáros uses the moment to comment critically on the hypocrisy of Stalinist pronatalist propaganda, with its anti-abortion ideology that idealized maternity and paternalism while claiming sexual equality.

Juli, too, is called to account by the Moscow Branch of the Hungarian Komsomol and accused, in a typical disciplinary session, of having a lover. She uses the occasion to vigorously defend her friendship with Anna Pavlovna, who insists afterwards that Juli must decide whether to be an adult or a child: "Don't worry about being understood—care about other people's feelings. Do you know what a film's director's job entails? I pay with my blood!" Here Mészáros seems also to refer to the courage she required and the opposition she encountered in her own trajectory as a filmmaker, as in a scene in which the head of the documentary unit offers Juli his help and compliments her on having a "magnificent comrade" such as Magda for a relative, all the while taking credit for the accomplishments of women directors.

At a lavish soiree for the party elite, Juli attracts the attentions of an older painter, a bon vivant who holds many official functions; "What a decadent world," she observes, as the champagne flows copiously. Unable to escape this hypocritical and stultifying situation, Juli dreams again of her father's studio and awakens in tears, comforted by her roommate, who offers the onions and mushrooms gathered by her own poverty-stricken family on a collective farm in Siberia and who urges her not to abandon her studies. But Juli leaves Moscow in search of András, János's son, who has been "relocated" (in the deformed parlance of the Stalinist lexicon) as an "enemy of the cause" through association with his imprisoned father.

At last, after eleven years, János is set free: the beautiful weather only underscores the years of imprisonment, torture, and lost opportunities shared by many others condemned to serve out their days for purported offenses that would come to acquire entirely different meanings under a gradually liberalized socialism. Like many who suffered a similar fate, his health is broken, and he cries out on behalf of the victims as well as the beneficiaries of Stalinism: "How could this have happened here? Our questions are not answered—instead it is only propaganda and autocracy." Nonetheless, Magda and her influential friends—among them perpetrators of some of the most vicious torture and imprisonment of their fellow citizens, one of whom spits in his face—do not forgive him his "betrayal." At a gathering in his honor, János at first refuses to allow Juli to touch him: later offering her a pair of earrings, he begins to discuss his experiences in prison, the changes in behavior of the guards, the beatings, torture, and death of his friends and comrades. János admits that Magda had warned him: "Those who don't consider the Party's interests virtually commit suicide"; Magda herself acknowledges that she would do anything, even sacrifice her life, for the party, a statement corroborated by the bereavement she had shown at Stalin's death. Juli and János embrace slowly and begin to dance as András looks on with tears in his eyes. János notices his son's distress and goes to him; they cry together as János confides that he has "no one but you."

Like others committed to liberal reform, Juli vows to work to end the Stalinist "cult of personality" in her own country, where she might now be able to live. For his part, János insists that he still believes in something. Watching with János a newsreel of the signing of accords between Yugoslavia and the U.S.S.R., Juli finds the material exciting and disturbing, and she vows one day to make a film about the tormented times which they have both survived. Eager to receive her film diploma, she plans to leave Moscow on October 21, 1956, only to learn that the "counterrevolution" (the uprising of Hungarian partisans against their Soviet-controlled leaders, later acknowledged to be a true "revolution") has broken out on the streets of Budapest. With *Diary for My Loves*, Mészáros deepens her inquiry into the consequences of totalitarian terror and hypocrisy while foregrounding a young woman's odyssey from grieving adolescent to nascent filmmaker. Perhaps more harshly polemical than *Diary for My Children*, this film's interrogative stance mirrors Mészáros's disaffection from the ideological stranglehold of the Stalinist moment it portrays.

Diary for My Father and Mother (1990)

Mészáros received permission to begin shooting the final segment of the trilogy, originally scheduled for release in early 1989, but again her project was delayed more than a year, ostensibly for financial reasons. *Diary for My Father and Mother* takes up at the conclusion of *Diary for My Loves*, in October 1956, with Juli begging for embassy permission to return to Budapest, where the uprising has just begun. The economic crisis and the course of historical events were, however, to alter Mészáros's project significantly, for in the interim, in uncanny resemblance to her cinematic interpretation, Hungary had become the first nation of the East bloc to declare itself a republic, setting in motion the historic transformations that were to follow throughout Eastern Europe. The death of János Kádár, prime minister for over thirty years, and the successes of oppositional forces reconfigured the contours of Hungarian history with an inexorability readable in her earlier texts.

"Father," the first word of dialogue spoken in *Diary for My Father and Mother*, is followed by a reprise of the black-and-white shot from *Diary for My Children* in which Juli's father caresses his wife's face for the last time before his arrest. The subsequent color sequence shows the Communist red star perched on a Budapest building in the center of the frame, followed by a cutaway to snow-capped mountains, and then to Juli as an adolescent watching her father working in his studio, his head shown in profile next to that of a bronze sculpture. The title reads "Moscow 1956" and, as the credits unfold, we see touristic views of the city's parks and fountains. A medium shot of Juli on a park bench precedes the next sequence in Budapest, again in black and white, beginning with a low-angle shot of a towering bronze statue of Stalin mounted on an immense concrete pedestal, with the title: "Budapest, October 23, 1956." It is a date of profound significance to Hungarians, marking the beginning of their brief and bloody uprising against Soviet domination.

A crane shot angles downward from the statue's head toward János standing below; the countershot of Stalin's face makes way for one of János tipping his hat toward the Stalin bronze, an ironic smile on his face. The assembled crowd begins to chant: "We want freedom!" as we glimpse János and his pregnant wife Ildi through the iron bars of a fence; their chants grow louder, intercut with documentary footage of the demonstrations being recreated here. A ladder is brought next to the statue and ropes hung round its head: "We want the rope," the crowd calls out, "We demand free elections of parties with a united front," as János beams at the euphoric mass of people. A truck pulls up and we see Stalin's enormous hand stretching out into the center of the frame, while a Hungarian flag, its Communist hammer-and-sickle emblem cut out in the middle, is brandished to the right.[23]

The screen fades to near-black, illuminated only by sparks from a blow-torch slicing from left to right; demonstrators fight for a chance to hold the rope in a scene that has since been repeated in reality countless times throughout Eastern Europe as, in slow motion, the statue comes crashing down to the accompaniment of the Hungarian national anthem. The crowd roars and swarms toward the supine figure; hands reach out to pound it, as shouts of "Long live freedom" punctuate the night air.[24] It is one of the film's strongest scenes, and if some audiences were less than enthusiastic about its subject by the time the film was finally released, it was surely a case of Mészáros's premonitory vision having been overtaken by world events.

In the next sequence, Tass announces over Moscow Radio in Budapest on October 24th that, encouraged by reactionary forces, a "counter-revolution" is underway in Hungary. The next cut refers back to Juli at the end of *Diary for My Loves*, her face pressed to the iron gate of the Hungarian Embassy, begging for a visa, as the official reproaches her for wanting to leave. Again Budapest, October 27: the point of view is from an army truck accelerating away from Magda as she tries desperately to climb up, only to be brutally pushed away. She falls on the road, sobbing, at last, Mészáros suggests, on the "wrong" side of history. Tanks roll through Heroes' Square, and it appears the Russians are leaving the city.

Meanwhile, in a Moscow restaurant, Juli and her actress friend Anna sip wine together while a band plays Russian folk songs: "I'm happy for all Hungarians," Anna says. "Now everything is all right." A week later, the setting is János's apartment, where he is asleep with Ildi as Russian tanks roll through the quiet Budapest streets. There is a color archival sequence of Imre Nagy, Prime Minister of the People's Repulic of Hungary, declaring "to the nation and the world" that Russian troops have attacked the city to over-throw its legal democratic government, as Magda confides to her comrade: "At last they're here [the Russians], peace again." Immediately thereafter, Tass insists on a radio broadcast that Hungarian reactionary forces and fascist gangs have been destroyed. Alternating between the two cities, Mészáros foregrounds their conflicting political perspectives, using the media to correct the historical record.

In the student dormitory in Moscow, Juli confronts each of her colleagues in turn, accusing Katya of betraying her parents in Siberia by taking as her lover an old party leader, and berating Natasha for her willingness to believe that her father, arrested in 1938, was a traitor instead of a victim. "Why must we always lie?" Juli asks, only to be told that she is merely "a Hungarian, and ungrateful [for Soviet support], like her nation."[25] She learns that the Central Committee has asked that she return to Budapest, and in a formal ceremony she receives her diploma with her fellow students, all dressed alike in beige suits, addressing each other ceremoniously as "comrade."

Street scenes in Budapest reveal a bombed city, clusters of flickering candles marking the places where revolutionaries have already died. Juli takes out her camera to film a grieving woman in prayer and is kicked away for intruding upon her grief. She visits her aunt Vera (Mari Töröcsik, one of Hungary's eminent actresses), who opens the door wearing a large hat decorated with a yellow chrysanthemum and a flowered shawl, carrying a cigarette holder, an apparition unmistakably at odds with the drab surroundings. With her throaty voice and bohemian manner, she explains that her husband was a Communist martyr killed by the fascist Horthy government, as Juli weeps for the injustice of having loved and lived in the country whose government is now killing her people. Vera consoles her with memories of her father, beloved by the Kirghiz people of Central Asia: "A lot of us are crying these days, very strange things are happening here."

In an editing room at the Moscow Film Academy, Juli looks at footage of the uprising taken by her friend Péter, especially the toppling of the Stalin statue. Mészáros thus casts the photographer and filmmaker in the role of reliable historical witness, suggesting that pictures alone retain the capacity to counteract the revisionist history already being written. There are dead bodies in the street and wooden coffins with "Magyar" scrawled in chalk, carted away to unmarked graves in the chaos of the moment. Seeing the footage, she realizes where János is, and in the next cut she is ringing his doorbell.

Sardonic at first that Juli has been away in Moscow while her countrymen are dying, János, wearing an armband of the Hungarian national colors, is reminded by her of his own guilty complicity. He joins the street fighting, hurling grenades at Russian tanks before crawling on his belly toward a young man who dies in his arms. Ever the silent witness, Juli observes his anguish before leaving for Magda's apartment, where she finds her broken and terrified. She forces Magda to read a declaration by the Soviet Supreme Court, dated Moscow, 1956, certifying that her father, László Kovács, was executed in September 1938 and is now "rehabilitated," and she demands to know what happened to the others for whose disappearance Magda is responsible. Juli is ordered to leave the house but remains in the dark, camera focused, as Magda points a gun to her temple. But Magda breaks down sobbing in the arms of her comrade; Juli leaves to warn János but is arrested in the street. Janos and Ildi see her taken away by the militia. The screens and sobs of bleeding victims resound in the interrogation room, where the patriots sing a haunting traditional melody, "I Left my Beautiful Country." When Juli tries to prevent a young man from being beaten, she is pushed to the floor, her film inspected by a police official as she is accused of breaking curfew under martial law. "I don't fight, I take pictures," she responds, her fluency in Russian an obvious factor in her eventual release.

Juli and her friends drive by an exhumation and stop to watch the wrenching scene of small children dead in their coffins. A camera rolls off-screen, while Juli, appalled, tries to prevent the operators from recording the mother's grief. Again in Vera's apartment, Juli is asked to accompany Russian soldiers to a concert by her schoolmate Natasha. Rows of men in uniform listen in silence to the soulful song, and when Juli goes backstage the friends embrace while arguing about who is responsible for the destruction of Budapest—Hungarian fascists or Russian tanks. Their differences are irreconcilable, their parting bitter. Mészáros is at pains to insist on the human toll of the suppression of the invasion: friends, family, and neighbors separated forever, lifelong ties irreparably broken. At a candlelight Christmas mass, a memorial service is held for the martyrs, and a mournful requiem—*Szózat*—is sung for them.

The old comrades gather for a final dinner before János is to leave for Vienna, drinking to "old companions—those who survived and those who didn't, Juli's father and those who disappeared, those who died in the fighting, and to ourselves." They speak of lives wasted in Siberia for the cause, of shattered families and fear of the future. Juli leaves for Vienna with János with Ildi's blessing; they stroll through streets strewn with sparkling lights, gazing at displays of fine jewelry in the shops, "All this only 250 kilometers from Budapest"—a reference as well to contemporary East European desires for Western living standards and consumer goods.

In a Viennese restaurant a Hungarian woman vows never to return to the country where her own brother was shot driving the wounded to the hospital. Her lament sounds again the theme of hopeless causes: "Small country, large sacrifice." János's son András begs his father to leave for Paris with him and his friends. There is a flashback of Juli's father in the stone quarry as János confesses that "they" killed his own father. The two return to Budapest together, where János leads the workers' council in prolonging their strike, if only to serve as an example of courage for posterity. Juli shows Péter, now her lover, photographs of her family and identifies János as "János, my father, my love."

It is New Year's eve and Juli prepares for the evening's celebration, dressed in a sophisticated red dress. In a Felliniesque sequence, the entire cast assembles for the party, some arriving in costume. János is rakish in white scarf and black hat: "I'll be a gigolo—I've had it with morals and ideology." He speaks for a generation whose lives were entirely overtaken with politics, and the evening becomes a ritual of collective mourning as Juli, in a lacy white hat, bends down in a conciliatory gesture to remove Magda's boots, lovingly this time. When János asks her who she wants to be in the masquerade, she answers, "Greta Garbo, can't you tell?," as she watches János guide Magda around the dance floor. The guests look on in amazement as János and Magda kiss passionately, while Ildi becomes hysterical at the hypocritical display. "Everyone is reporting on everyone," she cries: "Murderers, scoundrels, bastards, traitors."

Gunshots ring out in the streets during the night and the revolutionary flag is flown in the foggy morning. János suddenly begins to play a record of a Russian folk tune and the party comes to life again, revelers dancing in a circle of forced gaiety as if momentarily to hold at bay the national agony just outside. But even their strained merry-making is short-lived: Ildi gives birth to her baby while Juli waits outside, covering her ears to the woman's screams just as she did as a child waiting outside while her own mother died screaming in childbirth.

It is now May Day, 1957, in documentary color sequences of a massive gathering in Heroes' Square. As in *Diary for My Children*, Magda is once again in the crowd, chanting slogans and waving her flag for the new cause. Juli photographs the ceremony in 35mm, her face and camera now filling the screen. János pleads guilty to forming "counterrevolutionary" workers' councils, and in a theatrical speech goes on with a speech of his own accusing his accusers of being all the same "dirty murderers" and implicating himself as a spy for Horthy's police in 1939, for France in 1944, and for Tito in 1946. He is condemned to death and bound, blindfolded, and hanged: only his wrists twitch in Mészáros's clinical recording of his execution, and his body is removed and placed in a coffin. We see his blue eyes fixed skyward as a flock of birds passes overhead, the same birds seen first by Ildikó and then Juli.

In the penultimate scene, Juli sits in an armchair in Ildi's home: "I can't write a diary," she admits. "I don't even know what is happening around me—fear and suffering. I want to understand Magda, János, Ildi—why did my father have to die in 1929, innocent?" The diary—and perhaps the entire autobiographical trilogy, Mészáros means to suggest—has served its purpose, for the collective and individual mourning, always in some sense interminable, must turn once again outward, toward the future. Mészáros's Diary trilogy, spanning the decade of Hungary's transition from a post-Stalinist state to a postcommunist nation, is for everyone: children, lovers, father, and mother. As such, it serves to commemorate and remember those who had, and continue to have, the courage to speak the truth in the face of certain death, punishment, and deprivation. The trilogy's innovative autobiographical structure, its remarkable uses of documentary materials and personal journals, continues to suggest new possibilities for filmmaking in an era of global migration and the reconfiguration of Europe.

Hungarian critics of the younger generation, sympathetic to the unpredictable temporality through which history converged with cinematic representation, nonetheless acknowledge that *Diary for My Father and Mother* is incomprehensible without prior knowledge of the preceding segments of the trilogy, whose power resided in the novelty for local and international audiences of representing the Stalinist terror and the Muscovite cadre in Hungary.[26] Those of Mészáros's generation, on the other hand, recognizing the hostility with which Mészáros was met in Hungary after *Diary for My Children* was awarded Best Film at the Cannes Festival, praise her ambitious endeavor as a rare phenomenon in that country while confining their acclaim to unforgettable sequences such as János's performance before the tribunal.[27] Because the subject of 1956 was by the time of its release no longer new, Mészáros weighted the narrative in the direction of the moral and political conflicts of the protagonists—their personal choices rather than the larger historical scale.

When Juli visits the cemetery with Ildi and her son, the boy asks: "Which is Daddy's grave?" "I don't know," answers his mother, "but let's let it be this one." In perhaps the film's most violent scene, three mounted police appear on horseback as if from nowhere. Swooping down upon the small group of mourners huddled together in a vast untended field, they crack their whips with gusto against the helpless victims and then seem to ride off again as quickly as they came. The mourners cling together sobbing, and the mournful melodies associated with the time of János's imprisonment seem to echo in the autumn afternoon. In the next and final sequence, the same dreaded military police are seen unceremoniously placing János face down in his wooden coffin in a symbolic gesture reserved for those considered to have been traitors to the Hungarian motherland.

Poised between documentary and fiction, the Diary trilogy serves as a reminder that cinema is at once ideological and intimately personal—individual artistic intellect and memory, culture, economics, and private as well as collective fantasy all commingled. Mészáros's multigenerational narrative structure and her directorial decision to situate characters in a scenario that foregrounds their gendered connections as well as divisions owe a great deal to her East European heritage. In *The Velvet Prison: Artists under State Socialism*, one of Hungary's leading dissident writers, Miklós Haraszti, argues that post–Stalinist culture also effectively controlled criticism and dissent, whether in painting, cinema, literature, or theater. Through its preferential treatment of "successful" artists and their families, he argues, even oppositional art has become normalized and disciplined, and the artist, having too long enjoyed the privileged status of cultural worker within the party apparatus, has become an important creator of "directed culture."[28] To this charge, the Diary trilogy and, for that matter, Mészáros's cinema as a whole, stands as a testament to the contestatory possibilities of cinematic representation as *agent provocateur*.

Scenes from *Diary for My Children*

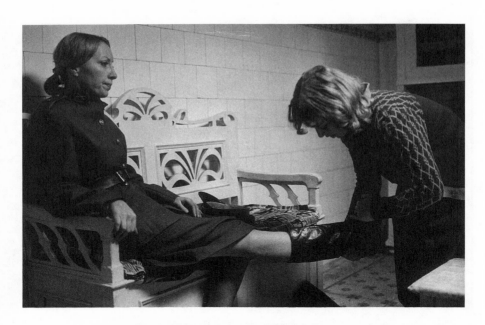

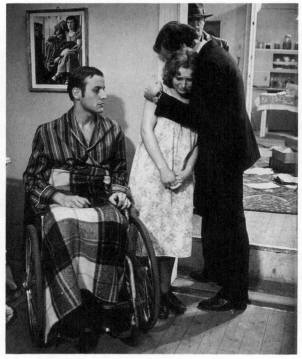

Scenes from *Diary for My Children*

Scenes from *Diary for My Loves*

Scene from *Diary for My Loves*

Scenes from *Diary for My Father and Mother*

Scenes from *Diary for My Father and Mother*

Scene from *Diary for My Father and Mother*

Mészáros Directing

Mészáros Directing

7 TALES FOR THE FUTURE

Filmed on location in Hungary and Montreal, *Bye Bye Red Riding Hood* (1989) is a retelling of the Grimm Brothers' classic children's fable. Part of a package of family entertainment in a series entitled "Tales for All," this Riding Hood, premiered in Montreal in December, 1989, is the first official Canadian-Hungarian coproduction in cinema history.[1] Yet despite—or perhaps on account of—its deceptive simplicity, Mészáros's version reclaims for its heroine the role of active agent in her own drama missing in other versions, demonstrating the influence of the Germanic folk tradition of the Grimm brothers in her narrative over that of the earlier French text of Charles Perrault.[2] At the same time, like most fairy tales, the film inscribes the anxiety, fantasy, and popular mythology of the society that produced it. Here, however, the filmmaker appropriates the cinematic strategy from the Diary films of combining factual document with reminiscence, transposing it to a level of the imaginary in which the fantastic—and the phantasmatic—is more fully articulated.

The film's genesis (it was originally entitled *Little Red Riding Hood/Year* 2000) thematizes the cultural and familial links that, as we have seen, characterize Mészáros's cinematic project as a whole.[3] Instrumental in connecting the principals for this production was Thomas Vámos, a Hungarian-Canadian cinematographer for the National Film Board and longtime associate of Mészáros, through whom she met the producer while serving on the jury of the Montreal World Film Festival in 1984. The designer for the film's innovative mise-en-scene was László Rajk, a Montreal-trained, Budapest-based acclaimed avant-garde artist and the son of the late László Rajk, whose funeral is depicted in *Diary for My Loves*. With this film, Rajk extends the illustrious screen credits he has earned with directors such as Péter Gothár and Pál Sándor, while Mészáros's long-time screenwriter, Éva Pataki, again collaborated on the script.[4] Among the actors, the ninety-seven-year-old Hungarian actress Margit Makay in the role of the great-grandmother is the oldest ever to appear on screen for Mészáros, this time opposite Fanny Lauzier, a thirteen-year-old Quebec native, whose "gorgeous red curls" inspired Mészáros to cast her as Red Riding Hood.[5] Closing the circle of intimate friends and colleagues working together is Jan Nowicki, "a helpful collaborator who gave us wonderful ideas to enhance the visual poetry of the forest . . . and to create a spiritual context for the forest through the presence of the great-grandmother," according to Mészáros.[6]

At first glance, nothing might seem further removed from the semi-documentary "realism" and personalized historiography of Mészáros's political Diary films than this folk tale, with its childhood resonance and escapist air. But on closer inspection we find that *Bye Bye Red Riding Hood* bears a more than superficial resemblance to those texts, for even its colorful narrative surface and pleasing visual style do not obviate a reading of the film's subversive possibilities. Such a reading of *Bye Bye Red Riding Hood* assures us that, while fairy tales are conventionally seen as enabling children and adults to indulge imaginative fantasy, they also have the capacity to serve as projective identification for collective desire. In response to those who greeted with surprise, laughter, and disdain the decision of an established Hungarian filmmaker to make a "children's" film, Mészáros counters: "Why *not* make this film?" For, in her view, its *raison d'etre* is far from humorous: "I think all my films are about girls who try to reach the other side of the forest unscathed. And, since I can't remember my father, I can give him any face I wish. So for me, Red Riding Hood is a perfect subject."[7]

Suggestive though it may be, this assessment nonetheless falls short of acknowledging the director's vision of this "perfect subject." Literary accounts of Riding Hood are, of course, plentiful, ranging from Charles Perrault's "Le Petit Chaperon rouge" (1697) to that of the brothers Grimm (1812) and beyond. Prose and verse adaptations abound, and there are folk versions as well, ranging from "A South African Red Riding Hood" (1889) to a Chinese "Gold Flower and the Bear" (1979). No other full-length feature film version of the story, however, has to my knowledge been produced in Eastern Europe, although there is an English film treatment based on Angela Carter's story "The Company of Wolves."[8]

In developing the scenario—originally constructed in a medieval setting—for its contemporary context, Mészáros and Demers sought to emphasize the core narrative's shifting stance between attraction and repulsion, domination and autonomy. The cinematic modernization, intended for general release, is told from the point of view of a cherubic, auburn-haired Red Riding Hood who lives with her mother, a blonde meteorologist in futuristic attire. En route to visit grandmother and great-grandmother on the other side of the forest, the young protagonist has four decisive encounters: first, with a friendly, talking silver wolf; second, with a magic tree in whose gigantic blossoms moving images of her parents reflect photographs on her bedroom wall of the "family romance" that evaporated with her parents' divorce; third, on a wilderness adventure with a group of classmates; and finally, with a dangerously handsome ornithologist dressed entirely in gray (like the wolf) who bears a striking resemblance to the adored father who abandoned the child and her mother long ago. Their instantaneous rapport marks the final stage of the girl's eventual separation from her family, rewriting her as an autonomous, pleasure-seeking subject instead of timidly passive prey.

This matriarchal family lives happily far from civilization, fiercely protective of an environment still unspoiled by urban encroachment, a variant of Mészáros's treatment of tensions between urban and rural life in her earlier features. When the city children invade her secluded forest, Riding Hood is initiated into the pleasures of play with human companions of her own age, and she soon reveals to the charming young Nicholas the secrets of her private world—the mysterious tree and the talking wolf. In turn he introduces her to the world outside—the symbolic order beyond pre-oedipal bliss—and to the circus where she sees the object of her father's affection, a circus performer dressed as a red bird.

Red Riding Hood's enclosure within and subsequent deliverance from a narrative universe ruled by women suggests the possible uses of fantasy as a fictional textual strategy for transforming the more naturalistic images of female experience. Red Riding Hood has been variously appropriated as cautionary tale, celebratory coming-of-age story, and seduction narrative for the delectation of the upper classes. Its folk motif is seen by some "as one of the few literary fairy tales to have been reabsorbed by the oral folk tradition,"[9] while others emphasize its interdictions against defiance of parental authority or stress its prohibition of indulgence in sensual pleasure. Whether French bourgeois or German peasant in sensibility, the tale's possible readings narrativize a persistent fascination with the consequences of a vulnerable young girl's solitary adventure in the unknown forest. Like the Grimm Brothers' character upon whom she is modeled, Mészáros's Riding Hood is ultimately saved from the belly of the beast, in contrast to Perrault's seventeenth-century, *haut-bourgeois* morality tale in which Riding Hood meets with certain death, or to pagan accounts of children attacked and killed by animals or grown-ups in the woods. Contemporary interpretations of the tale range from those insisting upon its ancient, anonymous status, presumably reflecting the "universal" psychic operations of women and men, to those describing a male European authorship projecting historically specific values onto a fictional, socially conventionalized genre. The girl is seen variously as guilty of "wild" inclinations to disobey her mother's interdiction against straying from the prescribed path, or as a victim of rape. Erich Fromm sees in both the Perrault and Grimm versions an expression of hatred toward males over whom man-hating females eventually triumph, while Bruno Bettelheim interprets them to signify the incipient danger of a pubescent sexuality that outstrips Little Red Riding Hood's capacity for emotional maturity.[10]

Enamored since early childhood of the story's richly suggestive possibilities, Mészáros did not fail to perceive its potential for ambiguity in the East European context:

> I have wanted to make this film for a long time because I love this story. Twenty years ago, it occurred to me to make a film about love, for children. But as an East European director, my whole life, unfortunately, has been filled with politics; it is a tradition that, good or bad, you must deal with politics, especially for those of my generation, educated under Stalinism. You can't, in Eastern Europe, simply make a love story or tale from the heart—honestly, truthfully—because people are continuously troubled by political, economic, and human changes. And as a result, artists tend to feel they cannot indulge their fantasy.[11]

As we have seen in previous chapters, Mészáros herself was until recently deprived of precisely such artistic freedom: prior to the glasnost era, her films were denied release or festival exposure in the Soviet Union, explicitly critical of Stalinism as they were. As love story or folk tale, Márta Mészáros had loved the story not least because, in the Grimm Brothers' version, the hunter rescues Red Riding Hood and her grandmother from certain death in the jaws of the beast. This tale of a fatherless adolescent girl, exiled far from home in unfamiliar circumstances, proved more attractive to Mészáros than she had imagined, perhaps in part because of her experience of exile and abandonment. As such, and despite its marketing as a commercial endeavor, the film nonetheless continues the autobiographical saga initiated by Mészáros's Diary cycle. Driven like her protagonist, Juli, by the fantasized rediscovery of deceased parents (especially her father), the director was in childhood and adolescence immersed in books and movies. "Children who have lost their parents fantasize what they look like," she explains. "These are the most profound relationships we have in our lives. . . . We idealize them."[12]

The designation "children's film," albeit commercially viable, ultimately misleads the spectator and detracts from other possible readings. The film's surreal, folk-tale elements, at odds with the more actively historiographical impetus of Mészáros's previous work, are, according to her, attributable primarily to the contributions of Jan Nowicki, his "quintessentially Polish" vision having provided a playful, imaginative freedom she finds generally lacking in Hungarian films—another version of "transitional space". Mészáros credits Nowicki with the film's original motif: a network of global communities representing the texture of modern life, and intended to include Budapest, Montreal, London, New York, and Moscow (a structure subsequently condensed for financial considerations). Addressing this point, the Hungarian film critic György Sas explains:

There is nothing more valuable on this earth than the tales passed from one generation to another. Frightening in its sweetness, *Little Red Riding Hood* obscures from us the reasons for our attachment to it. Márta Mészáros drinks from this source as if from a fresh-water well. Interestingly, the film is a part-Hungarian, part-Canadian production, just as it is part folktale with its idyllic scariness and visual effects, and part story of modern childhood with its stresses and anxieties. These are the signs of conflict in an urban family life for which the antidote can only be found in the harmony of nature.[13]

In spite of the financial constraints under which the film was produced, the collaborative screenwriting effort of Mészáros, Nowicki, and Pataki stands as an impressively original contribution to the substantial literature on Red Riding Hood and to the potential of fairy tales as subjects of narrative features. It indicates as well both the variety and consistency of Mészáros's vision in the two decades since the release of her first feature film.

The film opens with an aerial view of Montreal, skyscrapers intersecting the frame, in much the same way as *Diary for My Children* begins poised between cities, from the point of view of an airline passenger. In a vividly scarlet bedroom, a little girl's stuffed animal collection dominates the bed where she listens to her quarreling parents in the next room. Our first sight of her blonde mother is when she asks her husband to leave the house; as they sit together on the child's bed, the mother tells her daughter to say goodbye to her father. Together they set off for a new life in the forest.

There, ensconced in a bedroom decorated with family photographs, Riding Hood gazes longingly at the picture of her father, calling out: "Papa, where are you?," just as the Beast gazed at Beauty in Cocteau's version of that fairy tale. Riding Hood sets off to visit her grandmother with a white lamb running alongside, but instead of obeying her mother's advice to stay on the usual path, she follows her own inclinations and finds the magic tree, its red blossoms bearing locket-shaped images of the grandmothers awaiting her arrival. She meets the wolf, but no sooner has he promised to show her a marvelous place than he disappears, leaving her alone in the woods. The man dressed in grey cape and hat—an ornithologist, we learn—becomes her protector and as they walk, sharing stories of their love for animals, Little Red Riding Hood is struck by his resemblance to her father.

Arriving at the grandmothers' fantastically decorated peasant cottage, Riding Hood meets the schoolchildren who invite her to play, and when she tries to tell Nicholas of her adventures, he insists that they happen only in fairy tales.[14] The doubling of father surrogates recalls, of course, that of the Diary films, but in this version the hunter-father is transformed into a "good" scientist who has abandoned his family, while in the Diary films the "good father" is persecuted and ultimately put to death. Both, however, are once again portrayed by Jan Nowicki, whose eyes look suspiciously like those of the wolf.

Scene from *Bye Bye Red Riding Hood*

As in *The Two of Them* and the Diary trilogy, adults are here presented as fundamentally untrustworthy: when, for example, Riding Hood's mother pretends to be taking innocent walks at night with the ornithologist, her daughter responds: "All you do is lie!," just as Juli accused Magda of deception and dishonesty in *Diary for My Children*. And when the ornithologist pretends not to know her mother, Red Riding Hood lets the birds out of the cages in which he has kept them in retaliation for having deceived her.

Even the wolf is guilty of manipulation, keeping Riding Hood a prisoner in his lair after promising her freedom; like the Beast, he insists that she is his property, howling in fury when Nicholas rescues her. Although Mészáros claims to have wanted to make a film free of political overtones, the Stalin-era problematics of trust and lying reappear here in the cloak of a fable. In the final scene Little Red Riding Hood, now a beautiful young woman, looks down from the window of her sleek high-rise apartment in Montreal at the silver wolf meandering through the urban landscape below, "wild and free," in the lyrics of the song that concludes the film.[15]

The silver malamute Mészáros uses for the role of the wolf has the power to detect Riding Hood's unspoken desire, reminding the spectator of other films that privilege the relationship between humans and animals. Protagonists' unconscious feelings and thoughts are understood by bears, wolves, and other creatures in Jean Cocteau's *Beauty and the Beast* (*La Belle et la Bête*, France, 1945), with its respectfully sensual, poignant pre-oedipal eroticism, and Francois Truffaut's *The Wild Child* (*L'Enfant sauvage* France, 1976), based on the documentary account of a feral child raised by wolves. Truffaut's film, in which the director himself plays the role of a scientist—like Nowicki in Mészáros's version—who endeavors to rescue and socialize the wolf-boy into the presumably more "civilized" customs of eighteenth-century French bourgeois society, is also a meditation on debates between nature and nurture, between the relative merits of rural and urban values. Not unlike *Bye Bye Red Riding Hood*, Truffaut's and Cocteau's films bear out psychoanalytic assumptions that children make few distinctions between their humanness and the non-human qualities of the creatures to which they grow attached, and who are often their first—and most dependable—companions.[16]

Uncensored by conventional logic and unfettered by rational expectation, as Winnicott suggests, play and fantasy stand also for the forbidden, the ruthless logic of narcissistic desire. In an East European context, allegorizing the repressed part of the "double life" allows the imaginary to supervene, enabling the spectator to dream more freely and to forge unconscious associations that may in turn lead to new perceptions—and enactments—at odds with the prevailing order. Freud speaks of the uses of folklore for clinical purposes,[17] and Géza Róheim, the Hungarian folklorist, ethnographer, and psychoanalyst, extends his interpretation: "If we assume that all three protagonists of the story are one and the same person, the emphasis must be placed on the sleeping wolf. Red Riding Hood is swallowed into her own 'sleep-womb' which is at the same time the inside of her mother."[18] The ambiguous nature of the symbolic father—as in Mészáros's early features *The Girl* and *The Two of Them*—is evoked, with a somewhat different emphasis, by the Hungarian critic, Sas:

> The real drama is that Little Red Riding Hood's father is unfaithful to her mother, and ends up abandonding both of them. And this is the psychic wound she must bear. The father complex is intensified so that Little Red Riding Hood seems to see his image even in the wandering ethologist she meets in the forest. Or could it be he? . . . Woven into this tale are the very identity conflicts that characterize our lives. . . . Similarly, we may ask whether the film is truly an authentic tale, or whether it represents the retrieval of the psyche from the urban forest. But no, even in the forest, peace is not to be found. Where is it?[19]

The reference to peace by a Hungarian critic suggests as well the subversive quality of the fairy tale, recalling Alexander Kluge's postmodern cinematic archeology of history, *The Female Patriot* (*Die Patriotin* 1979), in which it is suggested that those who laugh at fairy tales have never suffered.[20]

The more striking link, however, between *Bye Bye Red Riding Hood* and Mészáros's prior feature *oeuvre* is to be found in the film's reconceptualization of the odyssey of an adolescent girl, Little Red Riding Hood, who, like her modern bourgeois counterparts, is left alone to fend for herself in foreign lands, her family dispersed or missing. In this way, according to Mészáros, she is more object of others' desire than subject of her own:

> *Little Red Riding Hood* tries to speak of love—the importance of love in our lives, especially in childhood. Everyone loves Riding Hood, but each in his own way. In other words, not exactly as she wishes. The wolf's love, for example, is possessive; the mother's love arises from her own loneliness and need for companionship; the little boy's love is that of an adventurer; and the grandmother's attachment meets her own needs. As we can see, then, love has many faces, and so, from this perspective, it is a political film that questions the nature of possessiveness.[21]

With regard to this apparent rupture with her previous cinematic concerns, Mészáros admits:

> After finishing *Diary II*, I felt I could allow myself the luxury of making *Little Red Riding Hood* because better times were ahead. I had a foreign producer for the story, knowing that I could only make it as an international coproduction . . . for the first time I could take up such topics as the nature of childhood and our adult relationship to it, the meanings of forests and animals . . . the importance of love in our lives, especially in childhood.[22]

This time, Mészáros's departure from the historical, political, and economic subjects with which she had become identified was greeted with rather less ambivalence than in her previous period of transition. The absence of direct reference to politics and history may account in part for the warmer reception, despite the fact that the film is far from devoid of political allusion. ''This is a movie about love, quite lyrical, with a sympathetic wolf!,'' the director insists, conceding nonetheless that some might (incorrectly, in her stated view) read it as an allegory of power, equating Hungary with Riding Hood and the Soviet Union with the wolf.

Enchanted by the German tale as a child, Mészáros acknowledges the sources of her interpretation in the same psychic configuration that defines her previous work. The image of a beloved absent father is here transmuted into a charming creature, at once human and animal, yet capable of the same deception as the father. Citing the Hungarian psychoanalyst Sándor Ferenczi, long a member of Freud's inner circle, Róheim's interpretation amplifies the tale's cannibalistic aspects, especially the theme of oral aggression exemplified in the Grimm story's dialogue:

> O Grandmother why do you have such big ears?
> In order that I can hear you better.
> Grandmother, why do you have such big eyes?
> In order to see you better.
> Why such big hands?
> To grab you. . . .
> Why such a big mouth?
> To eat you.[23]

Nevertheless, Little Red Riding Hood emerges victoriously independent of the seductive domination exerted by powerful forces, a dénouement that, like Mészáros's Diary trilogy, both anticipates and enacts the present odyssey of her own nation. "Tales for all," the increasingly global scope of Mészáros's work—and of Hungarian cinema as a whole—has the potential to appeal to a genuinely international audience. *Bye Bye Red Riding Hood* argues persuasively that East and West—Budapest and Montreal—are far closer than only a short time ago, anticipating the dramatic changes in the configuration of Europe since that time. The film is thus a cautionary tale that valorizes the interiority of a child's world as worthy of the same respect owed to small nations; it is also readable as a moral tale suggesting that the future of humanity is indistinguishable from coexistence with the natural world of animals and the environment:[24]

> I think European children will be interested, but Americans crave strong action. And then there is American television, which . . . is killing literature, culture and movies too. It's like Soviet propaganda. In Russia, they say "I love Communism, Socialism, building a new country." In America, it's "I love war, violence, money."[25]

By means of a narrative associated with childhood, Mészáros at once harks back to a historical culture of the European imagination and anticipates the interrogations of nationality and gender that are inescapably a part of the global agenda of the 1990s.

CONCLUSION

Mészáros's representation of the female subject at odds with social convention illuminates the larger question of the constitution of the self in an East-Central Europe which has favored group identity at the expense of the individual. Her emphasis on the moral categories of subject formation is anchored in György Konrád's notion of "antipolitics": "The culture of autonomy," he writes, "protests against making any human institution superior to the dignity of individual human beings."[1] Konrád's agenda finds its cinematic counterpart in Mészáros's *oeuvre*, in which the institution of Stalinism is seen as functioning to suppress the individual who has been forced to adopt the "mask" required to survive under that regime.

Formally and thematically, Mészáros's films are informed by a young woman's interrogation of the system and those who uphold it, from *The Girl* through *Diary for My Father and Mother*. Like most characters in East-Central European cinema, hers are divided subjects, split between an outwardly "correct" public persona and an inwardly repressed private self. It is not surprising that, among the future film projects she contemplates, Mészáros is especially drawn to making films about Marilyn Monroe and Anna Karenina. Her abiding interest in and command of Russian language and culture, are, to be sure, also demonstrated in the adaptation of Gogol's *Inspector General* as *The Land of Mirages*, and the three-part *Travel Diary* based in Moscow, Leningrad, and Frunze; these stand as a testimonial to the culture that played such an important formative role in her personal, political, and professional evolution.

Following the premiere of *Diary for My Father and Mother* at the Montreal International Film Festival and its selection to represent Hungary in competition in the Venice Film Festival, Mészáros is at work on several new projects: a long television series (and a separate feature film) on the life of the Empress

Elizabeth of Austria (affectionately known as Sisi); a biographical study of the young Marilyn Monroe; and a narrative of the woman who shot Lenin. Like the director herself, these are audacious and controversial subjects that challenge national, religious, historical, and gender expectations. And, in ways that both depart from and recall her previous work, these projects foreground the autobiographical within the historical by revealing the construction of the female subject through the unconscious and its engagements with language, material conditions, and the politics of location.

Similarly, the ethnography of the diverse cultures in which she has lived continues to interest Mészáros, all the more so in light of the ethnic and national questions that preoccupy East Europeans in the 1990s. To that end, she has embarked upon a sequence of documentaries and features concerning the Gypsy (Rom) peoples of Hungary, in particular their musicians, artisans, merchants, and intellectuals. Shakespeare's *Romeo and Juliet* serves as urtext for the feature project, "L'Amour fou"—a story of the love of a Gypsy boy for a Hungarian girl, and the inevitable familial opposition.[2]

Márta Mészáros's cinema—past, present, and future—takes up Andrzej Wajda's challenge to the ethnocentrism of Western viewers, inhabitants of a world perceived however illusorily to be more "permanent," for whom the concerns of Eastern European artists would appear to be at best irrelevant. The history of the Stalin era is now open to public discourse to a degree unimaginable only a short time ago. Creating and sustaining a climate of exchange for the cultural production to which Wajda alludes constitutes a challenge for Western film scholars, theorists, spectators, and distributors. The globalization of cinema, together with a greater interest in films made in the spirit—if not always the letter—of documentary perspective; the substantial and growing body of work by women filmmakers; and the undeniable importance of East-Central Europe in that reconfiguration, are evident in festival selections, joint ventures, and coproductions, pointing the way toward an inevitable hybridization and more collaborative production structures for the future.[3]

Both despite and on account of their firm grounding in regional, cultural, material, and historical realities, Mészáros's subjects—documentary and fictional—transcend their specificity. Problematizing national identity with the concerns of gender and sexuality, the re-reading of history through the lens of autobiographical experience that animates East European cinema owes much to Mészáros's bold paradigms. Her texts serve no less significantly to instantiate autobiographical cinema as a site of artistic autonomy and genuine cultural voice, hence an East European variant of the contestatory function of "women's cinema" for the West.

For Mészáros, approaching her fifth decade as a filmmaker,[4] there is little doubt that, as an East European director of her generation and accomplishment, cinema is inseparable from history, culture, and politics. Her cinematic practice, as I have shown in these pages, is driven by several lifelong concerns: first, the power of the film medium to record and interpret history through the interrelationship of textuality, spectatorship, and the autobiographical position of the speaking subject; second, the contextualization of a place for Hungary and Eastern Europe within the culture of politics and cinema, not only in a local but in a global sense; and third, the experience of a woman filmmaker that juxtaposes the significance of gender with that of sexual politics and the reworking of personal, familial history.

At once within and beyond the esthetic, ideological, and material framework of Hungarian production, Mészáros both transcends and is spoken by the documentary training that formed her early filmmaking experience. In her hands, the camera becomes an agent of individual and collective memory, an instrument of opposition to the "organized forgetting" and "collective amnesia" of Stalin-era esthetics. For "to articulate the past historically," according to Walter Benjamin, "does not mean to recognize it 'the way it really was' (Ranke). It means to seize hold of a memory as it flashes up at a moment of danger."[5]

Suppressed under the aegis of Stalinist internationalism, the culturally specific questions of gender, sexuality, and politics that anchor her work today invite renewed articulation, cloaked though these questions may be in the mantle of a Western "look" that bears little resemblance to the aesthetics of previous decades. Although economic constraints are likely to threaten temporarily the exploration of these issues, whether in the cinema or in other cultural media, an enduring (albeit seldom examined) dialectic of sexuality and nationality may well become the site of future representational enactments. Joining the ever increasing list of joint capitalist ventures and "limited corporations" that characterize Hungary's postcommunist transitional moment, the culture of cinema has been forced to reinvent itself if indeed it is to survive under a new order. (Nearly half of Hungarian film studios, for example, were acquired by controlling interests of foreign capital by the end of 1990). In Hungary, as elsewhere in East-Central Europe, filmmakers are responding to drastic structural, economic, and social transformations by endeavoring to reconceptualize—in public and private debate, through media laws and international coproductions, and in cooperation with television networks—the status, practice, and future directions of film culture.[6]

In the transitional space between collective discourse and individual subjectivity, between official narrative and private memory, gender-specific cinematic discourses in the Eastern Europe of the 1990s are thus at risk of foreclosure under the pressure of more "urgent" economic agendas. Just as the fragile economies of Hungarian, Czechoslovak, and Polish national cinemas are endangered by financial considerations increasingly determined by Western capital and entertainment priorities, so too are the concerns of East European women—and the foregrounding of such issues by women directors—likely to be subsumed by more "pressing" agendas of the new democracies' struggling for survival.

Thus far, no broad-based women's movements have emerged in Eastern Europe, and the absence of female representatives in the newly elected parliaments is noteworthy.[7] The employment security and generous maternity benefits guaranteed by the old order—issues interpreted and interrogated throughout Mészáros's films—may well be threatened by transition to the new.[8] Submerged under communism, gender discrimination—like nationalism and anti-Semitism—has grown more explicit as economic conditions impose cruel choices, resulting in renewed debates over the nature of women's "emancipation" over the last forty years. Taken together with the often painful costs of establishing a new democracy, such achievements, primarily of relative financial autonomy (significant in a country with the fourth highest divorce rate in Europe), are now viewed with suspicion by those still waiting for "results" from their sacrifices over the past four decades.

As Hungary prepares to enter more fully into European life, the completion of the Diary trilogy corresponds to the end of an era, opening new directions for filmmakers and spectators at the site of the border crossings between sexuality and nationality, identity and culture. Having proved herself to be an artist of vitality, integrity, and clarity of mind, and a filmmaker of enduring power, Márta Mészáros stands as a reliable, even prescient, witness to her century. A 1991 invitation to serve on the jury of the seventeenth Moscow International Film Festival honored her in the country that had both given her the chance to become a filmmaker and later banned her films under decades of artistic repression. Retrospectives of her *oeuvre*—documentaries as well as feature films—have been planned for 1992 by the Museum of Modern Art in New York City and by film festivals in Berlin and Florence, fitting tributes to Márta Mészáros's professional dedication, artistic independence, and political endurance.

INTERVIEWS WITH MÁRTA MÉSZÁROS

(Budapest: July 1988; June 1989; February 1990; July 1991;
February 1992)

On Women's Filmmaking

*You know, of course, that you are admired in the United
States, which is why you were among those directors
selected for this series. What is important to you about
being a filmmaker?*

You must understand that I love my profession enormously;
filmmaking is my life. But it's extremely difficult for me to
evaluate the quality or depth of my own films. I realize that
attention is being paid to my films around the world; that's how
I came to understand that I must continue in my profession, my
vocation. In everything I do, I strive for a maximum of honesty
and truthfulness. All my energies are directed toward avoiding
lies. Let's take American movies: a professional storytelling
industry. In contrast, our East European industry might be
called a "personal film industry." It's important to be able to
speak honestly about the era in which one has lived, and if you
can tell it in a way that attracts large audiences, then you are
successful.

When you write your book about me, it would be particularly
urgent for you to point out that, in Eastern Europe, films ought
to be made not only by male directors. I don't want to make
speeches about women's emancipation, because I'm not part
of that movement, but [filmmaking by women] represents a
different kind of sensitivity. If you interpret my films as strictly
political, you see that I approach power relations differently
from the way they are portrayed by male directors. Not be-

cause my films are necessarily better, and theirs worse, but they are simply different. One has to be aware of this.

How would you describe this difference?
It comes down to the ways a woman is different from a man. I think a woman has a different world view, a special sensitivity and relationship to people, to objects, to power, to children. . . . Biologically and neurologically, a woman has a different make-up. And if she can rework this difference truthfully and artistically, and convey it to the public, then the process itself is extremely exciting. I believe in this. I suggest you ask Jan Nowicki about this, because he has worked with many male directors, so he can compare this different sensitivity.

Does this different sensitivity translate into a film that looks different?
Yes. It bears a different form. Let's take a literary example, comparing Proust with Virginia Woolf. They may be working in the same form, but when you read them you are aware of the disparities. The same applies to film art. If you want to be a real artist—an "auteur"—then you must be able to confront the reality of this female sensitivity.

What is this female sensitivity?
We think the world otherwise, to a certain extent. Biologically, we are made to perpetuate the human race and not to pursue careers. We must give birth to children. You can also compare male creativity to childbirth. When a woman gives birth, it's also a creative act. Artists often equate the two: writing a poem or making a sculpture are comparable to childbirth.

One of the things that have been said in the past ten years or so about women directors is that temporality seems to be expressed differently in women's films. Would you say that is true for you?
Yes. We sense time differently. There is a problem, however, in talking about the connection between women and filmmaking. Film is related to money and propaganda, and money is power. This is why women have received so little money to make pictures. If you write a poem or a novel, it will either be published or not; it doesn't involve large sums.

But in our century women have achieved great gains, and I can say that in my lifetime I have seen immense changes. What previously has taken centuries to accomplish, in our century has taken only decades: ours is an accelerated century. Similar processes have taken place in Hungary in the relationship between women and the arts; women of certain intellectual strata have been able to attain the solid economic base that now permits them the luxury of being artists as well as mothers, where previously, this wasn't possible. Poor women confined to reproductive roles sometimes, secretly, produced diaries or verses; or, if they "married up," they catered to their husband's needs. All of this is undergoing change: it may be interpreted as a worldwide phenomenon, but the Hungarian situation is a bit more complicated than in the West, because here poverty is still rampant, and our moral values are backward, still rooted in tradition.

Are relationships between men and women changing in Hungary?
To a certain extent, yes, but there are still a great many obstacles. For example, material and financial conditions are so difficult that eighty to ninety percent of women are forced into the labor market. Otherwise, the family cannot survive. This, then, restructures the fabric of family life and, at the same time, exacerbates the exploitation of women. It's a very complex question.

And at the more intimate, personal level, are there significant differences in relationships between men and women in Eastern Europe—and Hungary in particular—in comparison with the West?
Here things are considerably worse than in the West, because we have had many layers of lies piled upon us. . . . The original promise of socialism was that we would all be equal, and they tried to fake, simplistically, an equality that didn't work. The same was to be the case for the "woman question": men and women were supposed to be equal, but it was never so. Women have been enslaved to serve both the factory and the family at once. Even in our government, you can see this imbalance; in some parts of Europe, you see a far greater participation of women in politics. In Hungary, it's only now beginning to change, but progressing very slowly. The party line was: "what do women want? we have already provided you with the official forum—the National Women's Council." But the NWC was a meaningless paper organization of the Hungarian Communist Party—and women working within it did nothing more than repeat official slogans, paying no attention to the real problems of Hungarian women: work, family, school, children. The Hungarian trade unions had the same relationship to power as the NWC. Obviously, we must fight to change all this.

Representation of Women in Mészáros's Cinema

Your films are often praised for their portrayal of female characters who are tough, strong, ordinary—"real" women who refuse to accept lies. What does this persistent demand for truth mean in your narratives?
I have always been interested in truthful personalities—the factory worker working eight hours, the artist, and the mother raising three children. In men, I look for individuals who possess their own firm standpoint and worldview, who can express both passion and anguish. As a woman director, I'm

especially interested in women with these same characteristics. What I want to work for is to help women become conscious of their being, the essence of their womanhood: this is what I try to express in my films, to make them aware of their own female personalities.

In The Heiresses, *you take up, among other things, a special kind of relationship between women of different classes in which infertility and surrogate motherhood are primary themes. I wonder if you would say something about that, because it seems to have been a film ahead of its time.*

Yes, maybe you're right that there is something special about it, because the film had a very strange odyssey. In certain countries it was adored, even by ordinary people; in others, including Hungary, it was hated. They described it as perverse, idiotic, "shit"; [the Hungarians] didn't know what to do with it, how to relate to it. To me, the important thing in the film was the meaning of friendship for these two women—not in its sexual but rather in its most noble sense. One woman knows that the other woman is "sick" [*beteg*], because a woman who is barren can be considered to have a physical disability, so why shouldn't she help her out? At the same time, however, the woman in need of help comes from the upper class in which money determines everything; consequently, she exploits the poor woman and, in doing so, betrays the friendship.[1]

This was, to me, the major interest of the film. Into that situation enters the man, the child's progenitor, who makes a statement by allying himself with the poor, exploited woman, the future mother—in my view an important element of the narrative. But I was shocked when people referred to the film simply as a story about a relationship between two women. On the contrary, this film is about three people, the third one being the man who impregnates the surrogate mother, taking a responsible step by finally joining her, and thus they *both* lose in the end.

Perhaps that's why Hungarians had such a difficult time with the film.

Yes, Hungarians couldn't really conceive of such a thing. My other film, *Just Like at Home,* met a similarly uncomprehending fate. In that film, the relationship between the girl (played by Zsuzsa Cinkóci, who epitomizes femininity) and the man (Jan Nowicki, an unfortunate character) was interpreted as an attachment based on suspect emotions. No! The little girl embodies the femininity and simplicity that he wasn't able to experience with adult women. But [critics] always tried to explain the relationship as fake, perhaps because the human mind is constructed always to suspect the worst. Even my colleagues referred jokingly to the film by arguing that if a strange man shows interest in a little girl, there can be no doubt that he's motivated by perverse desire. No, no, it's not about that: again, it is about friendship.

On the Diary Trilogy

What are the major differences and links among the three segments of the Diary trilogy?

It is important for us to know more about the period between 1948 and 1956, the Rákosi era, a time that has been erased from Hungarian history. For that reason, I felt obliged to provide that information [in *Diary for My Loves*] because young people now are almost entirely ignorant of who Imre Nagy was or how he came to power. I had to tell this story. The protagonist, Juli, carries a deep wound, as I do—her missing parents. We both feel the same way. Instinctively we detested the regime that forced people into compromising situations. My foster mother, who was a member of the AVO (internal security forces) was a typical representative of that regime, keeping people in a constant state of fear, not allowing them to enjoy life, love, and work. I didn't hate her; on the contrary, at the end I felt sorry for her because for her, the individual did not exist. I probably should have been more grateful to her, but I never made compromises in my life or in my films. And whether I have anything to eat or not never really bothered me. If I had wanted, I could have remained in the West, many many times. And now I would be living much more comfortably and could make movies more easily. As for János, he is a mosaic of figures. These people became communists in an age in which it was a common, basic philosophy. They truly believed in it, even when it became unfashionable. They remained faithful to it and therefore faithful to themselves. That is why they were always in conflict with the bureaucratic state apparatus. The character of János to a certain extent incorporates Imre Nagy, Szilági Ujhely, Miklós Vásárhelyi, and my grandfather Jenő Derkovitch.[2]

It must have been an extraordinary experience to make films with such personal as well as historical importance working together with your son as cameraman, and having been married to Miklós Jancsó. How did it affect your work as director?

For me it wasn't a problem. I never thought of Nyika as my son; he was my friend and cameraman. He knew my story and so it was easier to talk about things, rather than causing tension. I remember how nervous he was the first time, shooting in the Tatra mountains of Czechoslovakia! As for Jancsó, he made me Hungarian. He taught me about what this country is about. Without him my return to Hungary would have been much more difficult. We had a very close association: we thought about the same things, worked on the same things, helped to keep each other's souls intact. We were married for fourteen years, and this association was broken off by him—we divorced. And there I was with all the children who took up my time, and I had to bring them up. It wasn't easy, but if you have to, you can do it. Then came Jan

Nowicki [who I met] in 1975 [while] filming *Nine Months*. I went to Poland and talked to Wajda who gave me a list; the first name on it was Nowicki. The shooting followed, and from that, life together. Without him, I would never have completed the Diary. He was the one who always told me it's not worth making a movie "between two meals," because I love to cook, that you have to make a film from something inside of you.

And what of the third (and final?) segment of the Diary trilogy?
It was a very, very complicated time. For me, December 1956 was point zero, politically and psychologically, and for the Hungarian people as well. The revolution had been suppressed, the Russian army was occupying Hungary and now has remained, maybe for good. Everything seemed so uncertain: you didn't know what was going to happen, you heard nothing of Kádár but you knew Imre Nagy was out.

Every day, we hear more about 1956 and its re-evaluation in Hungary, just as other Stalin-era events are coming to light in the Soviet Union and elsewhere. How will the rapidity of liberalization now underway, and its impact on people's thinking about these issues, affect the completion and reception of your project?
In Hungary it's not at all clear now what will happen. Only yesterday, Prime Minister Károly Grósz still maintained that 1956 was a counterrevolution, that it was justified to call in the Russian tanks.[3] Imre Nagy was executed because he was against Russian intervention and wanted to give power to the workers' councils, to lead enterprises rather than the party. It's ironic that when I was working on the script for the next segment with my scriptwriter, Éva Pataki, about Imre Nagy's ideas of reform for Hungarian communism, we heard an announcement on television about Gorbachev's perestroika and glasnost that closely paralleled Imre Nagy's words in 1956. In spite of all these reforms, we still don't know where he is buried. This is such an open, festering wound that they don't dare touch it.

In *Diary for My Children*, there is a scene in which Juli goes into the rehabilitation office and asks where her father is buried. People interpreted this as *my* asking where Imre Nagy is buried. I didn't intend it to be so blatant, but even politicians made the association. Yesterday it was announced that, if the families of the buried president and his colleagues so wished, he would have them rehabilitated—the government is being evasive about it.

But an important contribution of the final chapter of the Diary trilogy is the way in which Juli is perceived in Moscow during that time. Nobody had ever before represented in film what the Soviets really thought about the 1956 revolution: that they considered it to be a fascist uprising by "hooligans." And when finally Juli is able to obtain her passport in Moscow and returns home, she sees something totally different taking place on the streets of

Budapest: a real revolution, her loved ones put away again, jailed or killed or forced to emigrate. The film ends with Juli coming back to Hungary, making a statement that this is her homeland; she takes the part of the revolution. János is executed, and his son decides to emigrate to the West with friends who take him along in a pickup truck. And Magda returns to her former, privileged position at Communist Party headquarters.

The moral of the film is that the figure of János is fused with that of the father in Juli's mind, and that the father's execution is mirrored in that of Janos. Juli's two loves—her father and János—become as one person, and with János's death, they both perish forever. Juli is now able to accept her past and her solitude, to begin her life anew.

How did the rapidity of political changes in Hungary before, during, and after the shooting of Diary for My Mother and Father *impinge upon your work? It was said by Western television crews present at the filming that the timing of the film coincided with the collapse of the Hungarian Socialist Workers Party.*

It's true, what we hear today has changed by tomorrow. But my own story doesn't change. When I completed the third installment, I planned to edit the three films into a final [fourth] version. And I'm still considering doing so. As for my timing, I wanted to shoot in early spring but there was no money available then. I had it in mind fifteen years ago. It was difficult shooting the scene of the toppling of the Stalin statue: there was enough budget for only three tanks—do you know how hard it is to simulate an occupation scene in Hungary with three tanks?[4]

Reaction of American Audiences to East European Film

Can an American understand an East European film? Is it possible for American audiences to comprehend at a deeper level what Hungarian films are about?

With great difficulty, because they have minimal information about Europe; that is, not only Eastern Europe, but Europe in general. When we were cutting *Bye Bye Red Riding Hood*, both my editor and my assistant were Canadians—two very intelligent women who told me that, during the three months we had worked together, they learned more about Europe, its people and history, than they had ever known. But all I did was to tell them stories while we were editing, chatting about one thing and another. They had an open mind toward the world, yet even for them this was a revelation; to them, I was a storehouse of knowledge. But let's face it, in Europe my level of knowledge would be considered only average. For instance, they knew very little about World War II—in fact, nothing: when it began and ended, how many were killed, how Europe became what it is, how many countries it contains—they hadn't the faintest idea.

This is one reason why I would like to make sure that, in our conversations, we take care not to exacerbate the misunderstanding of your work that can be found in the West. What is your sense of that cultural disparity?

It is extremely flattering that you are trying to understand my work and clarify these misunderstandings about my films. It is a responsibility of American intellectuals like yourself to understand and analyze these film narratives about Europe, mine included, because otherwise they can't even begin to measure the enormous contribution Europe made to the very existence of America. After all Canada and America came into being because of us, the Europeans. Now, their attitude is that everything that happened there is in the past, so let's forget it, even though their own origins include multiple nationalities . . . they have a lot to learn about their past, our culture. And so does American film. Take Spielberg, the quintessential American director: his is a Eurocentric way of thinking and expressing human emotions, and this is why his work is such a universal success. Because he talks about motherland, nation, country, the things he longs for. "I have a mother"—this feeling is the basic theme of *E.T.*, the little orphan trying to return to mother and homeland. It's an absolutely Eurocentric worldview, and this is why North Americans are so entranced by such films.

On Reconstructing the Past

From my perspective as an American with European roots myself (my father was Hungarian), I am struck by something else that is different in your films—the need to remember and the importance of reconstructing the truth of the past, which seems to be almost an obsession in East European cinema. Most Americans are without much sense of a past, or history. America is the country of the future.

Yes, but even that is not the whole truth, because America also builds on the past. But for the last two hundred years, American political and economic life have been so dynamic, acquired such momentum, that all the fine threads of emotion concerning the past were swept aside in the process. However, the "memory cell" of the human psyche is unique (because such emotions are inscribed within it). For example, right now Jan Nowicki is studying for the role of Shakespeare's Richard III, and if you look at the story—all right, it is in verse, written in the sixteenth century, about kings and regicide—it's very contemporary, about what's happening today in the world . . . our political, historical situation. The psychological structures mesh.

Your saying that your father was Hungarian is a good example: you might not even be aware of it, but it sets in motion a long process about your past. Society must look back on its own past and rework it; then we can build a future. A person can also break down because he doesn't rework the past. A person must know his or her past, nation, family situation, relations with others; you must be willing and able to analyze them, put them together, in order to build your personality for the future. If you don't do that, you get confused or sick, and then you run to a psychoanalyst, because Americans have discovered everything can be solved through psychoanalysis!

Parental Figures in Mészáros's Films

Especially in the Diary films, the role of the father is extremely important. And it is Jan [Nowicki] who plays these roles in a powerful way. Can you talk about your relationship to paternal and maternal figures as they are represented in your work—in particular, the child, the girl's, connection to these figures?

In *Diary for My Children*, the absent father is made manifest through lying. Because he was unjustly executed, he had to be denied at all times. This episode is not an exact equivalent or reconstruction of what happened to my own father, but I did have to contend with that kind of denial, and the characterization of him, throughout my youth, as a "bad person." He was represented to me as an "enemy" (*ellenség*), although I was never really convinced of that. That original lie and the subsequent denial of him as an enemy lies behind the father complex in my films, and it was that denial that determined both the emotional and rational aspects of my life in [Hungarian] society. Thus the importance of the father took precedence over that of the mother for me.

I was connected to my mother through sentimental, emotional bonds. But her image was never linked to politics. In Eastern Europe, you can't separate politics from life; it's impossible, especially if you are an artist and a film-maker. Today, at my age, having been through so much in my life, I know that in every relationship I've had I was searching for a "masculine" man, a man with a point of view. Obviously, this is also a part of my father complex. I always abhorred the kind of men who were too sentimental or fragile. I still believe that the father/man stands for controversy, argument, debate. Even in my private life, I reject a partner with whom I cannot argue or scream, who doesn't stand up strongly for what he believes; someone who is one-dimensional doesn't interest me much. I like a firm, opposing stance, a different opinion. . . . [With Jan,] whatever he knows, I don't know, and that's why I'm so attracted to him. I need a perspective other than my own, a different stimulus, an argumentative view from a man, someone who reminds me of who I imagine my father to have been. Even with Nyika and Muki [the sons she had with Miklós Jancsó], I respect them when they project their own individual selves and argue with me. I need to know that they can stand up for themselves and their point of view, even if it opposes mine.

In Diary for My Children, *Juli always seems to recoil whenever anyone refers to Magda as her mother. Each time I see the film it becomes more noticeable.*
Yes, because Juli imagines her mother very differently [from Magda]. In the final part of the trilogy, this whole relationship will be developed more fully. It's important and revealing to note who plays whom, the father-lover and the mother-lover figures, roles that blend together: Jan Nowicki plays both the father and János; Ildikó Bánsági plays my mother. In the second part she appears as János's wife, and in the third segment the same actress will be the wife who gives birth to a son, as she did to Juli in *Diary for My Children*.

Magda, the stern Stalinist woman—how do you see her, and what does she represent?
Well, Magda returns . . . these [people] always get back into power. Power is their life. She typifies a woman who gave up her life for an ideal.

Is she a particularly East European type of character?
Yes, I believe so. East European, including the Soviet Union.

Bye Bye Red Riding Hood *and* Anna Karenina

Why did you make this film? It seems so unlike anything else you have ever done.
I've never done a story for children, I suppose because I live in this political country and I have to make political films. When you do a film for children, people think: "what's happened to her? She won't be able to raise the money." There is always this political tension. For some twenty years, I've been wanting to do a project about the last day of Anna Karenina's life; maybe now I will, because the Soviet Union is finally open to me. They have never before seen or bought my films—it's been a closed market for me. Among the East European countries, only Poland and Yugoslavia buy my films; never Romania, Czechoslovakia or Bulgaria. And now China is buying several. By contrast, Poland has always been culturally and politically far more open.

I might be able to do a Soviet-Canadian coproduction of *Anna Karenina*. I love the story, and, in collaboration with Jan Nowicki and another woman, I've written a screenplay for it. But it's not only finances that stand in the way: you need the right actress—beautiful, but not a star. Meryl Streep, for instance, wouldn't work out, because the film wouldn't be about Anna Karenina but about about Meryl Streep, or, similarly, Jessica Lange. I might prefer a Russian actress, or perhaps Ornella Muti who's beautiful and a good actress with the right director, or even Isabelle Adjani.

Is there a role for Jan Nowicki in your Anna Karenina?
Maybe twenty years ago, but an old Karenin, I don't know. . . . He's in great form now, though.

Reception of Mészáros's Films

I have just seen The Inheritance *for the first time; it's a powerful film, and I wondered why it was never released in the U.S.*
Yes, I love it. Dan Talbot in New York usually buys my movies—he's very special.[5] But I don't know what happened with this one. I remember it being in New York. It's not for everyone, but still. . . . I wrote it with Ildikó Koródy, who also worked on *Nine Months*. After that I did another French coproduction, *Mother and Daughter*, that wasn't one of my best films; the choice of actress was a compromise, because I originally wanted Anouk Aimée who had promised a film to Bertolucci and so was unavailable, although she had wanted to do it. So finally I used Marie-José Nat, who is very popular with French audiences, she's "mignonne." But it would have needed an actress with more depth.

How did Hungarian audiences and critics receive the film?
They never like my films. Now, after the two Diaries, they acknowledge that they are successful, but they still don't like them. [Hungarian critics] don't want to see women succeed as I have; they think I've never really suffered the way a woman should. Hungarians love suffering, suicide, and alcoholics—they might have preferred it if I had become a depressed alcoholic! Now I'm an old woman, a classic, and they never really loved me. But the most important thing is that I have money for my next film. Maybe you should ask some Hungarian critics what they think. It's true that I have always been appreciated in Germany, France, and England. Perhaps you should talk to Jan Nowicki as well—there he is now! he speaks Polish and English!

Márta Mészáros on Jan Nowicki and Their Relationship

Would he talk to me about you? I'd be grateful, because it's rare, to my knowledge, that a woman directs so often on film the man who is also her partner in life. How does the collaboration affect the work, and vice versa?
We've had many conflicts about it, but after a while we arrived at a democratic solution. He is a very important actor in Poland, you know. He had always worked with great directors, and for him, being a director meant being a man. That was the first conflict. At first he thought it was something

of a joke, and then things began to change around the time of *The Inheritance*, when he realized, reading scripts, that he would never be the central character in my films, because only women can occupy that role.

What made that change possible?
We fell in love! We have been together thirteen years, and during the filming of *Nine Months*, our own love story began. But you know, in the beginning it was a man/woman question, not an artistic problem: he lived in Cracow and I lived in Budapest, it was very romantic meeting here and there, and then it seemed to be finished. I had my family, my country, I was sad but that's life. And then the relationship between us began another way, through friendship. He was often in Budapest as a tourist, here at the Hotel Gellért. And he began to feel that Hungary was his country too, as I felt Poland was mine.

That was the time of Solidarity in Poland: I was with him, it was very interesting. And now he plays in my films; he says, OK, I'll do what you want. When I finish the third part of Diary, his character, János, and Juli's father will have a very interesting and original dénouement: both will die at the same time by execution. As János is executed, Juli will have the image of her father before her eyes, and they converge. Nowicki is very excited by the prospect of playing what will be his biggest role, the condensation of lover and father. But to get back to Nowicki: he is one of the most liberal and democratic souls I have ever known.

Are there cultural differences as well that account for this?
Yes, but Jan Nowicki is especially open. He loves women: for him, women are supremely important in life—mother, sister, friends, lovers. And women love him.

Jan Nowicki on Collaboration with Márta Mészáros

Because you have been so important both as actor and collaborator in Marta's films, and because your relationship is rather unusual in the film world, would you be willing to comment on your view of her work, and yours, especially the Diary films and The Inheritance?
In my experience, working with Márta is a very, very good experience; as a matter of fact, I find women directors in general particularly interesting. People often say it's difficult to work with a woman, but I disagree. A good example is my current project with a West German film director, a fascinating and challenging coproduction. The atmosphere, the mood is positive and uplifting with a woman director; the reception of the final result is another matter. In all Márta's films, the main characters and themes are carried by women, and so as a male actor, I have never really been able to play a central role.

Is this a departure from your other experiences as an actor?
Yes, it's easier to work with male directors who are more intimately familiar with men's problems, and so they are able to put that knowledge into their filmic expression. For the record, let me clarify that I must fulfill my real artistic, theatrical ambitions elsewhere than in Márta's films. In any case, from the beginning it was quite clear to me that in her films, the main characters are neither female nor male, but Márta herself. This is not only the case for her autobiographically inclined films, but in general.

What do the Diary films mean to you as a Polish actor? How do you assess them as an East European?
I see them as laying the foundation for the new East European cinema; they touched upon themes wholly inconceivable before Gorbachev came to power, and broke a number of taboos in East European filmmaking. It's fascinating for me to see her cinema as a kind of *danse macabre;* with apparent ease, she resurrects the dead and buried in ways that others never dared to attempt. I've never played such roles nor seen such films before. Looking back on the fourteen years we've been working together, I compare the experience to tennis, in which you need good partners to bring out the best in each other. As an actor I have to be strong and determined, because Márta is like that too, and together we produce our best.

Then you see it as a collaborative effort.
I make every effort to bring about a fruitful collaboration to its fullest, but I'm not sure it can always be achieved.

I would be interested in your comparison between Hungarian and Polish cinema, having worked in both, and as a citizen of both cultural worlds.
I believe that Hungarians have a special talent for making movies. It's well known that Hungarians and especially Hungarian Jewish filmmakers conquered Hollywood, turned it upside down, and revitalized the film industry. Maybe the reason lies partly in the specific, isolated nature of the Hungarian language that helped to facilitate the emergence of related art forms such as film and music [in which Hungarians also excel]. On the contrary, Polish is a Slavic language, related to Russian, Serbo-Croation, Slovak, and Bulgarian, whereas Hungarian stands virtually alone. Because of this hermeneutic status, it is more inclined to create internal variations that are reflected in the artistic life of its people. Given the political situation in Eastern Europe, Hungarians have always had an extremely well-structured, well-functioning film industry, one that was the envy of Poland.

Were you aware of these disparities before you began working with Márta?
I only realized when I started working in Hungary with Márta and others that there is nothing in Poland that parallels the unique configuration of Hungar-

ian cinema. Hungarians are succeeding, whereas Poles are still only attempting to create such films. For example, Hungarians are very determined: when a director decides to make a film, he completes it in thirty-five days after the planning stage, whereas a Polish director spends a long time deciding, and then ninety more days shooting, and he's still not sure how the final cut will look. And when I play in Hungarian films, they pay me enough to live well, but when I'm invited to act in a Polish movie, sometimes I contribute my own money to the director to help complete the project. It's the Polish system. . . . In general, the Hungarian film industry has never tried to follow international trends and fads; it created its own terms and tendencies, based on its own life and history, and so it was able to make a special contribution to world cinema. Take the example of Andrzej Wajda, who is currently involved with French and Russian historical themes; in doing so, he is separating himself from his roots. I feel that it is the director's responsibility to rework his or her country's history and culture. He or she must do so with honesty and truthfulness . . . but that's only the beginning. You have to be able to *express* them. The Hungarian industry always tried to do that, and especially recently there has been greater possibility for doing so. But this must also be coupled with talent.

Mészáros on Documentary Filmmaking

It was remarkable to see how many of your documentaries were about artists. Those films seemed to have a more noticeably individual vision than some of your others. Did the fact that your father was a sculptor contribute to your interest in this subject?
Maybe unconsciously. At that time my family was so poor, I needed work, my children were small, Jancsó wasn't working, and it was absolutely necessary for me—I made a lot of educational and nature programs, pedagogical and scientific material. Some of the art documentaries displeased official circles because they were made in an era that did not recognize avant-garde art, such as the Szentendre school that was considered too controversial, and artists such as Jenő Barcsay weren't recognized. I'm amazed looking back now, in 1988, that people were so upset by films that are now considered classics in Hungary. The old hard-liners favored the realistic school that continued in many ways the socialist-realist directions.

I wondered whether you were working then in a direction similar to that of Agnès Varda, who also began in documentary and made films about artists.
No, I know her very well now, but the first movie of hers I saw was *Cléo de 5 à 7.* Later in Paris she showed me her work. She was very nice; there was always a kind of tension and competition between us, and when I got the

Berlin *grand prix* for *Adoption*, she came up and jokingly said: "I hate you because I did all this work and never won anything, and even though you deserve it I'm jealous!"

Now she's finally been widely recognized with Sans toit ni loi.
Yes. She always loved California, but Hollywood is not for me. . . . It's interesting, and if someone offered me ten million dollars, I might consider it! But I prefer Canada, it's enough for me.

On Marilyn Monroe as Film Project

[Perhaps reluctantly, Márta Mészáros acknowledges the lure of the West— and, in particular, the United States—in her desire to engage a topic close to her heart and quintessentially American: a cinematic study of Marilyn Monroe, her childhood and subsequent "discovery" by the Hungarian photographer André de Dienes, who emigrated to the United States during World War II. On closer inspection, as in the case of *Bye Bye Red Riding Hood*, a deeper continuity of interest connects this future film to those of Mészáros's past]:
One of my dreams is to do a film about the childhood of Marilyn Monroe. I have a script that deals with her life up until she became a Hollywood star. Of course it's from a European mentality, because none of the books about her really deal with the tragedy of her childhood. She was discovered by a Hungarian photographer, André de Dienes, who went to New York and Hollywood after World War II, and the Marilyn Monroe he met had never heard of Europe. They took a trip together for two weeks in the Southwest; he took pictures of her and discovered her great talent. She spoke of her mother, her life; he spoke of Hungary and fascism. His book about her is *Marilyn mon Amour*. In the film *Bye Bye Red Riding Hood*, the little girl has the same features. Maybe I'll wait a few years and I'll be able to make the film with her! She's beautiful, photogenic, erotic.[6]
[The "illegitimate" daughter of a schizophrenic mother, Monroe (Norma Jean Baker) was, like many of Mészáros's protagonists, the product of orphanages and foster homes. Her openly narcissistic sensuality, later callously marketed by Hollywood interests, hinted at the vulnerable innocence of an *enfant fatale* who was erotically attractive to spectators of both genders. Mészáros's fascination with Monroe's story centers on the actress's capacity for summoning the sustained energy required to prove herself after a tragic childhood, a life force not unlike that of Mészáros's female protagonists and, for that matter, her own]. It's as if she had wanted to take revenge on the world because of it, take everything she needed for herself. And of course she does get everything, but she pays for it with her life. No matter how great her stardom, she could never erase the childhood trauma. Her life was not unlike

the lives of saints, always in pursuit of love. That need determined the rest of her life to such an extent that she became ill and ultimately perished. She didn't trust men, and she never believed that anyone really loved her—neither men, women, nor money. Even success rang false for her, and I interpret her death as revenge for this deception. . . . She was really a woman (unlike Greta Garbo, who was exotic, bisexual, beautiful, mysterious, European). Marilyn Monroe was ordinary, beautiful, open, down-to-earth, unafraid of expressing her femininity. There has been no one like her since . . . even in Hungary, where the younger generation has produced very fine actresses.

Bye Bye Red Riding Hood

In that film, there seems to be a radical departure from everything that preceded. How do you explain this new direction?
Everything that has the element of folk tale in the film was suggested by Jan. I love the folk tale so much because it's about a little girl who lives in the forest and who loves her grandmother. One day she goes to visit her grandmother, and here are the questions that puzzle me: why must she cross the forest? why don't they live together? why does she meet the wolf? he loves her so much that he eats her up? Originally, I envisioned this love relationship in realistic terms; that's how I wanted to put it into the script. I had already conceived making it twenty years ago, and finally, when I met the Canadian producer, we discussed possible projects and decided quickly on this one. At first, my scriptwriter, Éva Pataki, with whom I had worked on previous films, objected, asking: "why would you consider making a movie from a folk tale?" Then I convinced her that it was an extremely likable story—because I love nature and animals—and that it would give me the chance to connect them. Together we imagined a realistic re-enactment of the tale for our film; I scripted the first version and when I insisted, Éva rescripted it.

When I told Jan about my exciting project, he immediately came up with new ideas, arguing that a forest with trees and animals was not so exciting! Why not, he suggested, present a forest with trees and flowers always in bloom? This resulted in the miraculous blooming tree. Next came the figure of the grandmother: why not make her into a seer? He thought that, instead of ending the story with the wolf eating the grandmother and Piroska, we might visualize them in the wolf's stomach. Even the motif of dual cities—Budapest and Montreal—was Jan's idea. His original notion was that the plane would take us over the major urban areas: Budapest, London, Montreal, New York, Moscow—suggesting a global community—ending up in the forest. But financial considerations prevented that. The final shot, when Piroska sees the wolf wandering through city, was also Jan's contribution. All in all, everything that is surreal about the film came from Jan. These suggestions made us decide to include him as one of the scriptwriters. Although Jan contributed to many of the scripts in our earlier coproductions, his work was never credited. This is the first time he has been acknowledged as coscript-writer.

Maternal Relationships

Let us return to the question of your mother.
In fact, my mother . . . since I absolutely didn't have a family . . . an interesting aspect of my background is that the first feelings of mother-daughter relationship I developed were with Miklós Jancsó's sister, who is no longer alive. She was extremely feminine and maternal toward me, and somehow she represented the world of my mother; that's why I loved her so much. Afterwards, I felt the same thing with Jan Nowicki's mother, who was a simple, down-to-earth—but wise—woman, and soon after our first encounter she became my surrogate mother. More and more now, the question keeps coming back to me: what was my mother really like? what should a mother be? This subject is acquiring a great interest for me. If I have any energy left, I would like to make a movie about it.

You seem to have always been interested in the younger generation, enabling young people to watch you at work, teaching, making films about them.
Yes, now I feel I want to surround myself with the young, even more than with my own generation—like Éva Pataki, with whom I've been writing scripts for a number of years, or my son, who is a cameraman and a young dramaturg whose work is very interesting.

As a youthful person yourself, are you close to colleagues of your own generation?
I don't know, it depends. I don't much like the way some of my colleagues lead their lives based so much on financial considerations. That bothers me: it's sad, because we no longer have real conversations. Everything is about money now, buying houses, cars, traveling. I'm fortunate that I've never been particularly enamoured of material things. Oh, I like as much as anyone to be able to buy things and to travel, but becoming a capitalist, no. And those things have never been very important to Nowicki or Jancsó either. We never talk about money in the family—it's an entirely different mentality. Here in Hungary, too, we have people who are obsessed by material things and those who have a more creative temperament.

Are your ideas about this shared by young people as well, or are young filmmakers also obsessed by money?
It's a very difficult philosophical moment for all of us, because everything has changed—ideas, daily life, perspectives on life—yet at the same time psycho-

logically nothing has changed, and many of the old guard are still in place. It's not a simple matter. For those who left Hungary, it's a complete revolution: their psychic and physical lives, their whole mentality is transformed. We need to find a new ideal, but I don't think it should be an economic one. It would be a shame if the East came to take on the worst aspects of the West in this fragile period of transition, but perhaps things will improve again after this very difficult time.

NOTES

1. Introduction

1. Usage of the term "Eastern Europe" itself is much contested: most of my Hungarian informants preferred "Central European" or simply "European," indicating a pervasive—and even passionate—desire to leave behind what many consider to have been an imposed identity that distorted their claims to having always been a part of Western culture, successive occupations by foreign powers notwithstanding. To respect this delicate and revelatory sense of cultural identity, I use the term "East-Central Europe" throughout this study where appropriate. See Timothy Garton Ash, "Eastern Europe: Après le Déluge, Nous," in *New York Review of Books*, August 16, 1990, pp. 51–57; and "Mitteleuropa?" in *Daedalus* (special issue on "Eastern Europe . . . Central Europe . . . Europe", Winter 1990), pp. 1–22; Tony Judt, "The Rediscovery of Central Europe," *Daedalus* (Winter 1990), pp. 23–54; and Endre Bojtar, "Eastern or Central Europe," *Cross Currents: A Yearbook of Central European Culture* 7, Michigan Slavic Materials 29 (University of Michigan, 1988), pp. 253–70.

2. Under the auspices of the Five College Women's Studies Faculty Project, I coordinated a symposium on "Gender and Visual Representation" at the University of Massachusetts in 1983 at which Mészáros's *Diary for My Children* was screened. Participating institutions in the consortium were Amherst, Smith, Hampshire, and Mount Holyoke Colleges and the University of Massachusetts.

3. C. Portuges, "Seeing Subjects: Women Directors and Cinematic Autobiography," in *Life/Lines: Theories of Women's Autobiography*, B. Brodzki and C. Schenck, eds. (Ithaca: Cornell University Press, 1988), pp. 338–50.

4. "Cinema and Psyche: A Psychoanalytic View of the Representation of Women in Three French Film Directors of the 1960s" (Ph.D. dissertation, University of California, Los Angeles, 1982). See also my chapter "The Spectacle of Gender" in *Gendered Subjects: The Dynamics of Feminist Teaching*, M. Culley and C. Portuges, eds. (London: Routledge and Kegan Paul, 1985), pp. 183–94.

5. Jacques Lacan, *The Four Fundamental Concepts of Psychoanalysis*, ed. Jacques-Alain Miller, trans. Alan Sheridan (New York: Norton, 1978). See also D. W. Winnicott, *Through Paediatrics to Psychoanalysis* (London: International Psychoanalytical Library, 1973), *The Maturational Processes and the Facilitating Environment* (London: International Psychoanalytical Library, 1963), and *Playing and Reality* (London: Routledge and Kegan Paul, 1986).

6. My interview subjects include Agnès Varda and Nathalie Sarraute (France); Jackie Raynal (France and USA); Anne-Claire Poirier (Canada); Myriam Abramowicz (Belgium); Ousmane Sembène (Senegal); Károly Makk, Pál Schiffer, György Szomjas, Judit Elek, and Márta Mészáros (Hungary); and Vojtech Jasny and Irina Pavlávskova (Czechoslovakia).

7. See my "Seeing Subjects: Women Directors and Cinematic Autobiography." A collection of interviews with these and other directors, accompanied by critical analyses, is in progress.

8. For a useful synthesis of some of these aspects of Soviet cinema, see Nancy P. Condee and Vladimir Padunov, "The Outposts of Official Art: Recharting Soviet Cultural History," *Framework* 34 (1987), pp. 59–106.

9. The twenty-seventh Karlovy Vary International Film Festival in Czechoslovakia in 1990 showcased an extensive retrospective of banned or blacklisted films entitled "Elective Affinities," including documentaries never before shown and works produced by Czech and Slovak filmmakers in exile.

10. Prizes were awarded at the Twenty-Seventh Karlovy Vary Festival of July 1990 to directors, including Milos Forman and Voytech Jasny, whose films had been banned or shelved and whose return was heralded as a triumph of the "Velvet Revolution"; the awards were officially sanctioned by President Vaclav Havel's presence at the Festival.

11. Included, for example, in the Los Angeles Film Festival were Krzysztof Kieslowski's made-for-television series *The Decalogue (Dziesec̆ Przykâzan, Poland)*, among which the expanded features *A Short Film about Love (Krótki film o milos̆ci)* and *A Short Film about Killing (Krótki film o zabijaniu)* won the first European Film Award for best film in 1988. Likewise, the 1990 San Francisco Film Festival and Washington, D.C. FilmFest featured long-banned films such as Jiri Menzel's *Lark on a Wire (Skr̆ivaci na nitích)*, which languished on the censor's shelf for twenty years, and Hungary's *Recsk 1950–1953: Story of a Forced Labor Camp (Recsk: Egy kényszer muukatábor története)*, while the New York Public Theatre's series "The Banned and the Beautiful" presented Czechoslovak films never before seen in the West, including many banned, shelved, and made in exile.

12. For recent book-length studies of male "auteurs," see, for example, Edward B. Turk, *Child of Paradise: Marcel Carné and the Golden Age of French Cinema* (Cambridge: Harvard University Press, 1989); William Karl Guérin, *Max Ophuls* (Paris: Cahiers du Cinéma Collection "Auteurs," 1988); Jeffrey Chown, *Hollywood Auteur: Francis Coppola* (New York: Praeger, 1988). Anthony Slide's *Early Women Directors* (New York: Da Capo Press, 1984) represents an effort to credit filmmakers such as Alice Guy Blaché and Margery Wilson, while Paule Lejeune's *Le Cinéma des femmes* (Paris: Editions Atlas, 1987) takes up 105 French-language women cinéastes from France, Belgium, and Switzerland.

13. See the sections "Positioning the Female Autobiographical Subject" and "Colonized Subjects and Subversive Discourses" in *Life/Lines: Theorizing Women's Autobiography*, B. Brodzki and C. Schenck, eds., for uses of autobiography by women writers in non-"privileged" contexts.

14. See, for example, Andrzej Wajda, *Double Vision: My Life in Film*, trans. Rose Medina (New York: Henry Holt, 1989); Andrei Tarkovsky, *Sculpting in Time*, trans. Kitty Hunter-Blair (Austin: University of Texas Press, 1989); Luis Buñuel, *My Last Sigh*, trans. Abigail Israel (New York: Knopf, 1983); François Truffaut, *The Films in My Life*, trans. Leonard Mayhew (New York: Simon and Schuster, 1985); Jean Renoir, *Ma Vie et Mes Films* (Paris: Flammarion, 1987); Yvonne Rainer, *The Films of Yvonne Rainer* (Bloomington: Indiana University Press, 1989).

15. Marguerite Duras's "Les Yeux Verts," a special issue of *Cahiers du Cinéma* 312/313 (June 1980), is among other things a fascinating compendium of essays, photographs, and first-person narratives of the writer's thoughts on filmmaking in comparison with literature. I refer in these pages to my own unpublished interviews with Agnès Varda and Yvonne Rainier. See also Paule Lejeune, *Le Cinéma des Femmes* (Paris: Editions Atlas Lherminier, 1987); Charles Ford, *Femmes Cinéastes ou le Triomphe de la Volonté* (Paris: Denoël Gonthier, 1972); and Anthony Slide, *Early Women Directors* (New York: Da Capo Press, 1984).

16. See, for example, Peter Hames, *The Czechoslovak New Wave* (Berkeley: University of California Press, 1985); Ella Shohat, *Israeli Cinema: East/West and the Politics of Representation* (Austin: University of Texas Press, 1989); Peter Besas,

Behind the Spanish Lens: Spanish Cinema under Fascism and Democracy (Denver: Arden Press, 1985); David Desser, *Eros Plus Massacre: An Introduction to the Japanese New Wave Cinema* (Bloomington: Indiana University Press, 1988); George Semsel, ed., *Chinese Film: The State of the Art in the People's Republic of China* (New York: Praeger, 1987); Patrice Petro, *Joyless Streets* (Princeton: Princeton University Press, 1989); Judith Mayne, *Kino and the Woman Question* (Columbus: Ohio State University Press, 1989); and Thomas Elsaesser, *New German Cinema: A History* (New Brunswick: Rutgers University Press, 1989); as well as my article "Lovers and Workers: Screening the Body in Post-Communist Hungary," in *Nationalisms and Sexualities*, ed. A. Parker, M. Russo, P. Yaeger, and D. Sommer (New York: Routledge, Chapman and Hall, 1992).

17. Andrzej Wajda, *Double Visions*, Graham Petrie and Ruth Dwyer, eds., pp. 131–32.

18. See Graham Petrie and Ruth Dwyer, eds., *Before the Wall Came Down: Soviet and East European Filmmakers Working in the West* (New York: University Press of America, 1990), pp. 1–14; and Graham Petrie, *Hollywood Destinies: European Directors in America, 1922–193* (London: Routledge and Kegan Paul, 1985).

19. Two books on East European cinema, both containing a number of important essays, are essential to the field: *Post New Wave Cinema in the Soviet Union and Eastern Europe*, Daniel J. Goulding, ed. (Bloomington: Indiana University Press, 1989), and *Politics, Art and Commitment in the East European Cinema*, David W. Paul, ed. (New York: St. Martin's Press, 1983).

20. Cases in point are Richard Roud, *Cinema: A Critical Dictionary* (2 vols., New York: Viking Press, 1980); and Karyn Kay and Gerald Peary, eds., *Women and the Cinema: A Critical Anthology* (New York: Dutton, 1977).

21. Mészáros states uncategorically in interviews with me in 1988–89 that she does not wish to be considered a "feminist," and sees no particular contradiction between that statement and the fact that most of her films foreground female protagonists. It is a concept she considers to be primarily a Western invention, too quickly applied without sufficient knowledge of the East European context, in particular of her generation.

22. From my interview with Mészáros, chapter 8.

23. Translations of films screened in Hungarian without subtitles were provided by László Kürti, as were reviews and interviews published or conducted in Hungarian.

24. As this book goes to press, the impact of restructuring of Hungarian national cinema—and of the economy as a whole—remains uncertain, even unstable. At the Twenty-Second Budapest Film Week of February 1990, in response to what some considered to be persistent self-interest on the part of the film establishment evident in proposed reforms, a group of "Young Hungarian Filmmakers" held a press conference to present a position statement calling for "democratic reform of Hungarian national film production and distribution." Among their demands were the development of a new "film law" protecting Hungarian national film culture; an audit of all studios to assess funding and disbursement; and the creation of a "financing system based on equal opportunity and a rational film production and distribution system that utilizes state funds in a market-oriented manner" (cited in *Hungarian Cinema 2* [1990], pp. 18–19). Since then, the future of Hungarian cinema has been debated in studios and other forums throughout the country, and in international symposia such as "Thirty-five Years of Hungarian Cinema," a symposium held in November 1991 by the Art Gallery of Ontario, Toronto, under the aegis of a two-month festival of Hungarian culture, "Hungary Reborn."

25. As the culture of East-Central Europe becomes better integrated into the world

of international cinema, there may be reason to expect a higher tolerance of—and, for that matter, desire for—difference. Nevertheless, it should be noted that American audiences are generally reluctant to patronize foreign-language films.

26. The role of the Hungarian film theorist Béla Balázs as head of the literary department in the Revolutionary National Council is noteworthy in this context. Believing that literature would gradually lose its traditional characteristics in a classless society, he sought a program of mass culture of the highest quality: "In the Communist society . . . life, worthy of man and assured for everybody, will no longer provide themes for the 'social drama,' and the innermost depth of the soul, the common roots of all of us, will come to flower upon the stage." Cited in Joseph Zsuffa, *Béla Balázs: The Man and the Artist* (Berkeley: University of California Press, 1987), p. 81, from Balázs's "A nép szinháza" (Theater of the People), *Fáklya* (Torch), April 22, 1919.

27. Nina Hibbin, *Eastern Europe: An Illustrated Guide* (London: A. Zwemmer, 1969). It should be noted that the political events of 1956 were reflected on the screen rather quickly after their occurrence in such films as *At Midnight* (*Éjfélkor*, 1957), *Yesterday* (*Tegnap*, 1959), and *Danse Macabre* (*A tettes ismeretlen*, 1957).

28. For entertaining and enlightening books on the "forgotten history" of Hollywood, see Miklós Rózsa, *Double Life* (New York: Wynwood Press, 1989), an autobiographical view of "Golden Age" Hollywood; and Neal Gabler, *An Empire of Their Own: How the Jews Invented Hollywood* (New York: Crown Publishers, 1988).

29. Interview with Éva Pataki, Budapest, July 1990.

30. According to *Variety* (May 23, 1990), Universal Pictures planned to schedule the release of some 200 American films on Hungarian screens in 1990 alone, more than eight times the total number of films produced in an average year by Hungarian studios.

31. Hungarian filmmakers and cultural workers express deep anxiety about the future of cinema; having grown accustomed to regular—if modest—government subsidies, few were prepared for the demands of privatization and fewer still possess the entrepreneurial skills required to succeed in the international coproduction marketplace. Several have abandoned projects approved for production under the pressure of unfamiliar conditions such as the pressure to raise private funding through limited partnerships.

32. All screened at the Twenty-second Hungarian National Film Festival in Budapest, February 2–8, 1990.

33. A pornographer is quoted in the *New York Times* (May 12, 1990) urging customers to "spend their sorrow" to enrich his business of sex magazines, massage parlors, and sex tours. A woman teacher, concerned about exploitation of women despite her understanding that these materials are spreading as a result of the years of repression, notes: "But what is missing from the debate is the articulation of the view that this is offensive to women. People are mixing liberty with bad taste" (p. 6).

34. According to István Várady, president of Hungarofilm/Budapest, funding for film projects and for the film bureaucracy under the Ministry of Culture is in doubt. The Hungarian film industry will inevitably become more internationalized, together with many other sectors of the economy. (Interview at Hungarofilm, August 19, 1990.)

35. David Paul, "The Magyar on the Bridge," in Goulding, ed., *Post New Wave Cinema in the Soviet Union and Eastern Europe*, p. 173.

36. István Nemeskürty, *Word and Image: History of the Hungarian Cinema* (1974; rev. ed. Budapest: Corvina, 1985), p. 216. It should be noted that the English translation of this important reference was recently updated to include films through 1985.

37. Graham Petrie, *History Must Answer to Man* (Budapest: Corvina, 1976), pp. 232–33; Karoly Nemes, *Films of Commitment: Socialist Cinema in Eastern Europe* (Budapest: Corvina, 1985).

38. While I shall take up aspects of its representation in later Mészáros films, its ramifications cross boundaries of history, psychology, economics, politics, and literature, and therefore exceed the scope of this study.

39. Progressively probing references to the events and political ramifications of the 1956 uprising may be found in films such as Péter Gothár's *Time Stands Still* (1981), Pál Sándor's *Daniel Takes a Train* (*Szerenesés Daniel*, 1982), Péter Gárdos's *Whooping Cough* (*Szarmárköhöges*, 1986), Pál Schiffer's *Magyar Stories* (*A Dunánál*, 1987) and Judit Ember's *Political Asylum* (Menedékjog, 1989).

2. A Cinematic Autobiography

1. Milan Kundera, *The Book of Laughter and Forgetting*, translated from the Czech by Michael Henry Heim (New York: Harper and Row, 1982).

2. István Deák, *New York Review of Books*, November 24, 1988, pp. 48–49.

3. See C. Portuges, "Retrospective Narratives in Hungarian Cinema," *Velvet Light Trap* 27 (Spring 1991), pp. 63–72.

4. I wish to acknowledge Jim Shedden's introduction to the catalogue for a series he organized, "Thirty-five Years of Hungarian Cinema," (Toronto: Art Gallery of Ontario, 1991).

5. See Vamik D. Volkan, *The Need to Have Enemies and Allies: From Clinical Practice to International Relationships* (New York: Jason Aronson, 1988) for a fuller discussion of the psychodynamics of mourning and international politics.

6. Quoted in Michael H. Seitz, "Remembering in Hungary," *Films and Filming*, January 1985, p. 36.

7. See C. Portuges, "Between Worlds: Re-Placing Hungarian Cinema," in *Before the Wall Came Down: Soviet and East European Filmmakers Working in the West*, Graham Petrie and Ruth Dwyer, eds. (Lanham: University Press of America, 1990), pp. 63–70.

8. See Timothy Garton Ash, *The Uses of Adversity: Essays on the Fate of Central Europe* (New York: Random House, 1989). The peculiar form of self-deprecation and alienated labor engendered by decades of communist rule in the East was often humorously captured in the joke: "We pretend to work and they pretend to pay us."

9. Sigmund Freud, "Mourning and Melancholia," *Standard Edition*, (London: Hogarth Press, 1953–59), vol. 14, pp. 238–60 quotation on p. 251.

10. See Jeffrey C. Goldfarb, *Beyond Glasnost: The Post-Totalitarian Mind* (Chicago: University of Chicago Press, 1989) for a cogent analysis of confusions in Western approaches to this issue, which also is useful to film theory.

11. *Ifiúsági Szemle*, journal of the Hungarian Communist Youth League, pp. 100–101; note also the effects of living abroad with her father in his travels to Italy and the Soviet Union.

12. I take up these questions in a book in progress on cinematic autobiography, considering especially the dramatic rise of testimonial, personal filmmaking by contemporary international feature directors such as Diane Kurys, Andrei Tarkovsky, John Boorman, Louis Malle, Nadine Trintignant, Chantal Akerman, and Euzhan Palcy. A recent panel of the Society for Cinema Studies on Autobiography and Film also addressed related issues (Jeffrey Ruoff, chair, May 1990, Washington, D.C.).

13. Catherine Portuges, "Seeing Subjects: Women Directors and Cinematic Autobiography," in B. Brodzki and C. Schenck, eds., *Life/Lines: Theorizing Women's Autobiography* (New York: Cornell University Press, 1988), pp. 338–50.

14. Georges Gusdorf, "Conditions and Limits of Autobiography," in James Olney, ed., *Autobiography: Essays Theoretical and Critical* (Princeton: Princeton University Press, 1980), p. 38.

15. C. Portuges, "Seeing Subjects: Women Directors and Cinematic Autobiography," in *Life/Lines: Theories of Women's Autobiography*, B. Brodzki and C. Schenk, eds. (Ithaca: Cornell University Press, 1988), pp. 338–50.

16. The work of such American experimental filmmakers and artists as Jonas Mekas and Maya Deren should not be overlooked in relation to that of contemporary filmmakers. More recently, Michelle Citron's *Daughter Rite* (1978), Jackie Raynal's *New York Story* (1984), and many other important contributions constitute a "counter-canon" whose influence has been substantial in the development of autobiographical film.

17. Roy Schafer, "The Fates of the Immortal Object," in *Aspects of Internalization* (New York: International Universities Press, 1968), p. 339.

18. See Michel Foucault, "What Is an Author?" in John Caughie, ed., *Theories of Authorship: A Reader* (London: Routledge and Kegan Paul, 1981); Roland Barthes, "The Death of the Author," in *The Rustle of Language*, trans. R. Howard (New York: Hill and Wang, 1986); Jean-Louis Baudry, "Ideological Effects of the Basic Cinematographic Apparatus," trans. Alan Williams, *Film Quarterly* 28, no. 2 (1973/74), pp. 39–47.

19. Michel Foucault, "What Is an Author?" p. 288. Foucault continues: "It would be as false to seek the author in relation to the actual writer as to the fictional narrator; the 'author-function' arises out of their scission—in the division and distance of the two. One might object that this phenomenon only applies to novels or poetry, to a context of 'quasi-discourse,' but, in fact, all discourse that supports this 'author-function' is characterized by this plurality of egos."

20. Quoted in Portuges, "Seeing Subjects," p. 339.

21. Although I cannot undertake here the systematic theoretical inquiry prompted by the magnitude of these concerns, my examination of Mészáros and her work is inevitably informed by an awareness of their importance to contemporary discourse.

22. As recently as 1989, Mészáros was described in film reviews as the ex-wife of Miklós Jancsó. She is, however, the proud grandmother of seven grandchildren, several of whom have been photographed with her on the set for film periodicals and newspapers. (With regard to her younger sister, Mészáros does not refer to her in the *Diary* films.)

23. Quoted in "A Napló Forgatása Közben: Beszélgetés Mészáros Mártával: az apjáról, a szerelmeiről, az esméről; a történelemről, a gyerekekeiről, Juliról, önmagáról . . ." (While Shooting the *Diary:* Conversation with Márta Mészáros," *Képes Hét*, December 16, 1989, p. 10.

24. See D. W. Winnicott, *Playing and Reality* (London: Routledge, 1989), p. 11.

25. The reactionary if covert program of Stalinism toward sexual difference is evoked in the Diary trilogy as elsewhere in Mészáros's work with reference to the "cult of personality" of Stalin himself, particularly in the documentary and pseudodocumentary segments.

26. Quoted in Annette Insdorf, "Childhood Loss Shapes a Director's Life and Art," *New York Times*, October 28, 1984.

27. Reluctant to dwell on autobiographical elements in conversation, Mészáros is characteristically reticent. Éva Pataki, screenwriter on the Diary trilogy (together with Mészáros), confirms the director's intensely private personality and her refusal to discuss certain aspects of her life. (Interviews, February 1990 and July 1990, Budapest.)

28. See Marie-Claire Ropars-Wuilleumier, *L'écran de la mémoire: Essai de lecture cinématographique* (Paris: Editions du Seuil, 1970).

29. For an excellent discussion of the place of the question of authorial voice, see Kaja Silverman, *The Acoustic Mirror: The Female Voice in Psychoanalysis and Cinema* (Bloomington: Indiana University Press, 1988), pp. 187–234.

30. With reference to the possibilities of the symbolic interpretation of the meaning of fog in Hungarian culture, the formulaic expression: "fog ahead, fog behind" suggests that the speaking subject is lost, literally nowhere. In popular parlance, *ködösítés* (fogging) means "lying."

31. This unsentimentalized positioning of the child is not rare in Soviet and East European cinematic representations of childhood experience, such as A. Tarkovsky's autobiographical feature film *The Mirror* (*Zerkalo*, 1966), in which the exigencies of war, occupation, and poverty deprive the youthful protagonist of innocence at an early age.

32. This gesture is repeated several times in flashback in the third film of the Diary trilogy; the viewer acquainted with Mészáros's own history is reminded of the director's homage to her father in the documentary *In Memoriam: László Mészáros* (1978).

33. This statement may also be read as an allusion to the lack of closure experienced by many Hungarians denied the ability to mourn their dead under Stalin's rule. The emotional sequellae of incomplete mourning are well documented in the psychoanalytic literature; see, for example, J. Bowlby, "Grief and Mourning in Infancy and Early Childhood," *The Psychoanalytic Study of the Child* 15 (1960), pp. 9–52; Sigmund Freud, "Mourning and Melancholia," *Standard Edition*, vol. 14; Edith Jacobson, "The Return of the Lost Parent," in *Drives, Affects, Behavior*, M. Schur, ed. (New York: International Universities Press, 1965), pp. 193–211. (I am grateful to Rita V. Frankiel, psychoanalyst, for suggestions on the clinical bibliography on mourning.)

34. Film screenings and festivals from 1988–90 testify to the urgency of this agenda, in particular in the work of Czechoslovak, Polish, Soviet, and Hungarian directors shown at the Hungarian National Film Week (Budapest, February 1990); the San Francisco Film Festival (April 1990); the Czechoslovak International Film Festival (Karlovy Vary, July 1990); the Montreal International Film Festival (August 1990); and the New York Film Festival (September 1990). Films previously banned, shelved, or censored continue to come to light, while others, primarily documentaries and features based on historical events, take up aspects of postwar Stalin-era life in detail.

35. Mészáros's interpolation of father/surrogate father, mother/surrogate mother, suggests the perturbation and even prevention of the work of mourning that results when a "path of illusion" remains open to the subject after loss of the object's love, whether by death or disappearance. See Catherine J. Parat, "Perte d'objet, perte d'amour," in *Revue française de psychanalyse*, tome 1 (mars-avril 1986), pp. 643–46.

36. Mészáros's documentary film *Travel Diary*, made for Hungarian television in 1989, is similarly reticent; the director's recollections are mediated by her characteristically self-deprecatory humor and irony, and her camera direction rejects the melodramatic in favor of a distanced—although powerful—style.

37. It is not unusual to find in autobiographical literature by filmmakers and writers evidence of an early obsession with movies as an escape from required school attendance. See for example Colette, *Colette au cinéma* (Paris: Flammarion, 1975); Jean Renoir, *Ma vie et mes films* (Paris: Flammarion, 1974); Marguerite Duras, *Les*

Yeux verts (Paris: Cahiers du cinéma, 1980 and 1987); Luis Buñuel, *My Last Sigh* (New York: Alfred A. Knopf, 1983); Jean-Paul Sartre, *Les Mots* (Paris: Gallimard, 1964); François Truffaut, *Les Films de ma vie* (Paris: Flammarion, 1975) and *Correspondence 1945–1984* (New York: Farrar Strauss and Giroux, 1988).

38. During this time, Mészáros also lived with a Romanian filmmaker, a relationship that she does not wish to discuss, but that, according to her associates, was formative in her personal and artistic life.

39. When I attempted to locate the film in Budapest, I was informed by officials at Hungarofilm that its whereabouts are unknown.

40. László Meszaros's background resembled that of the Hungarian tragic realist poet Attila József, whose "Curriculum Vitae" (written as part of a job application in 1937, ten months before he committed suicide) begins: "I was born in 1905 in Budapest; my religion is Greek Orthodox. My father—the late Áron József—left the country when I was three years old, and through the efforts of the Children's Protective Agency I was made to live with foster parents at Ocsod," (trans. Peter Hargitay, in *Perched on Nothing's Branch: Selected Poetry of Attila József* [Tallahassee, Florida: Apalachee Press, 1986]). Born in extreme poverty, haunted by schizophrenia, he sought treatment with several psychoanalysts and finally committed suicide at thirty-three, the age of Mészáros's father when he was arrested by the Russians. His *Curriculum Vitae*, a tersely powerful autobiographical essay, stands as a unique artistic achievement and a document of the material conditions that shaped his art. I am indebted to Antal Bókay for first bringing József to my attention in his presentation at the conference on Literature and Psychoanalysis at Janus Pannonius University, Pécs, in 1983.

41. The tensions between rural and urban life are visible in much of Hungarian cinema, reflecting the close ties many city dwellers maintain with families in small villages, including those of Transylvania, now a much-disputed part of Romania.

42. Autobiographical cinema resembles its literary counterpart in its potential for reworking material at successive stages of the life cycle, so that the subject may be represented in "versions" corresponding to current self- and object-perceptions. See Elizabeth W. Bruss, "Eye for I: Making and Unmaking Autobiography in Film," in *Autobiography: Essays Theoretical and Critical*, ed. James Olney (Princeton: Princeton University Press, 1980), pp. 296–320.

43. Such exhortations to remember have since acquired layers of meaning, as the horrors and secrets carefully guarded are exposed both gradually and with dramatic suddenness in Eastern Europe. See Hans Magnus Enzensberger, *Europe, Europe: Forays into a Continent* (New York: Pantheon, 1989); Vaclav Havel, *Disturbing the Peace* (New York: Alfred A. Knopf, 1990); *Eastern Europe . . . Central Europe . . . Europe*, special issue of *Daedalus*, vol. 119, no. 1 (Winter 1990); and *Lignes: Revue No. 10: Europe Centrale: Nations-Nationalités-Nationalismes* (Paris: Librairie Seguier, June 1990), among the many fine cultural studies of this transitional moment.

44. From "A Napló Forgatása Közben: Beszélgetés Mészáros Mártával" (While Shooting the Diary: Conversation with Márta Mészáros), *Képes Hét*, December 16, 1989.

3. Family Romances

1. Barbara Koenig Quart, *Women Directors: The Emergence of a New Cinema* (New York: Praeger, 1989), p. 193.

2. György Szabó, *A Magyar Film 1973–1977 Között* (Hungarian Film from 1973–1977). Budapest: Magyar Filmtudományi Intézet és Filmarchivum, 1980, pp. 218–23.

3. Quart, *Women Directors*, pp. 196–202.

4. Useful historical studies include Reg Gadney, *Cry Hungary! Uprising 1956* (New York: Atheneum, 1986); Jeffrey C. Goldfarb, *Beyond Glasnost: The Post-Totalitarian Mind* (Chicago: University of Chicago Press, 1989); Charles Gati, *Hungary and the Soviet Bloc* (Chapel Hill: Duke University Press, 1986); and Stephen Borsody, *The Hungarians: A Divided Nation* (New Haven: Yale Center for International and Area Studies, 1988).

5. *Nothing's Lost: Twenty-Five Hungarian Short Stories* (Budapest: Corvina Press, 1988). See especially Endre Vészi, "Chapters from the Life of Vera Angi," and Tibor Déry, "Philemon and Baucis." See also examples of contemporary Hungarian literature in translation in *Present Continuous*, Istvan Bart, ed. (Budapest: Corvina Press, 1985).

6. Max Schur, *Freud: Living and Dying*, (New York: International Press, 1972), p. 105.

7. Sigmund Freud, *The Interpretation of Dreams*, trans. James Strachey (New York: Avon, 1965), p. xxvi.

8. Among the excellent contributions are Constance Penley, *The Future of an Illusion: Film, Feminism, and Psychoanalysis* (Minneapolis: University of Minnesota Press, 1989); Mary Ann Doane, *The Desire to Desire: The Woman's Film of the 1940's* (Bloomington: Indiana University Press, 1987); and Teresa de Lauretis, *Technologies of Gender: Essays on Theory, Film, and Fiction* (Bloomington: Indiana University Press, 1987).

9. See, for example, Max Rosenbaum and Melvin Muroff, eds., *Anna O.: Fourteen Contemporary Reinterpretations* (New York: The Free Press, 1984); Jane Gallop, *The Daughter's Seduction: Feminism and Psychoanalysis* (Ithaca: Cornell University Press, 1982); and Shirley Garner, Claire Kahane, and Madelon Sprengnether, eds., *The (M)Other Tongue: Essays in Feminist Psychoanalytic Interpretation* (Ithaca: Cornell University Press, 1985).

10. Alexander Mitscherlich and Margarete Mitscherlich, *The Inability to Mourn: Principles of Collective Behavior* (New York: Grove Press, 1975). See also Sigmund Freud, "Mourning and Melancholia," *Standard Edition*, vol. 14, pp. 277–78; Vamik Volkan, "The Narcissism of Minor Differences in the Psychological Gap between Opposing Nations," *Psychoanalytic Inquiry* 6 (1986), 175–91; R. Furman, "Death and the Young Child: Some Preliminary Considerations," *Psychoanalytic Study of the Child* 19 (1964), 321–33; Edith Jacobson, "The Return of the Lost Parent," in M. Schur, ed., *Drives, Affects, Behavior* (New York: International Universities Press, 1965), pp. 193–211; Martha Wolfenstein, "How Is Mourning Possible?" *Psychoanalytic Study of the Child* 21 (1966), 93–123; M. Wolfenstein, "Loss, Rage and Repetition," *Psychoanalytic Study of the Child* 24 (1969), pp. 432–46.

11. Agnes Heller describes the devastating consequences of this legacy as a kind of national "schizophrenia": "The ravages of war, material damage can be repaired, but the moral havoc suffered by society in the past few decades has caused greater damage than anything else. I have in mind especially the injuries to a sense of identity and human dignity . . . people refuse to believe in something but pretend to believe in it. . . . They do not believe in the value of words, but they always use those words and ultimately do not even know what they actually believe in. . . . This leads to schizophrenia, to the development of split personalities and cynicism, which is the breeding-ground of dishonesty." *New Hungarian Quarterly* 30 (Winter 1989), p. 73.

12. Sigmund Freud, "Mourning and Melancholia," p. 251.

13. Ibid. In a turn of history that was unpredictable even at the time of *Diary for*

My Loves (1987), Mészáros and the Hungarian people experienced, on the anniversary of the 1956 uprising, the renaming of their country and the institution of a multiparty system at the very moment that the director completed the final part of the *Diary* trilogy. It is rare that history and cinematic representation mesh so dramatically: Hungarian participants in the uprising, many of whom have been in exile for nearly thirty-five years, have returned to witness these momentous occasions, often for the first time. For a technical exploration of the psychoanalytic concept of self-analysis, see Didier Anzieu, *Freud's Self Analysis* (London: Hogarth Press, 1986).

14. I am grateful to Mészáros for inviting me to be present in February 1990 at the studios of Mafilm, Budapest, for a looping of several scenes from *Diary for My Father and Mother (Napló apámnak, anyámnak, 1990)*, which provided the opportunity to observe her at work with a large number of the cast and crew.

15. Edit's character anticipates that of the somewhat younger widow in Polish director Krzysztof Kieslowski's 1984 film *No End (Kez Końca)*, an unsparing portrayal of the suffocating doom that characterized the period of martial law and the suppression of the Solidarity movement in Poland.

16. *Hiroshima mon amour* was scripted by Marguerite Duras, whose later novels and other texts interrogate the parameters of loss, usually from the point of view of a young woman unable to overcome a traumatic experience. See for example C. Portuges, "Love and Mourning in Duras' *Aurelia Steiner*" in *L'Esprit Créateur* 30:1 (Spring 1990), pp. 40–47. The French new wave of the late 1950s and early 1960s also influenced the stylistic innovations and preoccupations of Hungarian filmmakers such as István Szabó and Károly Makk.

17. The cycle of repetition and compulsion recalls the generations of families in Honoré de Balzac's *La Comédie humaine* and Emile Zola's *Les Rougon-Macquart* and the naturalist world of the Goncourt brothers, wherein the fate of a family marked by illness and madness cannot be altered. In *Wild Strawberries (Smultronstället)*, on the other hand, Ingmar Bergman too reworks this motif but reconfigures it by having the pregnant heroine insist on keeping a pregnancy initially rejected by her husband, himself the son of an unloving mother.

18. Mészáros's influence on this and other post-Glasnost East European films remains for the most part unacknowledged by film scholars and critics in East-Central Europe.

19. Members of underground rock groups such as the Galloping Morticians were often imprisoned for their performances, considered dangerously decadent by the authorities. See László Kürti, "Rocking the State: Youth and Popular Music in Hungary in the 1980s," in *East European Politics and Societies*, vol. 5, no. 3 (1991), pp. 145–64.

20. The poem continues:

Three days I haven't eaten
neither scarcely nor well,
all I have is twenty years,
twenty years I'll gladly sell.

If no one will take them,
then maybe the devil will.
I'll break in with all my heart,
and if need be, kill.

They'll catch me and they'll hang me,
cover me up with blessed earth,

and death-eating grass will start
growing on my lovely heart.

From *Perched on Nothing's Branch* p. 14.

21. A fuller analysis of the interconnections between Mészáros's critique of the state and the personal, autobiographical longing for paternal figures is taken up in chapter 6, where the Stalinist program offering party paternalism *in loco parentis* is seen as an important object of the Diary trilogy's interrogation

22. Mészáros's selection of untrained young actors and musicians for their debut movie roles proved to be judicious, and several thereafter became successful professionals.

23. In Jancsó's case, it should be noted that male nudity is also present. The erotics of spectatorship and visual pleasure are problematized in more recent Hungarian cinema in the context of a culture that celebrates sexuality and the body and that promotes its display substantially more than elsewhere in the East bloc.

24. Perhaps intimidating to the Western viewer unaccustomed to the discourse of Eastern European workers, this tone is at once intimate and direct; it bespeaks a lifetime experience of the uneasy equilibrium between solidarity and tribulation.

25. In Western cinema, similar moments privileging the quotidian gesture devoid of romanticism are found in Chantal Akerman's *Jeanne Dielmann*, where the protagonist (Delphine Seyrig) undergoes her daily, solitary ritual of dishwashing, cleaning, and receiving male visitors who pay for her sexual service; in Jean-Luc Godard's *Deux ou trois choses que je sais d'elle* (1966), where Marina Vlady addresses the camera directly when questioned by Godard's off-screen voice about the details of her domestic life; and in the lemon-juice bathing scene in Louis Malle's *Atlantic City* (1980). Among the outstanding collections of feminist film criticism in which such questions are taken up, see Judith Mayne, "The Woman at the Keyhole: Women's Cinema and Feminist Criticism"; Linda Williams, "When the Woman Looks"; Mary Ann Doane, "The 'Woman's Film': Possession and Address"; and Kaja Silverman, "Dis-Embodying the Female Voice," all in Mary Ann Doane, Patricia Mellencamp, and Linda Williams, eds., *Re-Vision: Essays in Feminist Film Criticism* (Los Angeles: American Film Institute, 1984).

4. Lovers and Workers

1. György Szabó, *A Magyar Film 1973–1977 Között* (Hungarian Film 1973–1977). (Budapest: Magyar Filmtudományi Intézet és Filmarchivum, 1980), pp. 218–23.

2. Mészáros's representation of ambivalence in mother/daughter relationships is a reminder that a child may experience abandonment and loss by at once idealizing and rejecting the lost object, a dynamic that may result in depression and feelings of guilt. Preoccupation with maternal rejection is also a persistent motif of Hungarian popular verse and folk music, expressing longing for the *édes anyám* (sweet, dear mother) and blaming her for abandoning or neglecting her child, such as: "Why did you bring me into this world / knowing that I would end up a soldier in battle?"

3. See Melanie Klein and Joan Riviere, *Love, Hate, and Reparation* (New York: W.W. Norton, 1964), for an elaboration of this notion from an object-relations standpoint. Kleinian views of an infant's destructive impulses toward the mother have been influential in feminist and other contemporary psychoanalytic and cultural discourses. In "Attachment and Separation in *The Memoirs of a Dutiful*

Daughter" (*Yale French Studies* 72 [1986], pp. 107–20), I offer a Kleinian reading of pre-oedipal features in the relationship of Simone de Beauvoir to her mother and her sister.

4. See Francine Duplessix Gray, *Soviet Women* (New York: Doubleday, 1990), for an excellent discussion of the deterioration of gender relations in the U.S.S.R. under Stalinism, aspects of which are relevant to Hungarian culture.

5. This ambivalence may be exacerbated when reproduction and aging are juxtaposed, as Mary Russo notes with regard to Bakhtin's model of the grotesque: "this image of the pregnant hag is more than ambivalent. It is loaded with all the connotations of fear and loathing associated with the biological processes of reproduction and aging." Mary Russo, "Female Grotesques: Carnival and Theory," in *Feminist Studies, Critical Studies*, Teresa de Lauretis, ed. (Bloomington: Indiana University Press, 1986), p. 213.

6. Agnès Varda's comment, from an unpublished interview with the author, on Mészáros's special mode of filming women's bodies also conveys something of the playful eroticism of the sequence: "she just needs the water." Varda herself was a long unacknowledged pioneer of the French New Wave in the mid-1950s. See Sandra Flitterman-Lewis, *To Desire Differently: Feminism and the French Cinema* (Urbana: University of Illinois Press, 1990), especially "Agnès Varda and the Woman Seen" and "Varda in Context."

7. Truffaut had also written a brief scenario for the story of Janine, a neglected adolescent of the 1950s, a character he had invented—and subsequently eliminated— more than twenty years earlier as Antoine Doinel's female counterpart in *Les 400 Coups*. La Petite Voleuse *(The Little Thief)* was to have been Truffaut's next film when he died in 1984; it was finally released, directed by Claude Miller, in 1989.

8. Quart, *Women Directors*, p. 200.

9. Bob Dent comments on the absence of women in the post-communist Hungarian parliament: "The point here is that while the new (and the old) parties in Hungary are falling over themselves in their proclaimed identification with Western democratic practices, this kind of under-representation of half the population would today be totally unacceptable in any Western party laying claim to be a party of the future," in "Interesting Times," *New Hungarian Quarterly* 34 (Summer 1990), p. 59.

10. While adoption of this kind is today far more common, at least in the West for single women (as well as older women in couples or alone), the director was virtually alone in bringing to the screen this sensitive subject with unflinching honesty and tact as early as 1977 in Eastern Europe. Quotation from Marguerite Duras from "Les Yeux vert," *Cahiers du Cinéma* 312–313 (June 1980), 23; my translation.

11. "The fact is that in spite of moving into the modern age, in spite of the relatively liberated status of women, the backward tradition of a wife's role remains firmly entrenched in the Hungarian male's psychology. Even in 1974, many of the free young women standing before the marriage registrar became overnight the appendage of men. From that initial act, the young women as *wives* were expected to serve and love their husbands, in spite of all the man's failings, for the rest of their lives, or as long as both could stand it." Iván Völgyes and Nancy Völgyes, "What Is a Wife," in *The Liberated Female: Life, Work, and Sex in Socialist Hungary* (Boulder: Westview Press, 1977), p. 125.

12. *Lázló Kü:* The root of the word is related to the notion of making a vow, hence to permanence.

13. *Cahiers du cinéma* 284 (January 1978), pp. 31–40; my translation.

14. Szabó, *A Magyar Film*, pp. 222–23.

15. Erszébet Magori, "Kilenc hónap," *Filmvilág* (Budapest), December 1976.

16. Szabó continues:

However, I cannot share the critic's enthusiasm concerning the closing sequence of *Nine Months:* in *artistic representations,* it is always the illusion of blood that conveys the truth, not the open wound itself. However, the close-up of childbirth—and especially the fact that the protagonist truly is giving birth to her own child—imbues the film with a *documentary* ending that re-casts the viewer's entire experience. Thus, of all Mészáros's films, *Nine Months* emerges as the epitome of quasi-documentary-feature. (However, in her next feature, *The Two of Them* (1978), she seems to diverge from this earlier direction.)

"It is important to note the way in which we are applying this 'quasi' concept: even in *Nine Months* with its natural narrative flow and serious effort to provide a broader social picture, there are many hypotheses that reveal Mészáros's characteristic perspective as well as its shortcomings, clearly demonstrated, for example, by the over-idealized figure of the heroine. Furthermore, as László Kelecsényi has aptly documented ("A feminizmus csapdája," [The Feminist Trap] *Filmtudományi Szemle,* 1977, pp. 35–40), the apparent stereotypes in Mészáros's films create barriers between the observer and the observed and thus overshadow social reality. As a result, Mészáros's work does not appear to be faithful to everyday reality." Szabó, *A Magyar Film,* pp. 218–19.

17. I spoke with Zsuzsa Czinkóczi in February 1990, during the post-dubbing of scenes from *Diary for My Father and My Mother,* in the commissary of the Mafilm studios. An atmosphere of camaraderie and rigorous professionalism was, she told me, typical of Mészáros's work. Without professional training, she developed into a remarkable actress under Mészáros's tutelage, and the rapport between the two women is extraordinarily successful.

18. Although Mészáros had written *The Two of Them* for Lili Monori and Jan Nowicki, partners in *Nine Months,* the project remained at an impasse until her discovery of Marina Vlady (who had worked in France for Jean-Luc Godard) for the role of Mari, and of Zsuzsa Czinkóczi for the child's part. Vlady is also a writer of distinction, and the former companion of a distinguished Polish poet. Quotations are from my 1989 interview with Mészáros.

19. "Entretien avec Márta Mészáros," in *Cahiers du cinéma* 284, (January 1978), p. 35, translation mine.

20. The scenario of a regressed male whose primary emotional attachment is to a little girl is reminiscent of Serge Bourguignon's *Sundays and Cybèle* (*Les dimanches de la Ville d'Avray,* 1982), in which a similarly ill-assorted couple finds enduring peace together, to the consternation and persecution of their peers.

5. Between Worlds

1. See D. W. Winnicott, "The Place Where We Live," in *Playing and Reality* (New York: Routledge, 1989), p. 107.

2. See D. W. Winnicott, "Transitional Objects and Transitional Phenomena," *International Journal of Psycho-Analysis,* vol. 34, part 2 (1953) and *The Child, the Family, and the Outside World* (Reading: Addison-Wesley, 1987); Adam Phillips, "L'Attente: Quand l'enfant s'ennuie," *Nouvelle revue de psychanalyse 34* (Autumn 1986); Linda Hutcheon, *Narcissistic Narrative: The Metafictional Paradox* (New York: Methuen, 1980).

3. International conferences such as "Winnicott and the Realm of the Imagination" (University of California, Los Angeles, 1990), and "Winnicott and the Objects of Analysis" (University of Massachusetts, Amherst, 1986) disseminate research that establishes these connections.

4. Masud Khan, "Connaissance de l'Inconscient," introduction to the French edition of Winnicott's *Therapeutic Consultations in Child Psychiatry* (London: Hogarth Press and the Institute of Psychoanalysis, 1971), J-B. Pontalis, ed. (Paris: Gallimard), pp. xvi–xvii. Khan considers Winnicott's concepts of transitional object, phenomena, and space to be what Nietszche calls "regulative fictions," rather than dogmatized abstractions from clinical experience.

5. From a letter from the poet Gyula Illés to György Lukács, *Népszabadság*, October 1970, cited in *György Lukács: His Life in Pictures and Documents*, Éva Fekete and Éva Karai, eds. (Budapest: Corvina Kiadó), p. 255.

6. See François Maurin, "Ciné-Spectacles: Racines Hongroises," *L'Humanité*, 31 janvier 1979, p. 5.

7. György Szabó, "Adatok egy identitászavarhoz: Magyar film és társadalom, 1982" (Information on Identity Conflicts: Hungarian Film and Society in 1982) in L. Kálmán, ed., *A magyar film 1982-ben* (Budapest: Magyar Filmtudományi Intézet és Filmarchivum, 1983/1, pp. 5–51. French critics are considerably more receptive. D. W. Winnicott addresses the issue of cultural relocation in "The Place Where We Live," in *Playing and Reality* (New York: Routledge, 1986), pp. 95–110.

8. Interview in the independent Hungarian journal *Hitel*, February 1989. The Hungarian film critic György Szabö takes up the question of Mészáros's unpopularity at home:

> All over the world, Márta Mészáros's films are enjoying attention and success. This is very likely attributable to the fact that they encompass an informative documentary content. Even at the beginning of her career, she declined to use visual effects and did not seek the possibilities of lyric imagery. Rather, she was interested in the problems of contemporary life, often illustrated by youthful protagonists. Quiet, tightly woven dramas characterized her work, as opposed to stylistic inventions. In her intellectual workshop, film is a subtle instrument of expression, its grammar dry yet widely appealing. Márta Mészáros does not enjoy creating an extensive tableau of the social world; instead, she tries to offer us "simple stories," particular pedagogical cautionary tales.

From *A Magyar Film 1973–1977 Között* (Hungarian Film from 1973–1977; Budapest: Magyar Filmtudományi Intézet és Filmarchivum, 1980), p. 218.

9. It is interesting to note how Mészáros compares her own treatment of that period with Gábor's: "[my films are] really my own experience, and Pál Gábor has a different style. *Angi Vera* is far from my films because it's constructed psychologically. Mine are constructed with less emotion: my characters have a more dry or enclosed look, and my actors practically don't 'act' " (from an interview with Annette Insdorf, *New York Times*, cited in the press packet from Artificial Eye Film Co. Ltd., London). In her conversations with me, Mészáros praised *Angi Vera* as one of the finest Hungarian films, a view with which I concur. Its director, Pál Gábor, was given a retrospective in Budapest in July 1988 shortly after his premature death, which confirmed the superiority of that film even within his own distinguished canon.

10. An unexpected death, as also in *Just Like at Home* and *The Two of Them*, is a favored narrative device of Mészáros, used to reveal the fissures lurking beneath the appearance of seamlessness in human relations, and perhaps also suggesting the disparity of the "double life": the gap between what one says and what one thinks in Stalin-era society.

11. I am informed by the anthropologist László Kürti that a formulaic epitaph on graveposts of native Hungarians buried abroad reads: "In this foreign soil lie the remains of . . . " (personal communication).

12. This was a 'transitional space' of an entirely different order by virtue of its

horrifying context. Nevertheless, according to some reports, a zone of manic denial and even hysterical frenzy described the experience of "the living dead"—Jews reduced to invisibility as their lives and apartments were taken over by greedy fellow-citizens even before their deportation. For a chilling account of this historical and psychological moment, see Jiri Weil's *Life with a Star*, translated by Ruzena Kovarikova with Roslyn Schloss (New York: Farrar, Straus and Giroux, 1989).

13. Mészáros comments on her portrayal of men in several interviews, including her interview with Annette Insdorf for the *New York Times* (see n. 9).

14. The problematization of maternity—and the interrogation of "true" as opposed to "surrogate" motherhood—woven throughout Mészáros's cinema invites reflection on the director's own experience as mother to Jancsó's two sons, whom she raised on her own after their divorce.

15. Whether this gesture should also be read as the director's commentary on her own film is ambiguous.

16. The viewer will note here similarities with regard to the treatment of Jews to István Szabó's film *Colonel Redl* (1984).

17. For a useful study of Hungarian Jewry, see William O. McCagg, "Jews and Peasants in Interwar Hungary," *Nationalities Papers* 15:1 (1987), 90–105.

18. See Catherine Portuges, "Retrospectives Narratives in Hungarian Cinema: The 1980s *Diary* Trilogy of Márta Mészáros," *The Velvet Light Trap Review of Cinema* 27 (Spring 1991), pp. 63–73.

19. The film thus refers indirectly to Hungary's alliance with Hitler and to the problematic consequences of its political alignments.

20. An important historical detail that could not be portrayed directly is conveyed through the director's commentary by means of this actual newsreel footage, doubling and at times contradicting the primary narrative and reminding viewers that it was on orders from Nazi Germany that the Hungarian army was posted to the Russian front.

21. "Long live Szálasi!"—a formulaic greeting referring to the former head of the Hungarian fascist Arrow Cross, the dreaded secret police.

22. This vast square, lined with statues of saints and leaders throughout their history, is imbued with special meaning to Hungarians, and is often the site of major political and ceremonial events.

23. For excellent historical documentation on these events, see Reg Gadney, *Cry Hungary!: Uprising 1956* (New York: Atheneum, 1986), and Charles Gati, *Hungary and the Soviet Bloc* (Durham: Duke University Press, 1986).

24. Szabó, "Adatok egy identitaszavarhoz," p. 15.

25. Other films especially pertinent to depiction of the events of 1956 are Pál Sándor's *Daniel Takes a Train* (1983) and *Whooping Cough* (1986).

26. This Kafkaesque nightmare is reproduced in *Diary for My Children* when Juli is similarly denied an exit visa from the Soviet Union, where she is studying, to her Hungarian home, suddenly in the throes of revolution and therefore inaccessible.

27. Although of a far greater magnitude, her generosity recalls Kata's symbolic gift of her nightgown to Anna in *Adoption*, which serves to cement their relationship.

28. Official terms of condemnation under Stalinism also included such charges as "incitement to suicide," an accusation leveled at the Georgian filmmaker Sergei Paradjanov. See Mark Le Fanu, *The Cinema of Andrei Tarkovsky* (London: British Film Institute, 1987), p. 9.

29. See Catherine Portuges, "Between Worlds: Re-placing Hungarian Cinema," in *Before the Wall Came Down: Soviet and East European Filmmakers Working in the West*, Graham Petrie and Ruth Dwyer, eds., (Lanham: University Press of America, 1990), pp. 63–70.

6. Re-Reading History

1. Films pertaining to the popular uprising of 1956 and to Stalinist practices, previously suppressed in Hungary, proliferated from the mid to late 1980s, growing more openly contestatory of official versions. Sándor Sára's *A Thorn Under the Fingernail* (*Tüske a köröm alatt,* 1979) directly criticizes party corruption, while Zsolt Kézdi-Kovacs's *Cry and Cry Again* (*Kíaltás és kiáltás,* 1987), from a novel by Gyula Hernadi based on a true story, underscores abuses of power that continued beyond 1956. Bálint Magyar and Pál Schiffer's *Magyar Stories* (*A Dunánanál,* 1987) represents the recollections of seven peasant men over forty years of Hungarian history, and the brothers Gyuula and János Gulyás's *In Keeping with the Law* (*Törvénysértés nélkül,* 1987) documents testimony by survivors of the notorious labor camps in the Great Hungarian Plain between 1950 and 1953.

2. For a sense of the theoretical debates with regard to the representation of history, see Michel Foucault, "Nietzsche, Genealogy, History," in *Language, Counter-Memory, Practice* (Ithaca: Cornell University Press, 1977); Hayden White, "Getting Out of History: Jameson's Redemption of Narrative," in *The Content of the Form* (Baltimore: Johns Hopkins University Press, 1987; Roland Barthes, "Introduction to the Structural Analysis of Narratives," in *Image, Music, Text,* trans. by Stephen Heath (New York: Noonday Press, 1977); and Marco Ferro, *Cinema and History* (Detroit: Wayne State University Press, 1988).

3. The Hungarian National Museum in Budapest (known under communist rule as the Museum of the Hungarian Working-Class Movement) mounted an exhibition entitled "Sztálin-Rákosi" from May through August 1990, devoted to an exhaustive itemization of this personality cult, and containing artifacts such as banners and posters, books, and crafted gifts "offered" to Rákosi in the name of the Hungarian people, together with elaborate texts created in his honor.

4. See Béla Kiraly, Barbara Lotze and Nandor Dreisziger, eds. *The First War between Socialist States: The Hungarian Revolution 1956 and Its Impact* (New York: Columbia University Press, 1984).

5. The election of men of letters as heads of state in Czechoslovakia and Hungary bears witness to a culture that regards the poet, playwright, and literary translator with particular esteem.

6. Ivan Sanders, "Budapest Letter: New Themes, New Writers," *New York Times Book Review,* April 10, 1988.

7. See *Before the Wall Came Down: Soviet and East European Filmmakers Working in the West,* Graham Petrie and Ruth Dwyer, eds. (New York: University Press of America, 1990).

8. See Mészáros's interview by János Palotai, in *Ijúsági Szemle,* October–November 1985, pp. 96–102, for a discussion of the influence of Lukács on her conception of history.

9. The viewer unfamiliar with Hungarian or Russian might miss that fact that Magda (played by the Russian actress, Anna Polony) speaks Russian with Juli, who has perfected that language during her film studies in the U.S.S.R. This linguistic bond signifies Magda's allegiance to Moscow and her manipulation of Juli's attachment to the past.

10. Mészáros insists in several instances on the solidarity and human bonds that link Russian and Hungarian people—for example, among students at the VGIK Film School in Moscow in *Diary for My Loves*—despite the deeply resented Soviet dominance in Hungary under Stalinism.

11. According to Mészáros, in her 1989 interview with me, this scene caused Hungarian censors to delay production of the film, because it was thought to embody

a reference to the unmarked grave of Imre Nagy, a hero of the uprising of 1956, executed in 1958 and subsequently given a hero's burial in June 1989. The whereabouts of his remains became a rallying point for the Hungarian opposition in its efforts to have him—and, by extension, all those who took part in the uprising—officially "rehabilitated."

12. Andrzej Wajda's Polish film *Kanal* (1956), for instance, is set during the Warsaw Uprising in September 1944, but may also be read as a commentary on the Poland in which it was produced.

13. See, for example, "Discourse of the Other: Postcoloniality, Positionality, and Subjectivity," a special issue of *Quarterly Review of Film and Video*, vol. 13, nos. 1–3 (1991), Hamid Naficy and Teshome H. Gabriel, eds.

14. S. Freud, *The Interpretation of Dreams*, "The Dream-Work," and "The Psychology of the Dream-Processes" (New York: Avon, 1965).

15. Elizabeth Bruss, "Eye for I: Making and Unmaking Autobiography in Film," in James Olney, ed., *Autobiography: Essays Theoretical and Critical* (Princeton: Princeton University Press, 1980,) p. 296; see also C. Portuges, "Seeing Subjects: Women Directors and Cinematic Autobiography," in B. Brodzki and C. Schenck, eds., *Life/Lines: Theorizing Women's Autobiography* (Ithaca: Cornell University Press, 1988).

16. For an excellent discussion of paternalizing symbolic role of the Communist Party and its masculinist indoctrination of East European youth, see Paul Neuberg, *The Hero's Children: The Postwar Generation in Eastern Europe* (London: Constable, 1972).

17. On *The Fall of Berlin*, directed by Mikhail Chiaureli, see Georges Sadoul, *Dictionary of Films* (Berkeley: University of California Press, 1972), p. 270; see also Jean-Pierre Jeancolas, review of *Journal Intime*, *Positif* 247 (October 1981), pp. 75–76.

18. Her treatment of the natural landscape and its inhabitants is later thematized more directly in *Bye Bye Little Red Riding Hood*, with its mixture of wildlife, forest settings and urban concerns. See also Graham Petrie, *History Must Answer to Man* (Budapest: Corvina 1978), pp. 5–6: "The film reveals a strong feeling for landscape and setting, the concrete environment typical of Hungarian cinema. It is story of class conflicts, the exploitation of forestry workers by the local landowner. When the wife dies from the landlord's ill treatment, the impoverished husband is forced to lie by pretending she is ill in order to bring her body home on the train for burial. Against the mist and trees of the Transylvanian landscape, he carries her body home, and murders the landlord, conveying a sense that such conditions are to be expected in an unjust social system."

19. Juli's story is reminiscent of that of Truffaut's, "delinquent" child, Antoine Doinel, in *Les 400 coups* (1958). The movies represent for him both escape and refuge, and the only moment of "familial" happiness. For Truffaut himself, the Paris Cinématheque virtually became a second home where, a delinquent child himself, he spent most of his days playing hooky from school.

20. Révai's speech refers, among other things, to a Hungarian proverb to the effect that "pigs dream of acorns and geese dream of maize." Freud cites the Hungarian psychoanalyst Sándor Ferenczi's quotation of this proverb, adding a Jewish proverb: "What do hens dream of? Of millet." *Interpretation of Dreams*, p. 165.

21. *Ditte menneskebarn* (*Child of Man*, Denmark 1946, dir. Bjarne Henning-Jensen). This celebrated film, based on the novel by the Marxist Martin Andersen Nexo, may have been considered acceptable by Stalinist standards because of its "realistic" portrayal of poor people living under harsh conditions.

22. Istvan Nemeskürty, *Word and Image: History of the Hungarian Cinema*

(Budapest: Corvina Press, 1974), p. 162. *Singing Makes Life Beautiful*, directed by Márton Keleti, an amalgam of propaganda and entertainment starring Violette Ferrari, is, according to István Nemeskürty and Tibor Szántó (*A Pictorial Guide to the Hungarian Cinema* [Budapest: Helikon, 1985], p. 108), a "workshop comedy."

23. The flag with its torn-out center was the symbol of the Hungarian uprising, and subsequently of other national independence movements in the East Bloc.

24. According to Éva Pataki, who wrote the script with Mészáros, when the night scene was shot in Heroes' Square (*Hősök Tere*) close to Pataki's apartment, neighbors fought to take part in the symbolic reenactment.

25. In *Diary for My Loves*, Juli is called "another anguished Hungarian."

26. Gyula Hegyi, "Film levél: Napló apámnak, anyámnak," *Magyar Hirlap*, June 23, 1990.

27. József Veress, "A Harmadik Napló," *Népszabadság*, June 21, 1990; László Zay, "Napló mindannyiunknak," *Magyar Nemzet*, June 16, 1990. Other critics see the film as on the whole disappointingly rigid, a realistic but soulless illustration of well-known events that at its worst revives a hidebound socialist realism. I am grateful to Lia Somogyi, Hungarian Federation of Film Societies and Hungarofilm, for providing me with documentation on the Hungarian reception of *Diary for My Father and Mother*.

28. Miklós Haraszti, *The Velvet Prison: Artists Under State Socialism*, translated by Katalin and Stephen Landesmann (New York: Basic Books, 1987). See also John Kadvany, "Anti-Samizdat," *The Threepenny Review* 34 (Summer 1988), p. 20.

7. Tales for the Future

1. The film was produced by Rock Demers, former president of the Montreal International Film Festival and a longtime admirer of Hungarian cinema.

2. These tales are reprinted in *Little Red Riding Hood: A Casebook*, Alan Dundes, ed. (Madison: University of Wisconsin Press, 1989) as Charles Perrault, "Little Red Riding Hood" (pp. 3–6), and Jacob and Wilhelm Grimm, "Little Red Cap" (*"Rotkappchen,"* pp. 7–12. Dundes's introduction begins: "The story of a little girl who wears a red hood or cape and who carries a basket of food and drink to her grandmother is one of the most beloved and popular fairy tales ever reported. The girl, called 'Le petit chaperon rouge' in French, 'Rotkappchen' in German, and 'Little Red Riding Hood' in English, invariably encounters a villainous wolf in European versions of the folk tale. Folklorists classify this folktale as Aarne-Thomspon tale type 333, 'The Glutton (Red Riding Hood)'. In Stith Thompson's 1961 revision of the tale-type index, the plot summary includes two segments: 1) Wolf's Feast. (a) By masking as mother or grandmother, the wolf deceives and devours (b) a little girl (Red Riding Hood) whom he meets on his way to her grandmother's. 2) Rescue. (a) The wolf is cut open and his victims rescued alive; (b) his belly is sewed full of stones and he drowns; (c) he jumps to his death' "(Dundes, ed., *Little Red Riding Hood*, p. ix).

3. Mészáros's sons Nyika Jancsó and Miklós Jancsó, Jr. have, as has been noted in previous chapters, been centrally involved in previous films as camera operator and director of photography. And the director is pleased to have directed scenes from *Bye Bye Red Riding Hood* with her granddaughter seated on her lap; although she dismisses such actions as "perfectly normal," Mészáros insisted, in her 1990 interview with me, that "movies should be a family affair . . . as in Italy where wives, husbands, and children are all over the set."

4. Pataki and Mészáros's second produced collaboration was the play "Edith and

Marlene," a treatment of the friendship between Edith Piaf and Marlene Dietrich. Its immediate success in Budapest assured the play a long run when it was discovered that three of the leading cast members were pregnant. Rajk, the son of the Communist László Rajk (who had fought fascism underground and was hanged after a forced confession in the bloody aftermath of the Stalinist takeover in Hungary), has recent screen credits including Péter Gothar's *Just Like America* (*Tiszta Amerika*, 1988) and Pál Sándor's *Miss Arizona* (1988). The Canadian art director Violette Daneau is also an imaginative designer, a longtime collaborator of Rock Demers.

5. Lauzier was cast first as the heroine of a previous episode of "Contes Pour Tous"; Mészáros met her in the Montreal production office during casting discussions casting with her line producer Ann Burke: "I saw her from behind . . . that gorgeous head of auburn red curls, and knew in my heart that I had found my Red Riding Hood." Rock Demers was also instrumental in creating the first official Canadian-Polish coproduction, "The Young Magician," which subsequently earned a number of international awards, as have all the tales in the series (production notes, Rock Demers/*Tales for All*).

6. One of Poland's most respected stage and screen actors and a veteran of some eighty films, Jan Nowicki has worked under the direction of such distinguished artists as Andrzej Wajda, Krzysztof Zanussi, and Jerzy Skolimowski.

7. Press packet, courtesy Les Productions la Fête/Montreal.

8. See Dundes, *Little Red Riding Hood*, for international versions. The English film treatment of "The Company of Wolves" was released in 1984. For a bold treatment of the film version based on Angela Carter's story, see "Lolita Meets the Werewolf: *The Company of Wolves*" in *The Female Gaze: Women as Viewers of Popular Culture*, Lorraine Gamman and Margaret Marshment, eds. (Seattle: Real Comet Press, 1989), pp. 76–85.

9. Jack Zipes, *The Trials and Tribulations of Little Red Riding Hood* (Bergin and Garvey, 1983), p. 14. Some thirty-one stories, ranging in date of composition from 1697 to 1979, have been collected in this volume. It should also be noted that, in Hungarian popular culture, obscene jokes about Little Red Riding Hood still abound.

10. Ibid., p. 220.

11. "XXI. Magyar Filmszemle: A harcos pihenője" (The 21st Hungarian Film Week: A Warrior's Repose), *Hitel* 3 (1989), pp. 33–34.

12. Cited by Gerald Peary, "Little Red Riding Hood Gets a Hungarian Twist," *Los Angeles Times*, February 7, 1989, p. 2.

13. György Sas, "Filmlevél: Piroska és a farkas," *Film Szinház Muzsika*, April 1, 1989, p. 7.

14. In Hungarian folk tales, a shaman climbs a magic tree to go into a trance, to travel to other worlds. Its flowers serve often to re-unite separated lovers.

15. The dog, Mookie, is a Canadian malamute, the Hungarian shepherd stipulated by coproduction contract having failed in the role; see Gerald Peary, "Little Red Riding Hood: Márta Mészáros and the Malamute," *Sight and Sound* 57, no. 3 (Summer 1988), p. 150.

16. See Bruno Bettelheim, "Little Red Cap and the Pubertal Girl," in Dundes, *Little Red Riding Hood*, pp. 168–91.

17. Freud refers to the tale in a 1908 paper "On the Sexual Theories of Children" with regard to the "cloacal" theory of creation presumably believed by children ignorant of the birth process: "The child must be expelled like excrement . . . if in later childhood the same question is the subject of solitary reflection or of a discussion between two children, the explanations probably are that the baby comes out of the navel, which opens, or that the belly is slit and the child taken out, as happens to the wolf in the tale of Little Red Riding Hood. . . . If babies are born through the anus then

a man can give birth just as well as a woman. A boy can therefore fancy that he too has children of his own without our needing to accuse him of feminine inclinations." In his 1913 essay "The Occurrence in Dreams of Material from Fairy Tales," Freud takes up the folk tale in more depth, with reference to the famous case of the Wolf-Man, a young male patient whose recurrent dream of white wolves in a tree leads to his recollection of being "tremendously afraid of the picture of a wolf in a book of fairy tales. . . . He thought this picture might have been an illustration to the story of 'Little Red Riding Hood.' . . . In both [referring also to the Grimm tale "The Wolf and the Seven Little Goats"] there is the eating up, the cutting open of the belly, the taking out of the people who have been eaten and their replacement by heavy stones, and finally in both of them the wicked wolf perishes." Sigmund Freud, *Collected Papers* (New York: Basic Books, 1959), vol. 2, pp. 68–69; vol. 4, p. 242. Freud also points out that the tale of Little Red Riding Hood may be about fear of the father in "From the History of an Infantile Neurosis," *Standard Edition* (London: Hogarth Press, 1955), 17:7–122. See also D. W. Winnicott, *The Child, the Family, and the Outside World* (Reading: Addison-Wesley, 1987), pp. 108–109.

18. Róheim continues: "The hunter would then be correctly interpreted as the father figure, as a rival for the inside (or breast) of the mother. In one of the German versions (Southern Tyrol) it is the father who chops the wolf's head off. . . . The point is that Little Red Riding Hood (as Wolf) eats the grandmother first and is then eaten by the grandmother-wolf." From "Fairy Tale and Dream: Little Red Riding Hood," in Dundes, *Little Red Riding Hood*, p. 162.

19. Sas, "Filmlevél," p. 7.

20. Born in 1932, Alexander Kluge is a writer, filmmaker, and activist of the New German Cinema, as well as a lawyer, media theorist, and teacher. He narrowly escaped death as a child during the American bombing of his home in Halberstadt. The unearthing of history, the film's controlling metaphor, takes place in *The Female Patriot* from the perspective of the living as well as the dead, and allusions to Grimms' fairy tales are among the film's prodigious accumulation of the artifacts of that history. The proverb "He who laughs best, laughs last" is known in many languages, including Hungarian.

21. In "XXI. Magyar Filmszemle."

22. Ibid.

23. According to Róheim: "The infant eats the breast, the infant eats and sees, and desires and is, therefore, the original aggressor. . . . The father imago is clearly recognizable as the rival for the inside of the mother. In other words, the oedipus complex goes back to the oral and to the uterine regressive organization." (In Dundes, *Little Red Riding Hood*, pp. 164–65). Róheim was a controversial figure in psychoanalytic circles; his contention that fairy tales come from dreams is considered extremely dubious by many, yet the breadth of his command of oral tradition is unparalleled. Nonetheless, it is worth noting that, inspired by Róheim, another critic argues that the wolf "is father and mother simultaneously . . . good and bad, giver and taker, sexual object desired and feared. . . . The wolf seduces, but the children invite seduction and danger" (Elizabeth Crawford, "The Wolf as Condensation" (1955), cited in ibid., p. 215).

24. See the most influential psychoanalytic critic of the literature of Little Red Riding Hood, Bruno Bettelheim, "Little Red Cap and the Pubertal Girl," in Dundes, *Little Red Riding Hood*, pp. 168–91, from *The Uses of Enchantment: The Meaning and Importance of Fairy Tales* (New York: Alfred A. Knopf, 1976). For other psycho-analytic views on the human-animal nexus, see *The Wolf Man by the Wolf Man*, with "The Case of the Wolf-Man" by Sigmund Freud and "A Supplement" by Ruth Mack Brunswick (New York: Basic Books, 1971); Patrick Mahony, *Cries of the Wolf Man*

(History of Psychoanalysis Monograph I, New York: International Universities Press, 1984).

25. Gerald Peary, "Little Red Riding Hood."

Conclusion

1. György Konrád, *Antipolitics* (New York: Henry Holt, 1984), p. 123.

2. Mészáros has had in mind a number of film projects on Gypsies which she was not encouraged to make, there having been an unofficial limit on productions on this highly controversial topic. Among her projects was a script written with Ferenc Grunwalski about Gypsy families living in the Hungarian Stalinist towns of Leninváros and Sztálinvaros (now Dunaujváros). According to Mészáros, when she lived and worked in Romania in the late 1950s, she made a film (deemed illegal by authorities) about the Csángó, a group of Hungarians living in the region of Moldavia. She considers that work, shot in a remote village, to have been of extraordinary beauty, based as it was on authentic songs and instrumentation of the Csángó. To Meszaros's regret, the documentary can no longer be found, if indeed the film still exists (personal conversation, Harvard University, Cambridge, April 1991).

3. No fewer than eleven East European or Soviet features and shorts were screened at the 1990 Cannes Film Festival, while the 1989 New York Film Festival boasted a record number of films labeled as "documentaries." See Andrzej Wajda, *Double Vision: My Life in Film* (New York: Holt, 1989), pp. 131–32.

4. Mészáros explains with pleasure in her 1991 interview with me that her age cannot be definitively established, given the fact that accurate records were either lost or not kept under the Stalinist conditions in which she entered the world.

5. Walter Benjamin, "Theses on the Philosophy of History," in *Illuminations*, trans. Harry Zohn, ed. Hannah Arendt (New York: Schocken, 1969), p. 255.

6. During the 1992 Hungarian Film Week, held February 8–12, no fewer than a dozen press conferences were held to debate issues including the rights of younger filmmakers; the loss of security and retirement benefits for older directors; the response of foreign journalists to Hungarian current films; support for film restoration and preservation; the meaning of being a "producer" for Hungarian cinema in the 1990s; and opportunities for funding from foreign capital.

7. "We tried to bring up the role of women during the campaign last spring," said Róza Hodosan, a member of the Hungarian parliament from the liberal Alliance of Free Democrats, "but we realized quickly that people were not interested. We did much better sticking to issues like land, real estate, and economics" (*New York Times*, "The Week in Review," November 25, 1990, pp. 1–2).

8. In a country where every woman is entitled to a twenty-four-week maternity leave at full pay, followed by a three-year leave at partial salary with the promise of returning to the same job, women are likely to be disproportionately affected by the changes under way.

Interviews with Márta Mészáros

1. Mészáros intimates here as well a sense of the presence of a sexual component in any intense friendship.

2. Mészáros indicates that other family members are illustrated as well by the character of the grandfather, played by Pál Zolnay in the Diary segments.

3. After this interview was conducted, and since the completion of the manuscript, Grósz was demoted and the Hungarian Socialist Workers' Party became the Hungarian Socialist Party; at the same time, the People's Republic of Hungary became the Republic of Hungary. Grósz had come to power only a few weeks before this interview was conducted. The status of the 1956 uprising—as revolution or counterrevolution—had not yet been officially decided, nor was it possible to predict that, scarcely a year later, Nagy would be officially rehabilitated and given a hero's funeral in the largest demonstration of popular sentiment in the country in thirty years. That Hungary would mark, on October 23, 1989, the thirty-third anniversary of the violent uprising against Soviet rule by announcing its status as a republic was still less imaginable. In a demonstration outside the Parliament building, some 100,000 Hungarians gathered to cheer the announcement and commemorate the rebellion that had, until recently, been labeled a "counterrevolution," and is now hailed as the wellspring of democracy (*New York Times*, Tuesday, October 24, 1989).

4. For more detailed discussion of Mészáros's thoughts on the third Diary, see "A Napló Forgatása Közben: Beszélgetés Mészáros Mártával" (While Shooting the Diary: Conversation with Márta Mészáros), *Képes Het*, December 16, 1989.

5. Dan Talbot is the owner of New Yorker Films, and an important force in international cinema; many of the films he distributes have been screened in the New Yorker Theatre.

6. Mészáros's screenwriter and collaborator Éva Pataki spoke of this unrealized project in Budapest, July 1990, as one of the director's favorite topics. For Andre de Dienes's account of his discovery of Marilyn Monroe, see his *Marilyn Mon Amour* (London: Sidgwick and Jackson, 1986).

FILMOGRAPHY

1957   *A History of Albertfalva (Albertfalvai történet;* fr. *Histoire d'Albertfalva)*
documentary (diploma film)

1959   *Life Goes On (Az élet megy tovább;* fr. *Et la vie continue)*
documentary (in Bucharest)

1961   *Heartbeat (Szivdobogás;* fr. *Battement du Coeur)*
short, popular-science documentary (Diploma of Merit at Padua)
Colours of Vasarhely (Vásárhelyi szinek; fr. *Couleurs de Vasarhely)*
short subject: painter

1962   *János Tornyai (Tornyai;* fr. *János Tornyai)*
short subject: artist
A Town in the Awkward Age (Kamaszváros; fr. *L'Age Ingrat d'une Ville)*
short documentary on the town Oroszlány, a one-time mining village suffering from the problems of rapid economic development.
Director of Photography: István Zöldi; screenplay: György Berényi; Production: Mafilm Studios, Budapest; world distribution: Hungarofilm, Budapest;
running time: 17 minutes; 35mm; black/white; without text. Awarded Diploma at Mannheim.

1963   *Saturday, 27th July, 1963 (1963, julius 27, szombat;* fr. *Samedi, 27 Juillet,
1963)*
short subject

1964   *Szentendre: The Town of Painters (Festők városa;* fr. *La ville des peintres)*
documentary on the artists' colony in the Danube town of Szentendre
Blow-Ball (Bóbita; fr. *Pissenlit)*
short feature
Director of Photography: István Zöldi; screenplay: Márta Mészáros; running
time: 22 minutes; 35mm; black/white; with dialogue.

1967   *Miklós Borsos (Borsos Miklós;* fr. *Miklós Borsos)*
short subject: sculpture
Synopsis: Presents the work of one of Hungary's foremost sculptors, Miklós
Borsos, at his home and studio on the picturesque peninsula of Tihany on the
shores of Lake Balaton.
Director of Photography: Tamás Somló; written by Márta Mészáros; running
time: 12 minutes; 35mm; Eastmancolor.

1968   *The Girl (Eltávozott nap;* fr. *Cati)*
feature
Screenplay: Márta Mészáros; Director of Photography: Tamás Somló; music:
Levente Szörényi; production: Mafilm Studio 4, Budapest; World distribu-
tion: Hungarofilm, Budapest; length: 2378 meters; running time: 86 minutes;
35mm; black/white
Cast: the girl (Kati Kovacs), Mr. Zsámboki (Ádám Szirtes), Mrs. Zsámboki
(Teri Horváth), Lajos, their son (Gábor Harsányi), Mari (Zsuzsa Pálos), Mr.
Papolczai (Gábor Agárdi), the boy (Gáspár Jancsó), the dark-haired young
man (Jácint Juhász), the fair-haired young man (András Kozák).
Special Prize of the Jury, Valladolid, 1969; Best actress award for Kati
Kovács.

1969   *Binding Sentiments (Holdudvar;* fr. *Marie)*
        feature
        Director of Photography: János Kende; music: Levente Szőrényi; screenplay:
        Márta Mészáros; length: 2423 meters; Agascope; black/white; production:
        Mafilm Studio 1, Budapest; world distribution: Hungarofilm, Budapest. Run-
        ning time: 96 min.
        Cast: Edit (Mari Törőcsik), her son (Lajos Balázsovits), the young girl (Kati
        Kovács).

1970   *Don't Cry, Pretty Girls (Szép lányok, ne sirjatok;* fr. *Pleurez pas, jolies filles)*
        feature
        Dramaturg/scenario: Yvette Biró; Director of Photography: János Kende;
        screenplay: Péter Zimre; music: János Baksa Sóos, Miklós Országczky, Zorán
        Sztevanovity, Károly Frenreisz, Levente Szőrényi, László Tolcsvay; produc-
        tion: Mafilm Studio 1, Budapest; world distribution: Hungarofilm, Budapest;
        running time: 91 minutes; 35mm; black/white.
        Cast: Géza (Lajos Balázsovits), Juli (Jaroslava Schallerova), Juli's fiancé
        (Márk Zala); Juli's brother (Balázs Tardy).

1971   *At the Lorinc Spinnery (A lőrinci fonóban;* fr. *La filature de Lorinc)*
        documentary
        Director of Photography: Lajos Koltai; screenplay: Márta Mészáros; produc-
        tion: Mafilm Studios, Budapest; world distribution: Hungarofilm, Budapest;
        running time: 17 minutes; 35mm; black/white; with dialogue.

1973   *Riddance (Szabad lélegzet;* fr. *Débarras)*
        feature film
        Director of Photography: Lajos Koltai; screenplay: Márta Mészáros; music:
        Levente Szörényi; production: Hunnia Studio, Budapest; world distribution:
        Hungarofilm, Budapest; running time: 84 minutes; 35 mm; black/white.
        Cast: Jutka (Erzsébet Kútvölgyi), András (Gábor Nagy), Zsuzsa (Mariann
        Moor), Jutka's father (Ferenc Kállai), Jutka's mother (Mari Szemes); An-
        drás's father (Lajos Szabó); András's mother (Teri Földi).

1975   *Adoption (Örökbefogadás;* fr. *Adoption)*
        feature
        Director of Photography: Lajos Koltai; screenplay: Márta Mészáros, Gyula
        Hernádi, and Ferenc Grunwalsky; dramaturg: Miklós Vásárhelyi; music: Gy-
        örgy Kovács; production: Hunnia Studio, Budapest; world distribution: Hun-
        garofilm, Budapest; running time: 89 minutes; 35mm; black/white.
        Cast: Kata (Kati Berek), Jóska (László Szabó), Anna (Gyöngyvér Vigh), Doc-
        tor (Dr. Árpád Perlaky).
        Awards: Berlin, 1975: Grand Prix—Golden Bear; OCIC Prize; Otto Dibelius
        Prize; Prize of the CIDALC Jury; Chicago, 1975: Gold Plaque.

1976   *Nine Months (Kilenc hónap;* fr. *Neuf Mois)*
        feature
        Director of Photography: János Kende; screenplay: Gyula Hernádi, Ildikó
        Kóródi, Márta Mészáros; music: György Kovács; production: Hunnia Studio,
        Budapest; world distribution: Hungarofilm, Budapest; running time: 93 min-
        utes; 35 mm; Eastmancolor.
        Cast: Juli (Lili Monori), János (Jan Nowicki), Professor (Djoko Rosic).
        Awards: Teheran 1976: Diploma; Best Actress Prize to Lili Monori; Cannes,
        1977: FIPRESCI Prize.

1977   *The Two of Them (Ők ketten;* fr. *Elles Deux)*
        feature
        Director of Photography: János Kende; screenplay: Ildikó Kóródy, József

Balázs, Géza Bereményi; music: György Kovács; production: Dialóg Studio, Budapest; world distribution: Hungarofilm, Budapest; running time: 94 minutes; 35 mm; Eastmancolor. Cast: Mari (Marina Vlady), Juli (Lili Monori), Feri, Mari's husband (Miklós Tolnay), János, Juli's husband (Jan Nowicki), Zsuzsi, Juli's daughter (Zsuzsa Czinkóczy).

1978   *In Memoriam: László Mészáros*
documentary
Director of Photography: János Kende; written by Márta Mészáros. 22 minutes; 35 mm; Eastmancolor. Not released in festival competition.

1978   *Just Like at Home (Olyan mint otthon;* fr. *Comme à la Maison)*
feature
Director of Photography: Lajos Koltai; screenplay: Ildikó Kóródy; camera: Tamás Somló; production: Hunnia Studio, Budapest; world distribution: Hungarofilm, Budapest; running time: 108 minutes; 35mm; Eastmancolor. Cast: Zsuzsi (Zsuzsa Czinkóczy), András Novák (Jan Nowicki), Anna (Anna Karina), Zsuzsi's mother (Ildikó Pécsi), András's mother (Kornelia Sallai), András's father (Ferenc Bencze).
Awards: San Sebastian, 1978: "Silver Shell".

1979   *On the Move (Útközben;* fr. *En cours de route)*
feature; a Hungarian-Polish coproduction
Director of Photography: Tamás Andor; screenplay: Jan Nowicki, Márta Mészáros, Marek Piwowski; music: Zygmunt Konieczny; production: Mafilm-Dialog Studio, Budapest and Zespole Filmowy "X" Warsaw; world distribution: Hungarofilm, Budapest; running time: 104 minutes; 35mm; Eastmancolor.
Cast: Barbara (Delphine Seyrig), Marek (Jan Nowicki), Barbara's husband (Djoko Rosic), Marek's wife (Beata Tyszkiewicz).

1980   *The Heiresses (Örökség;* fr. *Les Heritières)*
feature; a Hungarian-French coproduction
Director of Photography: Elemér Ragályi; screenplay: Ildikó Kóródy, Márta Mészáros; music: Zsolt Döme; lyrics: István Veredes; production: Mafilm-Studio Hunnia, Budapest and Gaumont-Partners Production, Paris; distribution: Hungarofilm, Budapest and Gaumont, Paris; running time: 104 minutes; 35 mm; Eastmancolor.
Cast: Iren (Isabelle Huppert), Sylvia (Lili Monori), Ákos (Jan Nowicki), Teréz (Zita Perczel), Sylvia's father (Sándor Szabó).

1981   *Mother and Daughter (Anna;* fr. *Une mère, une fille)*
feature; coproduction with Gaumont-Swan Productions/Port Royal Film, Paris.
Director of Photography: Tamás Andor; screenplay: Gyula Hernádi, Márta Mészáros; music: Zsolt Döme; production: Mafilm-Hunnia Studio, Budapest and Gaumont-Swan Productions/Port Royal Film, Paris; running time: 92 minutes; 35 mm; Eastmancolor.
Cast: Anna (Marie José Nat), János (Jan Nowicki), Péter, Anna's son (László Gálffy), Mr. Aubier (Lóránd Lohinszky), Mrs. Aubier (Teri Tordai), Marie Aubier (Marie Lebee).

1982   *Diary for My Children (Napló gyermekeimnek;* fr. *Journal Intime)*
feature
Director of Photography: Miklós Jancsó, Jr.; screenplay: Márta Mészáros; music: Zsolt Döme; production: Mafilm Studio, Budapest; distribution: Hungarofilm, Budapest; running time: 106 minutes; 35mm; black/white.

Cast: Juli (Zsuzsa Czinkóczi); Magda (Anna Polony), János (Jan Nowicki), his son (Tamás Tóth), Grandpa (Pál Zolnay), Grandma (Mari Szemes).

Awards: Budapest 1984, sixteenth National Film Festival Grand Prix and "acting award," Zsuzsa Czinkóczi; Cannes 1984, Special "Grand Prix" of the Jury; Munich 1984, "Interfilm" Prize; Chicago 1984, "Bronze Hugo"; Budapest 1985: Hungarian Film Critics' Prize for Best Direction.

1983   *The Land of Mirages (Délibábok országa; fr. Le Pays du Mirage)*
feature
Director of Photography: Miklós Jancsó, Jr.; screenplay: Balázs Vargha, based on a play by Nikolai Gogol, *The Inspector General (Revizor)*; music: Zsolt Döme; production: Mafilm, Budapest; world distribution: Hungarofilm, Budapest; running time: 87 minutes; 35mm; black/white.
Cast: the burgomaster (Jan Nowicki), his wife (Teri Tordai), his daughter (Kati Rak), Karikas (Marek Kondrat), his servant (Ádám Szirtes).

1985   *Ave Maria (Ave Maria, fr. Ave Maria)*
short documentary commissioned by the United Nations

1987   *Diary for My Loves (Napló szerelmeimnek; fr. Journal à mes amours)*
feature
Director of Photography: Nyika Jancsó; screenplay: Márta Mézsáros and Éva Pataki; music: Zsolt Döme; setting: Eva Martin; costume: Fanni Kemenes; Film editing: Éva Kármentő; sound: István Sipos; production: Mafilm, Budapest; world distribution: Hungarofilm, Budapest; running time: 130 minutes; 35mm; Eastmancolor.
Cast: Juli (Zsuzsa Czinkóczi), Magda (Anna Polony), János (Jan Nowicki), Grandpa (Pál Zolnay), Grandma (Mari Szemes), Erzsi (Erzsébet Kútvölgy), Anna Pavlovna (Irina Kouberskaia), Natasha (Adél Kovács).
Awards: Berlinale, "Silver Bear"; Budapest, National Feature Film Special Prize.

1989   *Bye Bye Red Riding Hood (Piroska és a farkas; fr Bye Bye Chaperon rouge)*
feature
Director of Photography: Thomas Vámos; camera operator: Nyika Jancsó; screenplay: Márta Mészáros, Éva Pataki; editor: Louise Coté; art director: Violette Daneau; chief decorator: László Rajk; music: Zsolt Döme; producers: Rock Demers & Gábor Hanák, Les Productions La Fête (Montreal), Hungarofilm/MOKEP (Budapest), with the participation of Téléfilm Canada. 35mm color, 94 min.
Cast: Fanny Lauzier, Pamela Collyer, Jan Nowicki, Teri Tordai, Margit Makay, David Vermes, Anna Blazejczak, Mouki (the wolf).

1989   *Utinaplo* (Travel Diary). Part I: *Moscow;* Part II: *Leningrad, the "Sick City" (Leningrad a "beteg" város)*, Part III: *Frunze.* Documentary of Mészáros's return to the Soviet Union in 1988–89. Broadcast on Hungarian television in three parts, fall 1989.

1990   *Diary for My Father and Mother (Napló apámnak, anyámnak)*
Screenplay: Márta Mészáros & Éva Pataki; Director of Photography: Nyika Jancsó; music: Zsolt Döme; sets: Éva Marting; editor: Éva Kármentő; costumes: Fanni Kemenes; sound: István Sipos. Cast: Zsuzsa Czinkóczi (Juli), Jan Nowicki (János), Mari Torocsik (Vera), Ildikó Bánsági (Ildi), Anna Polony (Magda). Production: Budapest Film Studio/Hungarofilm. 35 mm, 113 minutes, Eastmancolor.

1990   *My Preferred Opera: Portrait of Barbara Hendrix*

Director: Márta Mészáros; Documentary about an African-American opera singer.
Production: German Television, 60 minutes, color

1991 *Looking for Romeo (Keressük Rómeot)*
Documentary: interviews with Hungarian Gypsies—musicians and artists. 50 minutes.

1991 *Gypsy Romeo (Cigány Rómeo)* (feature film, in progress)
135 min. Based on Shakespeare's *Romeo and Juliet,* narrative of a doomed love between a Hungarian girl and a Gypsy youth.
The Last Soviet Star (project in progress)
Screenplay: Svetlana Boym, with M. Mészáros
A film about the making of a star in Soviet and American cultures, the story of Liubov, the blonde Soviet film goddess of the 1930s who was Stalin's favorite actress.

1992 *Sisi* (twenty-six-part television series in progress on the life of Empress Elizabeth of Austria, with possible additional feature film)

Sources for Rental and Purchase of Márta Mészáros's Films

Most of the films discussed in this book are available in Hungarian with English subtitles in 35mm from Hungarofilm, Budapest, V., Bathori u. 10, Hungary. North American sources include the following:

New Yorker Films, 16 West 61st Street, New York, N.Y. 10023; (212) 247-6110: *Nine Months* (1978); *Women* (1977); *Diary for My Children* (1984) (all 16mm)

Kino International, 333 West 39th Street, New York, N.Y. 10018; (212) 629-6880: *The Girl* (1968); *Riddance* (1973); *Adoption* (1975) (all 16mm)

Festival Films, 2841 Irving Ave. S., Minneapolis, MN 55408; (612) 870-4744: *Adoption* (1975); *The Girl* (1968); *Riddance* (1973) (all videocassette)

Les Productions la Fête, 225 est, rue Roy, Suite 203, Montréal, Qué., Canada H2W 1M5; (514) 848-0417: *Bye Bye Red Riding Hood* (35mm/16mm/video)

Other Useful Addresses

Ministry of Culture, Central Board of Hungarian Cinematography, Szalai utca 10–14, H–105 Budapest; Hungarian Film- and TV-Makers' Association, Gorkij fasor 38, H-1068 Budapest; Budapest Studio/Hunnia Studio/Dialog Studio/Objektiv Studio (feature film studios), Lumumba u. 174, H–1145, Budapest.
Cinemagyar/Hungarofilm Export Ltd., H-1054 Budapest, Bathory u. 10, Hungary.

SELECTED BIBLIOGRAPHY

Books and Articles

Allombert, G. "Découvrir le cinéma hongrois." *Image et Son* no. 335 (Jan. 1979): 21–22.

Ash, Timothy Garton. *The Uses of Adversity: Essays on the Fate of Central Europe* New York: Pantheon, 1989.

Auty, Martyn. "Staying On: Interview with Pál Sándor—The Climate for a New Hungarian Cinema." *Monthly Film Bulletin* 51 no. 105 (June 1984): 170.

Avisar, Ilan. *Screening the Holocaust: Cinema's Images of the Unimaginable.* Bloomington: Indiana University Press, 1988.

Balázs, Béla. *Theory of the Film: Character and Growth of a New Art.* New York: Dover, 1970.

Bazin, André. "The Stalin Myth in Soviet Cinema." *Film Criticism* 11, no. 1–2 (1987): 161–72.

Beke, László, and Biró, Yvette. *Béla Balázs Studio Budapest: Twenty Years of Hungarian Experimental Film.* Catalogue for film exhibition organized by the American Federation of Arts, 1985.

Bickley, Daniel. "Socialism and Humanism: The Contemporary Hungarian Cinema." *Cinéaste* 9, no. 2 (Winter 1978–79): 30–35.

"Bio-filmographie d'István Szabó." *L'Avant-Scène* no. 348 (March 1986): 65.

Biró, Yvette. "Landscape after Battle: Films from 'the Other Europe,' " in "Eastern Europe . . . Central Europe . . . Europe." *Daedalus* 119, no. 1 (Winter 1990): 161–82.

Biro, Yvette, ed. Film Kultura 1965–1973. Budapest: Századvég Kiadó, 1991.

Bisztray, George. "Activities of the Hungarian Film Institute and Archive." *Hungarian Studies Review* 9, no. 1 (Spring 1982): 55–58.

"Ciné-Perestroika: Le Rideau déchiré." *Cahiers du Cinéma spécial URSS*, supplement to no. 427 (January 1990).

Condee, Nancy, and Padunov, Vladimir. "The Outposts of Official Art: Recharting Soviet Cultural History." *Framework* no. 34 (1987): 59–106.

Daney, Serge. "Budapest 81." *Cahiers du Cinéma* no. 322 (April 1981): 49–50.

Deak, Istvan. *Beyond Nationalism.* New York: Oxford University Press, 1990.

Eagle, Herbert. "Color and Meaning in *Time Stands Still.*" *Cross Currents: A Yearbook of Central European Culture* 8 (1989): 127–42.

Elley, Derek. "In Camera: Beneath the Iceberg." *Film and Filming* 27, no. 7 (April 1979): 6–7.

———. "Tips of the Iceberg." *Film and Filming* 25, no. 3 (Dec. 1978): 22–25.

Estève, Michel, ed. "Miklós Jancsó." *Etudes cinématographiques* nos. 104–108. Paris, 1975.

Fargier, Jean-Paul. "Sept Films Hongrois." *Cahiers du Cinéma* no. 284 (Jan. 1978): 31–34.

Fisher, William. "Prague/Budapest: The Changing Film Industries of Eastern Europe." *Sight and Sound* 59, no. 3 (Summer 1990): 158–61.

Foster, Henrietta. "Eger: Péter Bacsó in Marlboro Country." *Sight and Sound* 54, no. 1 (Winter 1984–85): 3–4.

Gay, Richard. "Le cinéma hongrois d'aujourd'hui tourne surtout vers le passé." *Séquences* no. 122 (Oct. 1985): 23–24.
Geréb, Anna. "Selections from the Letters of Béla Balázs." *Move East* 1 (Budapest: 1991): 199–214.
Gergatz, Stephen. "An Interview with András Kovács." *New Orleans Review* 9, no. 1 (Spring-Summer 1982): 41–45.
Gervais, G. "Cinéma et révolution: vicissitudes du cinéma dans les pays socialistes." *Jeune Cinéma* no. 103 (June 1977): 13–24.
———. "En Hongrie, un cinéma sociographique." *Jeune Cinéma* no. 416 (Feb. 1979): 17–20.
Gillet, J. "Hungarian Cinema: Looking Good." *Film* 74 (June 1979): 10.
Giraud, Thérèse. "Entretien avec Márta Mészáros et sur trois films de Márta Mészáros." *Cahiers du Cinéma* no. 284 (Jan. 1978): 34–39.
Goulding, Daniel J., ed. *Post New Wave Cinema in the Soviet Union and Eastern Europe*. Bloomington: Indiana University Press, 1989.
Gyertyán, Ervin. "Let Down by Masters (Kovács)." *New Hungarian Quarterly* 23, no. 85 (Spring 1982): 193–97.
———. "Look Back in Compassion (Mészáros)." *New Hungarian Quarterly* 25, no. 96 (Winter 1984): 217–21.
Gyertyán, Ervin, and Jaehne, Karen. "Three Films by István Szabó." *New Hungarian Quarterly* 22, no. 84 (Winter 1981): 208–16.
Gyürey, Vera, ed. *Move East: International Film Quarterly* 1, no. 1. Budapest: Hungarian Film Institute. (Fall 1991).
Hoberman, J. "Mad Budapest." *Film Comment* 21, no. 3 (June 1985): 22–24.
Houstrate, G., et al. "Le Cinéma Hongrois." *Cinéma* no. 245 (May 1979): 12–29.
"Hungarian Cinema at the NFT." *Film* no. 66 (Summer 1972): 23.
Hungarian Films/Films Hongrois 1988. Published on the Occasion of the Twentieth National Feature Film Festival. (Budapest: Hungarofilm, 1988).
Hungarian Film Directors 1948–1983. Supplementary publication of the Hungarofilm Bulletin, ed. Lia Somogyi (Budapest: Interpress, 1987).
Insdorf, Annette. "Childhood Loss Shapes a Director's Life and Art." *New York Times*, Oct. 28, 1982, sec. 2, 21+.
Jaehne, Karen. "István Szabó: Dreams of Memories." *Film Quarterly* 32, no. 1 (1978): 30–42.
Jeancolas, J.-P. "Budapest 84." *Positif* no. 280 (June 1984): 50–52.
———. "Lettre à Budapest . . . mise à poste à Paris." *Positif* no. 214 (Jan. 1979): 41–45.
Jeancolas, Jean-Pierre. "Redl, ou l'ordre accepté." *L'Avant-Scène* no. 348 (March 1986): 3–8.
Kovács, András. "Controversies Surrounding Hungarian Filmmaking." *New Orleans Review* 11, no. 1 (1984): 83–97.
Kundera, Milan. "The Tragedy of Central Europe." *New York Review of Books*, April 26, 1984, pp. 33–38.
Kuttna, Mari. "Hungary: A Renewal of Energy." *Take One* 7, no. 9 (Aug. 1979): 2, 4.
———. "Letter from Hungary." *American Film* 7, no. 7 (May 1982): 23–25.
Langlois, G. "La Hongrie au temps présent." *Ecran* no. 76 (Jan. 1979): 15–16.
Lardeau, Yann. "Situation du Cinéma Hongrois." *Cahiers du Cinéma* no. 336 (May 1982): 35–38.
Liehm, Mira, and Antonin, J. *The Most Important Art: East European Film after 1945*. Berkeley: University of California Press, 1971.

Martineau, B. H. "The Films of Márta Mészáros or, The Importance of Being Banal." *Film Quarterly* 34, no. 1 (1980): 21–27.

Mesnil, C., and Petrie, G. "Entre cris et chuchotements: le cinéma hongrois (bio/filmographies)." *Revue Belge du Cinéma* no. 12 (Summer 1985): 1–63.

"Miklós Jancsó." *Etudes cinématographiques* nos. 104–108, Michel Estève, ed. Paris, 1975.

Nemes, Károly. *Films of Commitment: Socialist Cinema in Eastern Europe.* Budapest: Corvina Kiadó, 1985.

Nemeskürty, István. *Word and Image: History of the Hungarian Cinema.* Budapest: Corvina Kiadó, 1974.

"Le Nouveau cinéma hongrois." *Etudes cinématographiques* nos. 73–77. Paris, 1969.

Passek, Jean-Loup, ed. *Le Cinéma hongrois.* Catalogue Centre Pompidou, 5 déc 1979 au 7 janvier 1980, Paris, 1980.

Paul, David. "The Esthetics of Courage: The Political Climate for the Cinema in Poland and Hungary." *Cinéaste* 14, no. 4 (1986): 16–22.

Paul, David, ed. *Politics, Art and Commitment in the East European Cinema.* New York: St. Martin's Press, 1983.

Pederson, B. T. "*History Must Answer to Man—The Contemporary Hungarian Cinema.*" *Chaplin* 23, no. 4 (1981): 180.

Péter, Abel. *A forgalomban lévő magyar játékfilmek ajánlójegyzéke (1948–1978).* Budapest: Mokpép.

Petrie, Graham. "Hungarian Film Week 1986." *New Hungarian Quarterly* 27, no. 103 (Fall 1986): 228–33.

———. *History Must Answer to Man: The Contemporary Hungarian Cinema.* Budapest: Corvina Kiadó and London: Tantivy Press, 1978.

———. "Hungarian Film Week 1981: Dialogue or War, an Average Year." *New Hungarian Quarterly* 22, no. 83 (Fall 1981): 208–19.

———. "Hungarian Film Week 1984." *New Hungarian Quarterly* 25, no. 95 (Fall 1984): 210–20. 19.

———. "Just Movies? Hungarian Film Week 1985." *New Hungarian Quarterly* 26, no. 99 (Fall 1985): 200–205.

———. "New Cinema from Eastern Europe." *Film Comment* 11, no. 6 (1975): 48–51.

———. "Reconstructing Reality: The Hungarian Documentary and 'Pseudo-Documentary' Film." *Hungarian Studies Review* 9, no. 1 (Spring 1982): 39–54.

Petrie, Graham, and Dwyer, Ruth, eds. *Before the Wall Came Down: Soviet and East European Filmmakers Working in the West.* New York: University Press of America, 1990.

Polony, Csaba. "Film, Culture, Politics: A View from Hungary/Interview with György Szomjas." *Left Curve* no. 11 (1986): 3–19.

Portuges, Catherine. "Between Worlds: Re-placing Hungarian Cinema," in Petrie and Dwyer, eds., *Before the Wall Came Down: Soviet and East European Filmmakers Working in the West*, 63–70.

———. "Lovers and Workers: Screening the Body in Post-Communist Hungary," in A. Parker, M. Russo, D. Sommer, and P. Yaeger, eds., *Nationalisms and Sexualities.* New York: Routledge, Chapman and Hall, 1991, 285–95.

———. "Retrospective Narratives in Hungarian Cinema: The 1980s *Diary* Trilogy of Márta Mészáros." *The Velvet Light Trap* no. 27 (Spring 1991): 63–72.

———. "Seeing Subjects: Women Directors and Cinematic Autobiography," in B. Brodzki and C. Schenk, eds., *Life/Lines: Theories of Women's Autobiography.* Ithaca: Cornell University Press, 1988, pp. 338–50.

Quart, Barbara Koenig. *Women Directors: The Emergence of a New Cinema.* New York: Praeger, 1988.

Rainer, János, and Kresálek, Gábor. "Hungarian Society in Film, 1948–1956." *Move East: International Film Quarterly* 1, no. 1: 21–47. Budapest: Hungarian Film Institute (Spring 1991).

Riegel, O. W. "What Is 'Hungarian' in the Hungarian Cinema?" *New Hungarian Quarterly* 18, no. 65 (Spring 1977): 208.

Robinson, D. "Budapest Film Week." *Sight and Sound* 48, no. 3 (June 1979): 154.

Rubenstein, Lenny. "Politics, Art and Commitment in the East European Cinema." *Cinéaste* 13, no. 4 (1984): 54–55.

Sitton, Robert. "Hungarian Director Szabó Discusses His Film 'Father.' " *Film Comment* 5, no. 1 (Fall 1968): 58–63.

Stimpson, Mansel. *"Diary for My Children."* Film no. 139 (Oct. 1985): 6.

Stoil, Michael J. *Cinema beyond the Danube: The Camera and Politics.*

Szabó, István. "The Cinema Is Already Dead." *Film* no. 139 (Oct. 1985): 5.

"XXI Magyar Filmszemle: A harcos pihenője." *Hitel* no. 3 (1989): 33–34.

Wolf, William. "Blue Danube Diary." *Film Comment* no. 20 (May–June 1984): 6+.

Film Reviews

"Adoption." Hungarofilm Bulletin, Budapest no. 2 (1975): 9–10.

Alnaes, K. "Ungarn: frittalende om Stalintiden—enda en gang." *Film & Kino* no. 5 (1984): 174–75.

Andersson, W. "Varfoer just i Ungarn?" *Chaplin* 16, no. 29 (1974): 49–51.

Armatys, L. "Wszystkie Kobiece dzienne sprawy . . . o tworczosci Márta Mészáros." *Kino* no. 14 (Feb. 1979): 25–29.

Asahina, R. "Old Hat, New Voices." *New Leader* no. 60 (Nov. 7, 1977): 21–23.

Aubernas, J. "Journal intime." *Visions* no. 29 (May 1985): 39.

Aude, Françoise. "Journal intime: la mère menteuse." *Positif* no. 86 (Dec. 1984): 64–65.

———. "La menuisière et la sphynge" *(Adoption). Positif* no. 194 (June 1977): 65–67.

———. *"Une mère, une fille." Positif* no. 247 (Oct. 1981): 25–26.

———. "Le premier cri libre d'une petite fille hongroise" *(Neuf Mois* and *Elles Deux). Positif* no. 204 (March 1978): 64–66.

Barraclough, S. *"Diary for My Children." Monthly Film Bulletin* no. 52 (June 1985): 188–89.

Bassan, R. *Les héritières. Revue du Cinéma* no. 52 (July–Aug. 1980): 52–53.

Beerekamp, Hans. "Assapoester in Boedapest." *Handelsblad,* May 3, 1985.

Belmans, J. *"Neuf Mois." Amis* no. 261 (Feb. 1978): 32.

Bertin-Maghit, J.-P. "Journal intime." *Revue du Cinéma* no. 60, hors série 31 (1985).

Berube, R.-C. *"Neuf Mois." Séquences* no. 90 (Oct. 1977): 16.

Breton, Emile. "Les valeurs sûres et les autres: 'Comme chez nous' de Márta Mészáros." *La Nouvelle Critique* no. 121 (Feb. 1979).

Canby, Vincent. *"Diary,* or Hungary in the 1940s." *New York Times,* Sept. 30, 1984.

———. "Film: Márta Mészáros's *Diary for My Loves." New York Times,* Oct. 31, 1984, p. C21.

"Cannes 1980." *Céluloïde* 25: 7–9 July (no. 294–95); 12–15 Aug. (no. 296–97); 7 (no. 298–99), 1980.

Carroll, Kathleen. "A Child Torn by Politics." *Daily News,* Oct. 31, 1984, p. 63.

Clouzot, C. *"Adoption." Ecran* no. 8 (May 15, 1977): 59–60.

Clouzot, C., et al. "La Hongrie au coeur: Márta Mészáros" (filmography and interview). *Ecran* no. 76 (Jan. 15, 1979): 49–59.

Clurman, H. "Film Festival II." *Nation* no. 225 (Oct. 22, 1977): 412–14.

Codelli, L. *"Kilenc hónap." Positif* no. 195–96 (July–Aug. 1977): 90–91.

Daney, Serge. "Budapest, années 1950s." *Libération*, Oct. 1, 1984.

Dasen, René. *"Adoption." La Tribune de Genève*, June 13, 1976.

De Pooter, Maggy. *"Journal intime." Le Drapeau Rouge*, April 17, 1985, p. 12.

Decaux, E. *"Les héritières." Cinématographe* no. 58 (1980): 34.

Delacoup, Marie-Odile. "Comme chez nous de Márta Mészáros: un film de cowboy hongrois." *Libération*, Jan. 17, 1979.

Delmas. G. "Journal intime." *Jeune Cinéma* no. 163 (Dec.–Jan. 1984–85): 32–34.

"Diary for My Loves." Hungarofilm Bulletin no. 2–3 (1984).

"Diary for My Children." Time Out, July 18, 1985.

"Diary for My Children." London Weekly Diary, July 28, 1985.

Dignam, Virginia. "One Woman's Freedom Struggle." *Morning Star*, July 19, 1985.

Dimitrov, G. "Márta Mészáros." *Kinoizkustvo* no. 34 (Oct. 1979): 63–67.

Duarte, F. "Márta Mészáros e a defesa da dignidade da mulher." *Céluloïde* 26: 13 Oct. 1981 (no. 326–27).

Dwyer, John. "Intense, Exquisite Hungarian Film at Evans Art Theater." *Buffalo Evening News*, June 20, 1980, p. 34.

Elley, D. "Hiding under the Bushel." *Film and Filming* no. 20 (Feb. 1974): 30–32.

Elley, Derek. *"Nine Months/The Two of Them." Film and Filming* no. 26 (Nov. 1982): 37–38.

Elshens, M. *"Les heritières." Cinéma* no. 23 (Nov. 1980): 41–42.

Ember, M. "Az emberi kapcsolatok mér lyrétegeiben, Márta Mészáros *Ők ketten." Film Kultúra* no. 13 (Nov.–Dec. 1977): 18–22.

Fabricius, S. "Lad os se den igen." *Levende Billeder* no. 7 (June 1981): 34–35.

"Film: *Two Women* with Same Sorrow." *New York Times*, Oct. 6, 1977, C21.

"Un film hongrois pour finir l'année exigeant, austère," *Voix ouvrière*, Dec. 30, 1975.

Forslund, B. "Med andra ogen." *Chaplin* 18, no. 2 (143) (1976): 56–57.

Fsugan, I. "Mondom a magamét" (interview). *Filmvilág* 30, no. 2 (1987): 15–18.

Gino. *"Kilenc hónap." Variety* no. 288 (Oct. 26, 1977): 20.

Giraud, and Villain, D. "Troisième Festival de Paris; Deuxième entretien avec Márta Mészáros." *Cahiers du Cinéma* no. 284 (Jan. 1978): 34–37.

Goodman, Walter. "Diary for My Loved Ones: From Hungary." *New York Times*, Sept. 26, 1987.

Grant, J. *"Adoption." Cinema* 77, no. 224–25 (Aug.–Sept. 1977): 176–77.

Grelier, R. *"Une mère, une fille." Revue du Cinéma* no. 352, hors série 26 (1982).

———. *"Neuf Mois." Revue du Cinéma* no. 323 (Dec. 1977): 112–14.

Grelier, R., and Levieux, M. "Entretien avec Márta Mészáros." *Revue du Cinéma* no. 334 (Dec. 1978): 106–108.

Hardt, H. "Márta Mészáros." *Amis* no. 263 (April 1978): 21.

Harvey, S. "The 22nd New York Film Festival." *Film Comment* no. 20 (Nov.–Dec. 1984): 65–68.

Hatch, R. "Films." *Nation* no. 232 (March 28, 1981): 380–81.

"The Heiresses." Hungarofilm Bulletin no. 2 (1980): 3–4.

Herlinghaus, R. "Unter anderem zum Thema Frau" (interview and filmography). *Film und Fernsehen* 5, no. 1 (1977): 19–25.

Herman, J. "Just Like Home." *Film Quarterly* 34, no. 1 (1980): 56–59.

Hibbin, S. *"Diary for My Children." Film and Filming* no. 364 (Jan. 1985): 15.

Hoberman, J. "Film: Budapest Tales." *Village Voice* no. 29 (Nov. 6, 1984): 59.

———. "Film: Family Feud." *Village Voice* no. 29 (Nov. 6, 1984): 59–60.

Holl (R. Holloway). *"Örökbefogadás (Adoption)."* *Variety* no. 279 (July 23, 1975): 20.
Holthof, M. "Mészáros' vrouwenfilms." *Film & TV* no. 260 (Jan. 1976): 10–11.
Horosczak, A. "Sak przyszla?" *Kino* no. 18 (June 1984): 47–48.
"In Production: *The Land of Mirages."* *Hungarofilm Bulletin* no. 2 (1983): 19–22.
Insdorf, A. "Childhood Loss Shapes a Director's Life and Art." *New York Times*, Oct. 28, 1984, sec. 2, p. 22 + .
Jeancolas, J.-P. "Budapest 84." *Positif* no. 280 (June 1984): 50–52.
———. *"Les héritières."* *Positif* no. 232–33 (July–Aug. 1980): 112–13.
"Journal intime." *Séquences* no. 117 (July 1984): 14.
Kaiser, S. "Zuhause in einem fremden Land." *Film und Fernsehen* 19, no. 2 (1981): 40.
Kauffmann, Stanley. "On Films: Womanhood." *New Republic* no. 184 (March 28, 1981): 22–23.
Koch, Eric. *"Napló:* Hoe liberal een communistisch land kan zijn." *Desmet Amsterdam.*
Koole, C. *"Napló."* *SKoop* no. 21 (June–July 1985): 21.
Koskinen, M. "Kvinnofilm och kvinnofilm." *Chaplin* 24, no. 5 (1982): 231–33.
Kovács, M. "Az eltávozott hitelesség Márta Mészáros Örök befogadás." *Film Kultúra* no. 11 (July–Aug. 1975): 25–27.
Kreps, K. *"Nine Months."* *Boxoffice* no. 117 (April 1981): 25.
Kuttna, Mari. "Another Way." *Film and Filming* no. 338 (Nov. 1982): 25–26.
"Journal intime: adolescence à l'époque stalinienne." *La Libre Belgique*, April 17, 1985.
Lajeunesse, J. "Journal intime." *Revue du Cinéma* no. 398 (Oct. 1984): 28–29.
———. *"Neuf Mois."* *Revue du Cinéma* no. 332 (Oct. 1978): 199.
Laurendeau, F. *"Journal intime* de Márta Mészáros: un passé toujours présent." *24 Images* no. 21 (Summer 1984): 13.
Lederle, J.-L. *"Adoption."* *Cinématographe* no. 27 (May 1977): 36.
———. *"Neuf Mois."* *Cinématographe* no. 34 (Jan. 1978): 38.
Leeman, E., and Setz, I. "Fiction Conquers Reality." *Skrien* no. 142 (Summer 1985): 35.
Len (L. Borgen). "Anna *(Une mère, une fille)."* *Variety* no. 304 (Aug. 26, 1981): 26.
M. F. "Portrait de Femme: *Adoption* de Márta Mészáros." *L'Humanité*, April 30, 1977.
Malmkjaer, P. "Berlin." *Kosmorama* 21, no. 127 (1975): 181–83.
"Márta Mészáros" (interview). *Film* no. 45 (Dec. 1977): 8–9.
"Márta Mészáros" (filmography and interview). *Ekran* 3, no. 4, (1978): 28–29.
Martineau, B. H. "The Films of Márta Mészáros or, the Importance of Being Banal." *Film Quarterly* 34, no. 1 (1980): 21–27.
Maslin, J. "Movie: Hungarian *Just Like Home."* *New York Times*, April 13, 1979, C16.
———. "Screen: *Nine Months:* Hungarian Factory Tale." *New York Times*, March 16, 1981, p. C15.
Mass, D., and Slavich, I. "Márta Mészáros: vasskazyvaiu o sebe . . ." *Iskusstvo Kino* no. 5 (1979): 127–34.
Maupin, F. *"Adoption."* *Revue du Cinéma* no. 317 (May 1977): 84.
Maurin, François. "Racines hongroises." *L'Humanité*, Jan. 31, 1979.
Merckx, L. "Olyan mint otthon." *Film & TV* no. 274 (March 1980): 39–40.
Mérei, F. "Az élet minosége: Mészáros Márta *Kilenc hónap."* *Film Kultúra* no. 12 (Sept.–Oct. 1976): 5–9.

Mészáros, Márta, et al. *"Adopce"* (scenario extract). *Film a Doba* no. 22 (Feb. 1976): 84–91.

———. *"Unterwegs."* *Film und Fernsehen* 8, no. 7 (1980): 26–27.

Mosier, J. "Cannes 1984." *New Orleans Review* 12, no. 1 (1985): 58–89.

Moskowitz, G. *"Ök ketten (The Two of Them)."* *Variety* no. 289 (Nov. 16, 1977): 24.

———. *"Örökség (The Heritage)."* *Variety* no. 299 (May 21, 1980): 18.

———. *"Utközben (On the Move)."* *Variety* no. 298 (Feb. 27, 1980): 21.

"Mother and Daughter." *Hungarofilm Bulletin* no. 3 (1981): 7–9.

Murat, P. *"Adoption."* *Téléciné* no. 218 (May 1977): 46–47.

Nacache, J. *"Une mère, une fille."* *Cinema 81*, no. 273 (Sept. 1981): 74–76.

"Napló gyermekeimnek. Diary for My Children." *Sydney Film Festival*, 1985.

Napoli, T. *"Nine Months."* *Film Journal* no. 84 (March 23, 1981): 29–30.

"Nine Months." *Variety* no. 302 (Feb. 25, 1981): 20.

"O diario de Márta Mészáros." *Diario de Noticias*, July 23, 1985.

Oukrate, F. *"Neuf Mois."* *Ekran* no. 64 (Dec. 15, 1977): 60–61.

Palmer, J. "London Film Festival: 15 Nov.–2 Dec." *Stills* no. 14 (Nov. 1984).

Párkány, L. "Érvényes látlelet: Mészáros Márta: *Napló: gyermekeimnek."* *Film Kultúra* 20, no. 3 (1984): 7–11.

Peary, Gerald. "Little Red Riding Hood Gets a Hungarian Twist." *Los Angeles Times*, "Calendar," Feb. 7, 1989, pp. 2–4.

———. "Little Red Riding Hood: Márta Mészáros and the Malamute." *Sight and Sound* 57, no. 3 (Summer 1988): 150.

Pelacot, M. T. de. *"Adoption."* *Jeune Cinéma* no. 103 (June 1977): 36–38.

Picaper, Jean-Paul. "Un bon festival avec des films mediocres." *Le Figaro*, July 13, 1975.

Portal, M. *"Neuf Mois."* *Jeune Cinéma* no. 108 (Feb. 1978): 50–51.

Prochnow, C. *"Neun Monate."* *Film und Fernsehen* 6, no. 1 (1978): 11–12.

Quart, Barbara Koenig. *"Diary for My Children."* *Film Quarterly* 38, no. 3 (Spring 1985): 46–49.

"Qui sont-ils? Que font-ils? biographies/filmographies." *Revue Belge du Cinéma* no. 12 (Summer 1985): 42–63.

Ranzi, P. "Márta Mészáros 'Senza legami,' " *Cineforum* no. 156 (July–Aug. 1976): 470.

Renaud, I. *"Neuf Mois."* *Cinéma 78* no. 229 (Jan. 1978): 91–92.

Rickey, C. "Film: Hungarian Threnody." *Village Voice* no. 26 (March 18–24, 1981): 44 +.

Robinson, David. "Politics and Propaganda with a Personal Touch." *New York Times*, July 19, 1985, sec. C.

Rossi, U. *"Napló gyermekeimnek."* *Segno Cinema* no. 14 (Sept. 1984): 57.

Rother, H.-J. "Eine unmoegliche Frau." *Film und Fernsehen* 15, no. 3 (1987): 34–37.

Rouchy, Marie-Elizabeth. "Les exorcismes de Márta Mészáros." *Le Matin de Paris*, Sept. 26, 1984.

Sarlat, P. "Cannes: *Les héritières."* *CinéRevue* no. 60 (March 8, 1980): 28–29.

Sarris, Andrew. "A Hungarian Rhapsody." *Village Voice*, April 23, 1979.

Sas, György. "Filmlevél: Piroska és a farkas." *Film Szinház Muzsika*, April 1, 1989, p. 7.

Schick, Thomas. "32nd Sydney Film Festival." *Wentworth Courier*, July 3, 1985, p. 150.

Seitz, Michael. "The Quiet Integrity of Márta Mészáros." *The Chronicle Review*, May 14, 1979.

Serceau, D. *"Une mère, une fille."* *Revue du Cinéma* no. 365 (Oct. 1981): 51.

Siclier, Jacques. *"Adoption* de Márta Mészáros." *Le Monde*, May 2, 1977.

Sirca, M. "Intimni dvevnik." *Ekran* 10, no. 1–2 (1985): 23–24.

Stimpson, M. *"Diary for My Children." Film* no. 134 (Oct. 1985): 6.

Stratton, D. *"Délibábok Országa (The Land of Mirages)." Variety* no. 314 (Mar. 7, 1984): 216.

———. *"Diary for My Loves." Variety* no. 326 (March 20, 1987): 20+.

———. *"Napló." Variety* no. 314 (Mar. 7, 1984): 220.

Taconet, C. *"Les héritières." Cinéma 80* no. 258 (June 1980): 94–95.

———. "Propos de Márta Mészáros." *Cinéma 80* no. 258 (June 1980): 94–95.

Terreehorst, P. "Hangaarse Film." *Skrien* no. 69 (Nov. 1977): 36.

Tremois, Claude-Marie. *"Adoption." Telerama,* April 30, 1977, p. 89.

"The Two of Them." Hungarofilm Bulletin no. 4: 3–5, 1977.

"Ungarn: lyrisk varme." *Film & Kino* no. 4 (1980): 132.

"Útközben." Film & TV no. 309 (Feb. 1983): 43.

Van Bueren, Peter. "Pseudorealistische stije van Napló schept afstand." *De Volkskrant dozmei,* May 2, 1985.

Van Lierof, Pieter. *"Napló,* van Mészáros: hoogtepunt van zeitkritische Hongaarse gorf." *Utrechts Nieuwsblad N.Z.C.,* May 2, 1985.

Varène, C. *"Une mère, une fille." Cinématographe* no. 70 (Sept. 1981): 37.

Vecchi, P. *"Napló." Cineforum* 24, no. 235 (June–July 1984): 12–13.

Veress, József. "A Harmadik Napló." *Népszabadság,* June 21, 1990.

Wiinblad, A. *"Adoptionen." Kosmorama* 22, no. 129 (1976): 70.

Wisniewski, C. "Historia a los jednostki." *Kino* no. 19 (Feb. 1985): 45–46.

Zay, László. "Napló mindannyiunknak." *Magyar Nemzet,* June 16, 1990.

INDEX

CATHERINE PORTUGES is Professor of Comparative Literature and Director of Film Studies at the University of Massachusetts.

DATE DUE

#26160858